"*The Do-Over* is a beautiful and inspirational journey of struggle, hope, grit, passion and faith. Diving into the depths of alcoholism, ascending the heights to recovery and labouring the path to super-achievement, Karlyn's story will hit you in the heart. A truly moving read."
KELLY ARMATAGE, THERAPIST AND INVENTOR OF A.S.K. A SERENITY KIT

"Every coach dreams of getting that super-gifted, talented athlete. Karlyn was my gift. Unfortunately, she was not in the 'I am willing to put in the time and effort to maximize my ability' phase of her life. If she had trained as seriously as Tracy Caulkins, who at that time held an American record in every stroke, Karlyn could have made it to the Olympics and had that very same level of success. Over the years, I have looked back and felt that somehow I failed her. Unaware of her personal demons, I can now truly appreciate what she has accomplished today. May she enjoy the success that she *now* wholeheartedly deserves."
MIKE TROY, TWO-TIME OLYMPIC GOLD MEDALIST

"This is such a wonderful testimony of a woman so heavily decorated with so many awards and achievements in the swimming world, yet behind the cap and goggles was a soul lost in the darkest and deepest depths of despair. Karlyn channels the demons that once haunted her and uses them to resurface as a champion both in and out of the water. Her story inspires us to believe that anything is possible with hope and desire, and that it's never too late to turn your life around."
SUZY DEGAZON, 15-TIME ULTRAMAN HAWAII COMPETITOR
AND RECOVERING ANOREXIC

"*The Do-Over* is a wonderful story of addiction and recovery with the sport of swimming as the backdrop. Karlyn Pipes' unembellished description of her childhood and life in the grips of alcohol addiction made me cheer for each of her hard-won victories, and her quest for wholeness. Karlyn's description of our sport is spot-on; both its torments and joys."
NANCY HOGSHEAD-MAKAR, J.D., CEO CHAMPION WOMEN AND
OLYMPIC GOLD MEDALIST

"*The Do-Over* is a must read about the true definition of success in life. Karlyn got to where she is today not from innate talent, dumb luck or a magic formula, but by taking responsibility for her shortcomings and doing something about it. Her book is an inspiration to everyone who wants to live a more purposeful life."
MIKE WIEN, FOUR-TIME IRONMAN WORLD CHAMPION COMPETITOR
AND AUTHOR OF THE SPECIFIC EDGE

"Karlyn's a fierce competitor, a gifted competitive swimmer—and an alcoholic. She misses practices, loses a college scholarship and work opportunities, and her portrayal of these mishaps is brutally honest and disturbing. Just when her illness seems destined to win, she's given a second chance. Once she is released from the rehab facility, instead of hiding from the pool like she's done before, the water becomes a place for healing, a place where she can forgive herself and others and move forward and reach for new amazing possibilities for her life."
SUSAN DAWSON-COOK, SPORTS AND FITNESS WRITER AND AUTHOR

"The Do-Over is both illuminating and inspirational. Without glamorizing either alcoholism or eating disorders, Karlyn Pipes writes about these and other difficult topics with honesty, courage, authenticity, and conviction. Her story is gripping, raw, at times uncomfortable, and beautiful. It is ultimately triumphant and transformative. For those of us who have also struggled, Karlyn's story puts words to experiences and feelings that many of us have shared. Karlyn's triumph comes not just through athletic victories, but through an awakening of the soul. Karlyn gives us all the permission and encouragement to have our own 'do-over,' no matter our age or station in life. She lets us know it's never too late to be our very best selves."
ELLEN HART PEÑA, THREE-TIME IRONMAN WORLD CHAMPION AND SUBJECT OF DYING TO BE PERFECT: THE ELLEN HART PEÑA STORY

"In The Do-Over, Karlyn reveals the essence of a true champion in the pool and in her toughest competition—life! Gut-level honest and inspiring for anyone facing life's challenges."
CAROL LEBEAU, MASTERS SWIMMER AND FORMER ABC10 NEWS ANCHOR

"Most great athletes, I've discovered, after writing about them, training with them and now coaching them, are not only passionate about their sport, but addicted—both to exercise and to the adulation they receive from winning. How Karlyn Pipes survived her destructive addictions as a youth and focused her energy into becoming an elite level swimmer at an age when most swimmers have long retired, creates a fascinating and enlightening story for any athlete who's been reminded by friends and family of their own addictions."
KIM MCDONALD, FORMER EDITOR OF TRIATHLETE MAGAZINE, SPORTS WRITER, AND UCSD TRIATHLON COACH

"When I took my first private swim lesson from Karlyn in 2007, I thought she had it all—beauty, talent, a gorgeous husband, and a lovely home in paradise. But behind her bubbly personality was pain that causes you to cringe and cry as she digs deep to face her turmoil in *The Do-Over*. There is a little bit of Karlyn in all of us. In telling her story, her talent for teaching emerges, as you also take a look at your own shortcomings."
CATHY TIBBETTS, 11-TIME HAWAII IRONMAN WORLD CHAMPIONSHIP FINISHER

"As a recovering alcoholic and member of the swimming community, I found Karlyn's story both truthful and inspiring. I believe her journey will resonate with others that have been exposed to alcoholism, or are facing this disease themselves, and will hopefully give guidance and support to those in need."
STEPHEN PICKELL, OLYMPIC SILVER MEDALIST AND SWIM COACH

"At times heartbreaking but ultimately heartwarming, Karlyn's story will inspire you to rise above your own challenges and realize your greatest potential."
MALI APPLE AND JOE DUNN, AUTHORS OF *THE SOULMATE EXPERIENCE*

"In *The Do-Over*, Karlyn Pipes swims far beneath the surface to reveal both the pain and the motivation that drives an extraordinary elite athlete. While she initially—and for some time—seeks escape from her personal demons through alcohol, Karlyn eventually finds a way out, thanks in large part to her lifelong companion: the sport of swimming. With beautifully evoked memories and exacting honesty, *The Do-Over* shows us what it really takes to be a world champion. It's a powerful memoir that both swimmers and non-swimmers alike will not be able to put down."
W. HODDING CARTER, DIE-HARD SWIMMING FAN AND
AUTHOR OF *OFF THE DEEP END*

"Karlyn is one of the most inspiring humans I have ever encountered, and *The Do-Over* is a testament not only to her own personal courage and perseverance but to the resiliency of the human spirit and the power of swimming to heal, transform and provide endless joy."
LISA CONGDON, ARTIST AND AUTHOR OF *THE JOY OF SWIMMING:
A CELEBRATION OF OUR LOVE FOR GETTING IN THE WATER*

THE
DO-OVER

Aloha Trevor & Heather,

with your amazing
attitude & athletic
strength & power you inspire
many! Including me ☺
Thanks for the swims.

Hugs,

Karly

Kelowna 2012

THE DO OVER

My Journey from the Depths of Addiction to World Champion Swimmer

KARLYN PIPES

with Tito Morales

Aquatic Edge

Honolulu, Hawaii

Margo Migatz Morales

TITO MORALES studied at both the University of California, Berkeley, and the University of California, Los Angeles, where he earned his Master of Fine Arts degree in writing. He is the author of *Forward Swim* and *Meb, Deena, and the Return of the Great American Marathoner.* A former contributing editor for *Swimming World* magazine, Morales is a U.S. Masters Swimming All American and a member of the American Society of Journalists and Authors. Several of his stories have been recognized in *The Best American Sports Writing* anthology.

DEDICATED TO NANCY STERLING

While ALS imprisoned your body,
your dreams set you free to swim,
sing, and soar with the angels.

Contents

Acknowledgments   i

Prologue   1

1   I Never Set Out to Become an Alcoholic   5

2   The Alcohol Gene and the Swimming Gene   8

3   I Adapted as Best I Could   14

4   Every Second We Dropped, We Earned a Dime   21

5   The Security Was Worth the Pain   24

6   My First Taste of Fame   27

7   "So . . . How'd You Do?"   31

8   Fighting to Survive   35

9   Recovery: Zero Hour   40

10 Life Without the Elephant   46

11 A Desire for Love and a Hunger for Speed   50

12 It Was Easier to Stay Under Water Than Face Reality   59

13 The Moments You Wish You Could Freeze in Time   66

14 Recovery: Days 1 and 2   69

15 This Isn't My Dream   74

16 You Don't Deserve the Talent You Possess   80

17 Instant Gratification   84

18 Down the Rabbit Hole   90

19 Eating Disorders Flourished Here   95

20 The Drinking Permeated Everything   101

21 Was I Driving—or Was My Addiction?   105

22 One Day Closer to Oblivion   110

23 Where Had the Time Gone?   117

24 Recovery: Days 3 to 10   121

25 Searching for Something Beyond the Next Drink   127

26 Water Reveals the Truth   134

27 It Felt Like Home   137

28 A High-Maintenance Lifestyle ... 143

29 Taking Care of Daddy ... 151

30 Recovery: Day 11 and Beyond ... 171

31 A Natural High ... 178

32 Life on Life's Terms ... 182

33 Seek Progress Not Perfection ... 188

34 Attitude Is the Mind's Paintbrush ... 193

35 Working My Way Into a "Do-Over" ... 198

36 My First "Birthday" ... 203

37 Just Grateful to Be on the Blocks ... 207

38 Racing with the Kids ... 215

39 From Recovery to Rediscovery ... 222

40 When You Swim, You Swim for Yourself ... 230

41 A Perfect 54 ... 233

42 Is This Life Just a Test? ... 243

43 The Exclamation Point on My College Career ... 249

44 Taking the Right Kinds of Risks ... 256

45 The Do-Over Took On a Life of Its Own ... 263

46 Baby or Bust ... 266

47 Why Do We Act the Way We Do? ... 271

48 You Never Have to Go Solo in Swimming or Sobriety ... 274

49 The Big Island Exudes a Spiritual Energy ... 277

50 In the Water, You Are Ageless ... 280

51 Just Keep Swimming, Just Keep Swimming ... 288

52 The Day That Everything Changed ... 294

53 No More Stopping the Tears ... 305

54 The Island Whispers Truth to Your Heart ... 308

55 It's a Break, Not a Breakup ... 315

56 What Good Was Enlightenment with No One to Share It With? ... 327

57 My "Happily Ever After" Fantasy ... 334

58 Seeking Out Lessons from the Pain ... 340

59 You Gave Me Life Not Once, but Twice ... 346

60 The Courage to Be Myself ... 353

Epilogue ... 356

Be not the slave of your own past . . .
Plunge into the sublime seas, dive deep,
and swim far, so shall you come back
with self-respect, with new power, with
an advanced experience, that shall explain
and overlook the old.

RALPH WALDO EMERSON

Acknowledgments

HELEN KELLER ONCE SAID, "Alone we can do so little; together we can do so much." I owe a debt of gratitude to the many people who helped this story come to life and turn a dream into a reality.

First, I would like to thank writer Tito Morales. Tito beautifully translated my words and thoughts into a compelling story that authentically captures my energetic spirit and tattered soul.

My mom, Adrienne Pipes. You inspire me every day to be my very best and to never give up. Eric Neilsen, who loved me even when I didn't know how to love myself. Maggie Schwindt Roepke and Laurie Miller Voke, who over the years have provided a safe harbor when my life was adrift.

My amazing mentors, authors Mali Apple and Caroline Adams Miller. Thank you for your precious gifts of time, expertise, experience, wisdom, and the occasional kick in the pants.

My angelic editors Kim Aiken, Anna Embree, Jerry Trump, and Phil Whitten. Your insight, awareness, and talent helped to weave together the words that I hope will inspire many do-overs worldwide. I will forever be grateful you swam into my life just when I needed you.

Photographer and graphic designer Angy Chesler; author and lawyer Jonathan Moore; John Kilbank; and contributors Joe Dunn, Jim Grant, Christopher Hromek, Sid Orrik, Dave Pratt, and Bill and Grace Spore. I appreciate your help and input.

And finally, my Higher Power. You waited patiently, never gave up, and, when it was time, embraced me with open arms and a love I could never have imagined possible.

Prologue

I WAS SITTING IN THE READY ROOM at the Janet Evans Invitational swim meet waiting for the finals of the 200-meter backstroke, surrounded by swimming royalty. On my left was Leah Loveless, who had captured gold and bronze medals at the 1992 Olympic Games in Barcelona. On my right was Nicole Stevenson, the Australian national record holder who had also won a bronze in Barcelona, and next to Stevenson was Lindsay Benko, the high school phenom with the bright future from Elkhart, Indiana.

A meet official came through the doorway and announced, "Okay, ladies. It's time." We all got up and moved in single file toward the door.

As we emerged into the bright daylight of the McDonald's Olympic Swim Stadium and began to parade around the pool deck to the starting blocks, the speakers dotting the complex started to blare thumping, bass-heavy music. The spectators who filled the stands took the cue and rose to their feet to applaud, cheer, and whistle loudly in anticipation of what promised to be one of the most contested races of the afternoon.

I scanned the facility and tried to take it all in. The Southern California sky was vibrant and cloudless. The surface of the pool was still, and the lane lines were as colorful as sticks of candy. I felt the familiar pre-race nervous flutter in my stomach, the dryness in my mouth, and the warm tingling in my hands and feet. But mostly what I felt was a tremendous sense of gratitude. It wasn't gratitude for having performed so well in the preliminary heats, nor for having been steered into this beautiful sport as a child by my mother, nor even for having been blessed with a talent that offered me an opportunity to compete against these other skilled young women. I was grateful just to be alive.

When we reached our positions behind the blocks, I couldn't help but grin inside. At thirty-four, I was by far the oldest swimmer in the field. Some of the girls who had swum against me in the preliminary heats in the morning were young enough to be my daughters. Yet here I was, behind Lane 4 as the top seed, at one of the most important meets of the summer. I glanced over at Eric, my husband and coach, standing shoulder-to-shoulder on the pool deck with some of the best coaches in the country, including Stanford and Olympic coach Richard Quick. Earlier that day, Quick had approached Eric and said, "Karlyn had a nice swim this morning." Eric beamed. As I prepared to race, I flashed him a slightly nervous smile. The announcer began to introduce the swimmers one at a time, detailing a few notable achievements for each. The realization came to me that my path to the blocks on this day had been anything but normal and straightforward.

In contrast to the accomplishments of the other swimmers, my bio was, by Olympic standards, woeful. You would expect that, given my age, I would have had a fair share of swimming-related honors to report. When asked to prepare a media information sheet, however, I had struggled to come up with even a few items of note. All I could say was that I was from Coronado, California, and that I still did most of my training there. That was easy enough to jot down. What else could I add? Did results from U.S. Masters swim meets count? If not, I didn't have anything else to list; no major titles, records, or medals. Sure, I had plenty of stories to share, that was true, but the majority of my accomplishments were only tangentially related to competitive swimming. How could I possibly summarize the circuitous route I had taken to reach this moment? If they only knew the darkness I had survived to make it here. "If they only knew," I mused to myself, as the announcer introduced me. I gave the crowd a quick, sheepish wave.

The race starter, dressed formally in white, stood like a sentry on the side of the pool deck. He reached for the whistle that hung from his neck and delivered two rapid tweets, a nonverbal command indicating it was time for us to remove all clothing but our swimsuits. A second, longer whistle blew, meaning it was time to enter the pool. Because backstroke is the only stroke that starts in the water, the swimmers began to hop into the pool feet first, bobbing up and down a few times before rising to the surface and maneuvering themselves onto the handgrips underneath the blocks. I gazed down at the alluring, clear blue water, drained my thoughts, and jumped.

CHAPTER 1

I Never Set Out
to Become an Alcoholic

I WAS A THIRTY-ONE-YEAR-OLD ALCOHOLIC consuming up to a liter of vodka a day and my life was in complete free fall. I felt as if I had been swept into a watery, cavernous hole and was swirling wildly out of control in the void. I was blind. I could not see the angry water around me, but I could feel the turbulence and hear it roar. The noise was *deafening,* so deafening I couldn't think straight. I knew that once I hit whatever lay below it would be all over. I looked forward to that moment. I welcomed it, in fact, because it would mean an end to the pain. I was plummeting toward my rock bottom.

I never set out to become an alcoholic. It is not like trying to become an Olympic swimming champion. There is no blueprint to follow. There are no coaches to commission and no training protocol to follow. The one thing these two pursuits have in common, however, is that neither is achieved overnight. My descent into the abyss had been years in the making.

I knew the finish line of my slide into oblivion was nearing, but I had no idea how much longer it might take to reach it. If I could just be asleep when it happened, maybe, just maybe, I would not feel anything. Sleep. That's all I needed. Just a little bit of sleep. It seemed like such a simple request. The truth was I had not really slept in weeks. My brain wouldn't let me. I couldn't eat either. I craved one thing and one thing only: alcohol.

A liter of vodka a day—*a liter*. I would buy half-gallon plastic jugs and store them in the freezer. Sometimes I would mix the vodka with a little grape Gatorade. That was the only nutrition I was getting. For the most part though, I was drinking it straight, right out of the jug. I hadn't left the house in weeks. I would completely lose track of night and day. I wasn't sleeping. I was passing out. I wasn't waking up. I was coming to, and the only time I would come to was when my body alerted me it was time for yet another drink.

The cycle kept repeating itself, like the tides. Drink, pass out, come to. Drink, pass out, come to. Around and around and around. There was nothing I could do to stop it. Because if I tried—if I tried to *not* drink—I would start to get the shakes. *Delirium tremens,* also known as "shaking frenzy." The DTs.

When you are wracked with DTs, you feel as if your body has been possessed. You are feverish, disoriented, nauseated, and utterly powerless to control your convulsions. As any good alcoholic knows, the only way to keep the DTs at bay is to have another drink.

My brain was like a little cartoon flipbook where each page is a picture and the picture changes just a little bit on each page so that rifling the pages makes a charming figure dance. The problem was, someone had shuffled all my pages. They had pulled them out of the binding, tossed them into the air, kicked them as they hit the floor, and then crumpled them all together. They had not even tried to put them back in order. Flipping through my book was not charming at all. It was an incomprehensible nightmare. And that someone who had pulled the pages out was me.

My body had become a pool filled with alcohol. In a swimming pool, the water level shouldn't be too high or too low. If it's too high, surface debris like leaves or twigs cannot get into the skimmer, and the pool becomes filthy and unsightly. It is worse when the water level is too low. That causes havoc with the pump. A constant flow of water is necessary to ward off algae and bacteria. My body had become the same way. I needed to keep a certain level of alcohol in my system, but I couldn't maintain the balance. If I didn't drink, I'd get the shakes. If I drank too much, I'd get sick and pass out. I took the safer course and always drank too much. So I just continued to fall. Tumbling uncontrollably in the darkness, praying for sleep, and waiting for the end.

How did things ever get this bad? For a while, my future had looked so bright. As a young teenager, I had had the world at my feet. I had competitive swimming superstardom written all over me. I had *potential*. My face was going to be on the Wheaties box. I was going to be Natalie Coughlin before there was a Natalie Coughlin. Then it all went to hell.

Was there anything I could have done to prevent this, or had my fate been decided long ago, before I was even born?

CHAPTER 2

The Alcohol Gene
and the Swimming Gene

M Y FATHER, HOWARD "RUSTY" STANLEY PIPES, was number eight of ten kids. With a last name like Pipes, I am sure at one time or another every one of his seven brothers went by the same nickname.

The Pipes family is part Nordic and part English. I take after my Grandma Emma, my father's mother. Out of the five kids in my family, I was the only one to inherit her tall stature and blue eyes.

The Pipes were a Salvation Army family. Most people know the Salvation Army from the bell ringers and red kettles that collect donations during the Christmas season. If not, they may recall Salvation Army donation trucks wheeling through neighborhoods scooping up used furniture or bags of old clothing.

If you look past the red kettles and donation trucks to the history of the Salvation Army, you'll learn it's a Christian organization formed in England during the 1860s. Members were taught to abstain from drinking, smoking, and taking drugs. Member-based brass bands were a way of drawing attention to the organization and its teachings. The group has always been a welcome refuge for addicts attempting to get their lives in order. When you worked for the Salvation Army, as my grandparents did, it was almost like being in the military. After marrying in 1913, my grandparents entered officer training school, and in 1914 they became probationary captains, stationed in first Minnesota and then Colorado. Captains were sent into communities to establish a presence and serve as faithful officers "in the war against sin and its consequences." After Colorado, my grandparents were posted in Fresno, California; Phoenix, Arizona; and Prescott, Arizona. Life in the Pipes household was strict and very regimented.

By 1941, the now very large Pipes family relocated to their final post in El Centro, an agricultural hub located some one hundred miles east of San Diego, California. To support the cause, everyone in the family was put to work. The girls were relegated to the kitchen to prepare food or clean, and the boys were sent out to the street to play music. They would be out under the broiling sun for hours at a time with their brass instruments trying to entice the drunks to come in for a free meal and a sermon. The kids were never allowed to come inside to eat until everyone else had been fed. No matter how miserable the weather, the drunks always came first. The Salvation Army fed and clothed the Pipes family, but the family was very poor.

Grandma Emma was a hard-working, no-nonsense kind of woman. Maybe it was because she had married an alcoholic and did not realize what she had gotten herself into until it was too late. Or maybe it was because, when you're surrounded by alcoholism day in and day out, there is not much room left in your world for nurturing your offspring. My father was most likely overlooked as a child, as were his brothers and sisters. How could he have possibly gotten much love or affection in such an environment? There just was not enough to spread around among ten children.

Grandma Emma herself never drank, but no matter how devoted she was to the Salvation Army's message of abstinence, she could not stop the disease from trickling down and saturating her children.

While the Salvation Army may have rescued my grandfather, it did not save the next generation. Of the ten kids, at least six were afflicted with alcoholism or struggled with alcohol use. My Aunt Ruthie died after falling and hitting her head, and it was rumored that she was drunk at the time.

The Pipes, however, were not without merit, and most became musicians and teachers. But the disease ran through nearly every one of them, which speaks to the strength of alcoholism's grip. Here my father and his siblings were raised in a strict household and witnessed firsthand the ravages of alcoholism every time a lost soul came teetering through the Salvation Army's doors, yet many of them still succumbed to the disease.

My mother, Adrienne Wade Spore Pipes, was the first-born child to Eugenia and Jim Spore. Mom was born in 1934, and her brother Bill joined the family a mere thirteen months later. Jim first worked as a state trooper and then later made a living as a claims adjuster for Travelers Insurance, initially in Syracuse, New York. Mom's side of the family is Dutch and English. My grandmother, whom we all called Ga'mee, was diagnosed with multiple sclerosis in 1942 at the age of thirty-nine and confined to a wheelchair for as long as I knew her. The family moved to San Diego in 1943, in large part because the icy winter sidewalks in New York made walking hazardous for someone with her condition, reliant on a cane. Ga'mee was very controlling, especially of my mother. Both were headstrong, which led to a miserable mother-daughter relationship. My mom would do just about anything to avoid coming home from school because she knew that as soon as she walked in the door, the hypercritical Ga'mee would be barking orders or on her case about something. Instead of subjecting herself to her mother's tyranny, she would escape by volunteering to babysit many of the kids in the neighborhood or, significantly for me, walking to the local pool to swim.

When the Spore family moved to San Diego from upstate New York, it was the middle of World War II and the whole region was in full war-time production supporting the defense industry. Food and fuel were rationed and housing was extremely scarce, so the Spores lived in the

Ramona area until they managed to buy a small house on Alabama Street in the Balboa Park neighborhood. It was one canyon over from the San Diego Zoo and down the street from a public pool where Mom and Uncle Bill used to swim. The water quality was not great back in the late 1940s and early 1950s, and Mom used to get severe ear infections. For her, it was still better than being at home.

Uncle Bill grew up to be a big, gregarious, good-looking guy, and did not seem to be affected by the situation at home like my mother was. He went on to swim competitively for the San Diego Swim Association for many years alongside his good friend and 1956 Olympian David "Daisy" Radcliff. While not quite Olympic caliber himself, Uncle Bill did go on to swim and play water polo at the University of California at Berkeley. While the alcoholic gene I inherited may have come from the Pipes side of the family, the swimming gene definitely came from the Spore side. It is strange to think that two different liquids, one toxic and the other therapeutic, would come to play such huge roles in my life.

Good girl falls for bad boy is an old cliché, but it rings true for my parents. They met at San Diego State University, where she was a straight-A, baton-twirling majorette and he played in the marching band. He was ten years older than she was and, at the time they met, had enrolled in and dropped out of college numerous times. That in itself didn't make Rusty a bad boy, but the fact that he had been married previously and was now divorced did. Back then, dating a divorcé was downright scandalous. Rusty, being quite a bit older than the more naïve Adrienne, also liked to party it up. As a musician, he had plenty of opportunities to drink and carouse when he and a few of his brothers and college friends formed a band called the Ten Men of Swing. By all accounts they were pretty good, and they stayed busy playing at dances and local night clubs.

I can see how Mom became smitten with Dad. He was good-looking, with dark hair, sparkling blue eyes, and adorable dimples, and he was definitely the life-of-the-party type. But what made him irresistible to her was that he played her very favorite instrument, the trombone. She, on the other hand, was a bit introverted and bookish, and she loved science. In a different era, Mom would have become a doctor. In fact, even today my Uncle Bill, who enjoyed a long and successful career as an OB/GYN physician, insists that his older sister should have been the doctor in the family because she was the one with all the smarts. Since female physicians were a rarity back then, she instead earned her degree in medical technology and eventually became a clinical laboratory scientist. By dating Dad, Mom was acting out against her tyrannical mother, who was unabashedly vocal in her opinion of the unsuitable pairing.

Mom and Dad first moved to Los Angeles, and my brother Mark was born shortly thereafter. Dad took a job working for Standard Brands for the summer. After less than a year in LA, Mom, Dad, and Mark moved to Laguna Beach, where Derek was born. Dad taught at Laguna Beach Junior High School for the next two years. Then he moved the family again, this time to San Jose, where he attended San Jose State University with high hopes of earning a Masters degree in music education. Mom worked full time at a local hospital, while Dad dutifully completed all of his coursework. However, when it was time to finish his thesis to complete his degree, he dropped the ball and never turned one in.

The next move took the Pipes family to Petaluma, where Kirsten was born in August of 1960. That fall Dad began teaching band at yet another junior high school. While he had a gift for teaching, he was also an accomplished musician. He could play just about every instrument and was especially strong on the trombone and string bass. But conducting was his true gift. Whenever he conducted, his bands performed exceptionally well. They would receive more recognition and higher honors than all the other junior high school bands in the area. The problem was, Dad couldn't handle the success. Instead of parlaying a great performance into something better, he'd respond by going on a bender.

And then everything would snowball out of control and it was time to move again.

That's one of the common things about alcoholics: they tend to attribute their unhappiness to their situation or surroundings. With Dad there always came a point when he was convinced that life would be much better somewhere else. There's a term in Alcoholics Anonymous (AA) for alcoholics who roam: "geographicals." Geographicals are always trying to run from their problems, desperately hoping the problems don't follow. Like most addicts, alcoholics never want to acknowledge that *they* are the problem. And you can't run from yourself.

CHAPTER **3**

I Adapted as Best I Could

I WAS BORN IN LOMPOC, CALIFORNIA, the "flower seed capital of the world," located about fifty-five miles north of Santa Barbara. That's where we moved in 1961 and where my little sister, Kerri, was born as well. We girls were the three Ks. In the household laundry, our underwear and socks were labeled K1, K2, and K3. With five kids under the age of seven and both parents working, one can only imagine the constant chaos under our roof.

As a child growing up, I rarely heard my parents express their love for one another. Words of affection just weren't used much in our household. Dad would come into our room to say good night to us, always smelling of alcohol and cigarettes. He'd draw cartoons in the darkness with the orange tip of his burning cigarette, then give us each a brief hug. That was the extent of his affections as far as I can recall. I can't remember crawling into his lap for a cuddle or catching a piggyback ride across the front lawn. I never saw him playing ball with my brothers. Even as a little girl, I had a sense that he didn't seem to like us very much.

Mom worked hard to give her kids the love and support they needed, but she was in what can only be described as constant survival mode. It must have taken all the energy she had just to keep her head above water, living with a drunk husband, five active kids, and an income that never seemed to be enough. To make ends meet, Mom worked nights as an on-call medical technologist in the laboratory at Lompoc Community Hospital. The job also gave her a brief respite from our crazy home life.

I adapted as best I could and learned to "self-soothe" long before that idea became a named parenting technique. My mid-March birthday made me a Pisces, and people born under this sign are believed to be dreamy and sensitive and often find reality to be harsh, cruel, and confusing. I often felt this way when I was little. My solution was a baby blanket I had had from the time I was born, which I dubbed my "Nightnight." Night-night was the most important thing in my small world, the anchor in my emotionally turbulent life. Whenever I needed comfort or reassurance, instead of going to Mom or Dad, I would retreat to my bedroom to hold Night-night tight against my cheek and suck my index finger, upside down. When I held that warm, silky blanket, magically the cold, hard edges of the world became soft. I felt safe.

All the Pipes kids began swimming as youngsters. The indoor pool in Lompoc was twenty-five yards long and six lanes wide. My introduction to swimming came through the YMCA's Learn to Swim program. First the instructors showed us how to be safe in the water, and then they taught us how to swim. The lessons I learned about healthy living, community service, and tackling challenges were invaluable. The Y made me feel as if I belonged.

I remember how safe and warm I felt walking into that natatorium for the first time. It was like walking into a protective bubble. For some reason the smell of chlorine seemed familiar and comforting to me, as did the sounds of kids splashing around, playing, laughing, and having fun. For a kid who wasn't getting much attention at home, it was all so appealing. I was only four years old, but I could already tell I felt happier in the water than I did anywhere else. Being in that pool and holding my Night-night were the two things that gave me the greatest sense of security and belonging.

Some of the other kids weren't too keen about getting into the water, and some even seemed petrified of it. They had to be coaxed, coddled, and prodded to put their heads under the water to simply learn how to blow bubbles. But I couldn't wait to try to stroke and kick toward the instructor's outstretched hands. I was an energetic kid to begin with, and my enthusiasm for the sport created a great outlet for all the excitement and energy I possessed. That combination served me well, and my swimming improved quickly, particularly my backstroke. When I swam backstroke, bystanders on the pool deck often took notice of my smooth and effortless stroke and would ask Mom how long I had been swimming. Due to my ability to execute near-perfect technique, when I was just five years old I was asked to join the Lompoc Marlins swim team.

That same year, I swam in my very first race, the 25-yard freestyle. We didn't wear goggles back then, so having your face in the water meant peering into a universe that was blurry and undefined. There were three girls in the race. I took second place, earning a bright red ribbon. Everyone was so excited by how I'd done, especially Mom. From the moment I saw the reaction I received from her, as well as from friends and family, I was hooked. Next time, I decided, I'd try to win the blue ribbon.

I didn't realize it at the time, but one of the main reasons I took to swimming was that it filled so many voids in my life. Unlike my life at home, swimming was structured and offered acceptance and approval. I may not have been getting much attention at home, but I was sure getting it in the pool. I was getting it from coaches, from other children's parents, and from my peers. They'd always tell me what a great job I had done after each of my races. I flourished under all this attention. I also quickly recognized the payoff—the better I swam, the more attention I received.

One of my first coaches was Mr. Cully. He was a big, burly man whom we all thought of as a second father. He spent a lot of time with us working on the basics. So much of swimming is technique. Yes, you have to be physically and aerobically strong and well trained, but if you don't have sound fundamentals, you're never going to get very far in the sport. There's a reason why when you watch the Olympic Games, all eight swimmers in an event are using a similar technique, no matter what part of the world they're from. Generations of great coaching minds have reached a consensus about what works and what doesn't work in elite swimming.

One of the best things about competitive swimming is that all the rewards are objective and tangible. The starter fires a pistol, and you swim across the pool as quickly as you can. If you record the fastest time, you're the winner. It's as simple as that. Unlike figure skating, diving, or gymnastics, there's nothing subjective about it. It doesn't matter if you're from Lompoc, Mission Viejo, Manhattan, or Mars. It doesn't matter whether your coach is world-famous Olympic coach Teri McKeever or an unknown John Smith. And it makes no difference whatsoever whether your parents drove you to the meet in a brand-new Bentley or a beat-up VW Bug. Just touch the wall first.

Another great thing about swimming is that each time you swim a race, your time is recorded. It's right there in black and white. In minutes, seconds, and tenths and hundredths of a second. And Mom dutifully jotted down each of our race results in little spiral notebooks, one for each of us. I still have mine. Each entry, written in her best penmanship, includes the date, the event, and my time. It's easy to chart your progress in swimming, and there's something exhilarating about trying to swim faster today than you did last month.

Competitive swimming must be one of the most orderly sports ever invented. Everything about it is neat and organized. There are only a few standardized strokes. Races and competition pools are uniform in length. There are black lines along the bottom of each lane that help guide the swimmer in a straight path, no bends or corners to negotiate. There are even black targets to alert the swimmers to the location of the walls. The brightly colored lane lines divide the width of the pool into equal sections. The fastest swimmers are positioned in the middle of the pool; the slower ones occupy the outside lanes. There is no team strategy here. Nobody trying to hold you back. No offense and no defense. No fancy plays or secret signs. You just swim.

When you are the parents of a brood of rambunctious youngsters, you try a variety of activities to engage them. Mark and Derek played instruments like tuba, trombone, and trumpet, and were also involved with 4-H. Kirsten was a Campfire Girl and I was a Bluebird. We also went to the Episcopal church every Sunday. But we were destined to become a swimming family. It would become our religion for a time, no doubt in large part because of Mom's love of the sport.

One of my favorite memories is from when I was about seven. The highlight of the Pipes kids' summer was to go to a YMCA camp in Sequoia and Kings Canyon National Parks. In the spring we'd go door-to-door selling cans of butter toffee peanuts for fifty cents to raise funds for tuition. The camp was in a beautiful setting with hundreds of acres of mature forest and a sprawling lake. Mom worked as the waterfront director and Dad ran the camp store selling soda, chips, candy bars, and bait.

While the YMCA Learn to Swim classes at home had challenged me to be a better swimmer, the lessons at camp took on a whole new dimension as they were held in the open water. As with all Y programs, you are given an opportunity to progress through the ranks, in this case from pollywog to guppy to minnow to flying fish to porpoise to shark. Everyone, of course, wanted to be a shark. In order to earn that distinction, you had to swim across Lake Sequoia. As an added incentive, any kid who also managed to swim back across the lake earned a big chocolate candy bar.

I tackled that lake crossing challenge as soon as I was old enough. There was a rowboat escort for me, with Mom paddling alongside, cheering me on. The lake was brilliant in the sunlight, glowing like a green gemstone. It seemed as far across as an ocean, but I kept swimming. And I made it. I could have stopped at that point, already having become one of the youngest campers to earn the shark patch, but I wanted more. After a brief rest, I made a decision. I was going to swim back and earn that big chocolate candy bar.

As I eased back into the water I wondered to myself, *Could I do it? What would happen if I failed and had to be pulled up into the boat? Would Mom be disappointed?* I pushed my fears aside and began stroking across the lake, seeking the safe harbor on the opposite shore. It seemed to take three times as long to get back, but just as I was about to give up I heard cheers from a small crowd waiting for me on the beach. I experienced a burst of energy and worked as hard as I could until I touched the sandy bottom. The crowd went wild. I had just become the youngest person to accomplish this feat in the history of the world! The scene overwhelmed my seven-year-old mind, and I reveled in the feeling of accomplishment and validation. I also knew I wanted to feel like that again.

Swim meets were one of the best ways to get our family together for a big outing. For transportation, we had a bright blue Volkswagen bus and a black VW Bug. To save money on gas, sometimes all seven of us would pile into the Bug and hit the road. Dad would be driving, Mom would be in the passenger seat, Mark and Kirsten and Derek would be in the back seat, and Kerri and I (the two smallest) would squeeze into the narrow space behind the back seat. It was fun for the two of us, our own secret world. We'd be tickling each other and squealing as the car bumped along the road and the radio blared out Top 20 hits like The Archies' "Sugar, Sugar" and Sly and the Family Stone's "Hot Fun in the Summertime."

But these trips weren't always all fun and games. Once we were heading up a steep hill on our way back to Lompoc from Santa Barbara when the car broke down. Late at night, we found ourselves stranded by the side of the road. It was freezing cold, and the darkness was terrifying. Mom and Dad started arguing about whose fault the breakdown was. They seemed to be arguing a lot more at that time, about everything from the scarcity of money to Dad's excessive drinking. At night their voices were so loud they often woke me. Sometimes I would get out of bed, creep halfway down the stairs and, with a knot in my stomach as big as a basketball, listen to them scream at each other. I wanted to make them stop fighting, but I didn't know how. *Maybe I needed to be a better daughter. Maybe I needed to ask for less and not cause any problems. Maybe then they would stop.*

Sitting there cold and stranded on the side of the road, I kept thinking about the way they argued. In the past they had kept the fights private, at home. But now they were doing it in public. One time I even heard Dad threatening Mom with leaving. And on this night, Dad's anger reached a new level, and it was aimed directly at Mom. I can still see the veins bulging on the side of my father's neck as he shouted at her, "If you're such an expert at everything, figure it out yourself!" Mark and Derek were off to the side of the car, eyes downcast and feet pawing the ground nervously. Kerri started to cry, and Kirsten tried to shush her.

I was scared to death we'd never get back home, and I feared my father would abandon us right then and there. All I wanted was to be at home where I could crawl into my warm bed and clutch my Night-night; then everything would be okay. Just then a stranger stopped, and we were rescued. It was one of the last times I can remember my family all being together, and it was one of the scariest experiences of my childhood.

CHAPTER 4

Every Second We Dropped,
We Earned a Dime

S WIMMING HAD BECOME THE CENTERPIECE of the Pipes' family life. When it became clear that we had talent, Mom introduced us to a rewards system: for every tenth of a second we took off of our best time, we would earn a penny; for every second we dropped, we earned a dime. That seemed like a lot of money to us at the time, and we knew we had the opportunity to really cash in because just about every meet would bring personal records, or PRs. When I was a teen-ager, the rewards changed. If we broke such-and-such record we'd get something we really wanted, like a pair of tennis shoes or a cool pair of ski glasses, the kind with the reflective lenses that were all the rage back then.

Those memories are good ones. But they are few and too far between. The arguing. How I remember the arguing. Children of alcoholics, find-ing the memories painful to recall, learn sooner or later that it's often safer to forget. It seems Mom was in the same boat. She later told me that she has almost no memory of our time in Lompoc. I, however, have lots of memories of my swimming life there. Like the time I swam five events in a meet for the Lompoc Marlins and won four first-place blue ribbons and one second-place red ribbon. I must have been all of six or seven. I was already an "all or nothing" competitor, so I asked my friend Lori Krebs if I could buy her first place award so I'd have all five. She politely declined. No amount of persuasion or negotiation would get her to change her mind.

I also remember the first time Mr. Cully told us to swim a mile. At the time I had no understanding of what a mile meant. I went ten 100s, which seemed to take forever, and I stopped.

"Is that a mile, Mr. Cully?" I asked.

He shook his head and said, "No, Karlyn. Keep going."

I put my head back down and swam some more, struggling back and forth across the pool one laborious length at a time. Finally, convinced I surely must have swum far enough, I stopped again.

"Is that enough?" I asked, huffing and puffing.

"No, Karlyn. You're almost there—keep going."

I don't know how I did it, but I finally swam enough laps to make a mile. I hadn't known how far a mile was or how long it would take, but I knew I wasn't going to get out of that darn pool until I was done. I was going to rise to the challenge.

I distinctly remember the first time I ever saw an Olympic-length, 50-meter pool. The whole family had driven up to Lemoore to race at the Navy Wings of Gold swim meet. That pool seemed almost as far across as Lake Sequoia. It was a pretty big meet, and the racing lasted well into the long summer's night. I swam the 50-meter breaststroke, and it must have taken me a good seventy strokes to make it to the other end. Our Lompoc pool felt like a backyard kiddy pool compared to this one. The top eight swimmers won custom-made medals, not ribbons like we earned back at home. After the race was over, the results were announced, and all the kids who had won awards were gathered together for a group photograph. The winner got to stand on the highest spot on the podium, second place the next highest, and so on. I placed seventh, putting me near the end of the line, but still earning me a beautiful medal. I was accustomed to winning most of the time back home, so this was a new experience. It motivated me to try harder and swim faster. I wanted gold.

A few years later, I remember watching the 1972 Summer Olympic Games. Every night, my sisters and I would sit on the living room floor glued to our brand-new color TV set. It was inspiring to see Australia's Shane Gould win three gold medals and be recognized as the top female swimmer of the meet. I decided I wanted to go to the Olympics too. Not for the gold medals and the glory like most kids with an Olympic dream. I had a different dream. I wanted all the free stuff they got. The swimmers who made the Munich team were outfitted from head to toe with brand-name sweats, tennis shoes, hats, cameras, and all sorts of cool freebies. I was sold. This was taking Mom's reward system to a whole new level.

CHAPTER 5

The Security Was Worth the Pain

S WIMMING WAS GOING WELL, but I was still looking for ways to feel secure at home. One day when I was seven, I went into my room and noticed Night-night wasn't there. My first thought was that it must be in the wash. I went down to look for it in the laundry room, but couldn't find it. I started tearing up the house looking for it. "Mark, have you seen my blanket?" He shook his head. "Kirsten, do you know where my blanket is?" She also shook her head no. I even asked the babysitter. I fretted about it for hours. Finally my parents came home, and I accosted them in a panic as soon as they made it through the front door.

"Mom and Dad, I can't find my blanket," I said. "Have either of you seen it?"

They glanced at one another before looking back at me.

"We gave it to the trash man," Dad said. "We told him to give it to his daughter."

"Y-you gave away my blanket?" I asked, my eyes welling.

"You're a big girl now, Karlyn," Mom said. "You don't need it anymore."

"But you didn't even ask me," I said.

"His daughter needs it more than you do," Mom said. "Don't worry. I'm sure she'll take good care of it."

At this point, my Night-night wasn't my parents' only concern about me. They'd spent years trying anything they could to get me to stop sucking my finger as well, including having the dentist place a metal apparatus with four prongs on the roof of my mouth. It made eating a challenge and tore up my tongue, but I stubbornly figured out a way to get my finger in anyway. The security it brought was worth the pain. Even Mom's pleas to stop it because "you are wrecking your teeth" had no effect.

Giving away my blanket must have been a last-ditch attempt to stop what they considered childish behavior. They didn't know that when I held my Night-night it helped me feel safe and secure in our unpredictable home. I begged, pleaded, and cried, but my parents stuck to their story. I was a sensitive child to begin with, but this turn of events crushed me like a bug in a gutter. I was devastated. My blanket had buffered me from the hardness of the world, and now it was gone. They'd given away my security.

The next week I lay in wait for the garbage truck to come back. When I finally heard it rumbling up the street, I ran outside and explained my dilemma to the trash man. I told him how important that blanket was to me. I told him maybe we could give his daughter one of my stuffed toys in exchange for it. I invited him to pick out any one he wanted. He didn't know what in the world I was talking about. Heartbroken, I felt my anchor was gone and I was set adrift. I now doubted the validity of my parents' story, and I retreated back into the house. I tried sleeping with a towel, but it never had that same ability to shield me from the pain of the world, the ability to help me disappear.

Desperate to find something to give me some semblance of the security that Night-night had represented, I knew that I had to adapt. I had to change.

Boys, from what I could see from observing Mark and Derek, could be detached. They didn't feel. They didn't hurt when someone took their blankets away. If I could become more like a boy, then I could put boy-like armor around myself too. I was already athletic and strong from all the swimming I'd been doing, and I could run fast and jump high. That was atypical of little girls back then. Although my hair was already short, I had it cut over my ears. I took to wearing hand-me-down jeans, Chuck Taylor sneakers, and Hang Ten t-shirts. Mom tried to get me to wear dresses, but I refused. At swim meets, I'd walk into the women's locker room only to be stopped by women saying, "I'm sorry, little boy, but this is the girls' bathroom." Instead of feeling embarrassed, I took it as a huge compliment. I had achieved my goal. I had become a tomboy.

Life went on as usual for us until the day when Mom had had enough. After a particularly volatile shouting match with my father, she hastily threw some things into an old suitcase and stormed out of the house. I heard the door slam behind her. From my upstairs bedroom window I could see her walk down the driveway and get into the Bug. I started to tremble. I was so scared. My eyes got misty, but I didn't cry. Tomboys don't cry, no matter what. Even if Mommy was leaving. I had already sensed Dad emotionally abandoning us, but now Mom was leaving us too? She started the car and backed it up. But when she got to the end of the drive, she stopped. In horror, I watched as she started to bang her head against the steering wheel. She sat like that for what seemed an eternity, just banging her head. She couldn't do it. She couldn't bring herself to leave us kids behind. For the first time in my life, I saw that I wasn't the only one who was unhappy. For the thousandth time, I wished I still had Night-night. Even a tomboy can't disappear.

CHAPTER 6

My First Taste of Fame

I N THE SUMMER OF 1970, when I was eight, we moved to Chula Vista, at that time a midsized town, located south of San Diego and only a few miles north of the Mexican border. Once again, Dad felt that life would magically be better somewhere else. We always seemed to have a difficult time making ends meet, even with both of my parents working, and I'm sure that factored into the decision. Too much money, I can see now, was going toward my father's liquor bills. All I knew then was that I'd need to make new friends and join a new swim team. Mom went kicking and screaming. I remember listening through their bedroom door early one Sunday morning as they argued about the move. Mom liked Lompoc—or Lom*puke*, as my father would derisively refer to it. She disliked the weather, but enjoyed the small-town feel, the close-knit community, the schools, and her job at the lab. Besides, moving to Chula Vista meant we would be closer to Ga'mee, and that was the last thing she wanted. But as much as Mom managed all the details of our daily lives, Dad had final say on any big decisions, so Chula Vista it was.

Once settled, we joined a swim team called the Chula Vista Aquatics Association, or CVAA. Our team trained at Loma Verde, a brand-new 50-meter outdoor pool. Since it was fall and we'd recently turned our clocks back for the end of daylight savings, the after-school workouts were in the dark. I hated it. I've never liked being cold. And the pool's cavernous locker rooms were always damp and chilly. But worse than that, I knew what was coming after I suited up. It would be time to get wet. Swimmers can have an odd relationship with the water. While most of us love swimming, we dread getting in. There's something about the initial shock when your body hits the water that is intrinsically unpleasant. And it doesn't seem to get any easier, no matter how long you have been in the sport. I have watched teammates stand on a freezing-cold pool deck wearing nothing but a skimpy bathing suit and shivering for long stretches before mustering the courage to dive in, even though they know it's much warmer in the water than out. You also know that once you're in, it's going to get uncomfortable. You didn't show up to swim leisurely laps or to play sharks and minnows. You came to train and to work, and it's going to be hard. There might even be some pain involved. Even as an eight-year-old I knew this. From the beginning, I found my new situation intimidating before I even swam a stroke.

Compounding my angst was the fact I didn't know any of the kids, and it quickly became apparent that they were bigger, stronger swimmers and much more competitive than I was. I'd been accustomed to being a shark in Lompoc, but now I was a minnow again. I felt completely out of my league. I was cold all the time and, truth be told, swimming at night scared me. I started making excuses to get out of practice. I'd tell the coach, Ricky Evans, I had a headache or a stomachache. He bought into it the first few times, but eventually said, "Karlyn, this is the third time you've pulled this stunt. If you get out of the pool right now, I'm kicking you off the A Team and you'll be relegated to the B Team." That sounded fine to me. I just wanted a hot shower, which I got. I must have stood under that warm stream of water for twenty or thirty minutes while the rest of the team continued to practice.

But my grand plan was pretty shortsighted because the B Team swimmers were a lot slower and the workouts were boring. I wasn't challenged at all. Plus, the only kids I'd befriended, Suzy Kovac and Heidi Lagergren, were both on the A Team. So I had to pay my dues on the B Team, swallow my pride, and ask to please be promoted back up. It took almost six months, but I made it.

Mark and Derek swam for CVAA for a season, but then lost interest. We girls, however, were swimming up a storm, and Mom was the first to praise us for our accomplishments. Since we were dropping our times at just about every meet, she was digging into her purse and doling out monetary rewards right and left. I used my earnings about as wisely as can be expected for an eight-year-old: to buy candy and soda at the meet snack bars. On her end, Mom learned to be resourceful with her limited budget. When Lycra "speed suits" came into fashion, we couldn't afford to buy them so she made them for us using the new material. The three Ks were treated to special meals too. Mom would prepare hamburgers before we swam. It became a tradition, and my sisters and I ate hamburgers all the time, even for breakfast. Not Mark and Derek, though. It seemed this was to be the price they paid for quitting the team. Derek later resentfully griped, "If you don't swim in this family, you ain't shit."

The assistant coaches at CVAA, Steve Yamamoto and Ken Thiltgen, were such positive influences that by age ten I rarely missed a practice and often had perfect attendance. They both made swimming fun, and I wanted to swim well for them. Our girls 10-and-under 200-yard free relay broke the Southern California Age Group record. Each of us on the relay squad swam under thirty seconds, and together we dipped under the two-minute barrier. It was the first time in my swimming career that I got a taste of what true teamwork could accomplish. To celebrate, we went to Farrell's Ice Cream Parlor and gorged on a thirty-scoop sundae called The Zoo. Sirens sounded and bells clanged as a team of employees paraded around the restaurant with our mountainous dessert (appropriately topped with miniature plastic monkeys, giraffes, and elephants). I don't think I've ever eaten so much ice cream, whipped cream, and cherries in my life.

A few months later, my teammates and I couldn't wait to open up our issues of *Swimming World* and see our names in print as a result of our record-breaking feat. When the magazine finally arrived, I couldn't stop beaming. There we were, in the same publication that wrote about swimming superstars like Shirley Babashoff, Rick DeMont, and John Naber. We were famous!

CHAPTER 7

"So . . . How'd You Do?"

K IRSTEN AND I WERE GETTING ACCOLADES from just about every-where and everyone, with one exception: Dad. In the beginning, he'd come to the occasional meet, but never sober. My friends and I would be underneath the bleachers, playing card games like Slap and Crazy Eights and eating space food sticks and dry Jell-O out of the box, killing time between races. Then one of them would say, "Hey, what's wrong with your dad? He's acting really silly." I'd try to laugh it off, but it made me feel ashamed.

Eventually Dad just stopped having much to do with our swimming. Mom shuttled us back and forth to practices and drove us to all the meets. Not one to sit around and do nothing while we competed all day long, Mom made herself useful by volunteering. She started as a timer, then moved up to clerk of course at the registration table. After becoming certified, she began officiating as a stroke and turn judge. Eventually she became so involved and proficient that she moved up the ranks to become meet referee. In later years, she advanced even further, officiating at Junior and Senior Nationals and at the Olympic Trials.

Not Dad. Since our move to Chula Vista, he seemed to just want to stay home and sit. On weekdays, when he came home from work, which was usually when school let out around 3:30, he'd plant himself on a stool in the garage and while away the hours smoking cigarettes and drinking beer.

On weekends, he'd sit in the same spot doing the same thing all day long. We would burst into the garage all excited from a meet, and he'd look up at us with a glassy expression on his face and ask, "So . . . how'd you do?" We'd fall all over ourselves as we told him all about it, giving him the blow-by-blow of what events we'd swum and where we'd placed. We'd show him our medals and ribbons and he'd smile and nod and say, "Great job! Great job!" And, for a split second, he seemed really proud of us. But then, a little while later, after we'd put our swim stuff away and settled down, he'd wander into the house and ask, "So . . . how'd you dooooooo?" Kirsten and I would give each other furtive glances and, in an attempt to be good sports about it, we'd repeat the whole story all over again. By the time he questioned us a third time, though, we just rolled our eyes and walked away.

I didn't have many close friends, and those I did have were never invited to play or sleep over, because I never knew what was going to be there when I walked through the door. It's embarrassing to see someone completely smashed in the middle of the day like my father would be. And later on, when my brothers started getting into drugs and alcohol, having friends over was even more risky.

Everyone in the alcoholic's family becomes adept at tiptoeing around the elephant in the middle of the room. The amount of dissimulation that goes into trying to conceal the truth from the outside world is emotionally draining. You assume roles as if you were actors in the alcoholic's play. In my family the roles played out as follows: Kirsten was the oldest girl, and she became the "good" child, never disappointing and always taking on responsibility beyond her years. Mark and Derek became the slackers, the ones who got attention, but for all the wrong reasons. I was the athlete, trying to make everyone like me and entertaining them with my feats of aquatic excellence. Kerri, the youngest, was literally a performer, taking up theatre. And Mom. She played the sensible one, the one who tried to ensure that all of our needs were taken care of in a very practical way.

Fortunately, Dad wasn't much of an angry drunk, so there weren't too many violent public displays that I can recall. There were, however, the frequent shouting matches with Mom and the boys, and sometimes there'd be slapping and threats of violence like "getting the belt." But he was not habitually physically abusive. As I look back on it, Dad was mostly just an impassive, hollow drunk.

While often indifferent, he could still be very controlling. Once I came home from swim practice to find him and Mom sitting in the living room together in complete silence. Just sitting there, with Dad reading the paper. When Mom tried to retrieve her sewing, he snapped, "No! You just sit there!" So she sat there for another ten minutes or so. Then, no doubt getting restless again, she tried to turn on the television, but he snapped, "No! Turn it off, damn it! Just sit there!" Maybe it was a way to punish her. Whatever Dad's motive, I could see sometimes it was better for all concerned for Mom to just take it rather than fight back.

Another day we all went to Mission Bay for a barbecue. My father, as was usually the case, manned the grill. He juggled a can of beer in one hand and an oversized fork in the other. My brothers and sisters and I were all having fun, splashing and playing games in the water, looking forward to eating marinated flank steak, a family favorite. My father was drunk even before the charcoals had been doused with lighter fluid, so we probably should have foreseen what happened next. While we were swimming, he accidentally dropped the steak onto the sand and then tried to wipe it clean with a paper towel to cover up what he'd done. We didn't know it at the time, of course, but we put two and two together when lunch was finally served and we kids, with mouths watering, took our first sandy bites. No one dared say a word. No amount of grape soda could wash away the grittiness or my disappointment.

I was too young to understand it at the time, but Dad was drowning. He may have seemed harmless enough as he planted himself on his stool every day, but the truth was he was in just as much peril as someone who couldn't swim pitching themselves overboard. Early on my mother tried to throw him a life preserver, but he failed to accept it. Just as I found out in my own life, you cannot help someone who doesn't want to be helped.

CHAPTER **8**

Fighting to Survive

M Y FATHER'S BIG FAMILY WAS SPREAD far and wide across the country; we rarely saw any of them. Sometimes we'd get together with Aunt Doris and her kids, Patti and Misty, up in Escondido. On very rare occasions, we'd make a trip up to Anaheim to see Uncle Don, his wife, Yvonne, and their four kids. We did go to Disneyland once, but that was a rare family vacation. We did, however, spend the holidays with Mom's brother, Uncle Bill, and his wife, Auntie Gracie. Uncle Bill loved that we'd become competitive swimmers just like he had been. Every time we got together he wanted to hear all about how we were doing in the pool. Uncle Bill and Aunt Gracie and their kids—Eric, Brock, Dain, and Ingrid—lived in Point Loma. On Christmas the kids would be outside playing games or riding skateboards and bikes, while the adults would be inside, drinking and socializing. Whenever we were together like this, it felt as if I were finally a part of a normal family.

I had a very different feeling at my house. Even in our big family, I never felt as if I had anyone to turn to or anyone I could count on. I felt alone. One memorable example of this dates from when I was ten. We had developed a flea problem in the house, and for some reason I was the one who was getting bitten the most. My ankles and legs were covered in flea bites. The constant itching was so bad, I had made myself bleed from scratching. I went to Mom and told her, "Mom, we have fleas. Look!" I showed her my welts and scabs. She gave me some ointment to put on them, but she didn't offer to do anything about the infestation, and neither did Dad. Looking back, I realize we probably didn't have the money. At the time, however, their apparent lack of interest in my welfare felt telling.

I retreated to my room and started to cry, mostly out of frustration. The lack of action from my parents made me feel helpless. That's when I realized I would need to take matters into my own hands. I went to the kitchen, got a plastic cup from the cabinet, and filled it with water. Then I went back to my room, locked the door, and took off all my clothes. I sat naked in the middle of the room and waited for the fleas to start jumping on me. I was using myself as bait. My skin was sensitive enough to feel when one of them landed on me. I'd pick it up, angrily squeeze it between my fingernails, and drop it into the cup. One after another after another. By the time I was done, the surface of the water was covered with dead or dying fleas. *Take that!* I thought as I watched the ones still alive struggle sideways with their tiny legs as they tried to escape their doom. I had taken matters into my own hands. I was destroying those menacing little bastards. My strategy proved so successful that I did it more than once. But more importantly, I had reinforced in my mind that no one was going to protect me. If I wanted to survive, I'd have to do it by myself, no matter what it took.

I was fighting to survive at the pool, too. CVAA had a big shake-up when I was twelve. Coaches Steve and Ken moved on, and a new guy was brought in. Mom decided we'd be better off swimming for the Coronado Navy Swim Association (CNSA), because it had a stronger program and was coached by Olympic gold medalist Mike Troy. The move was a big deal, for a number of reasons. At CVAA, I'd been able to ride my bike to practice because the pool was only a mile or so from our house, but now

Mom would need to drive us thirty minutes each way to Coronado. We were upping the ante big time, because the dues were more expensive too, and the commitment also entailed midweek early morning workouts for the first time.

CNSA was making a name for itself and attracting a lot of the best swimmers in San Diego County, yet only a few actually lived in Coronado. Some of the kids were coming in from La Jolla, others from Point Loma or Clairemont Mesa, and now a whole bunch of us were commuting from Chula Vista. The Kimura family drove the farthest, coming more than forty miles all the way from Oceanside.

So now the alarm clock went off at 4:20 a.m., and Mom would drive Kirsten and me to practice in our VW bus. It is pitch black at that hour, no matter what time of year it is. While we were swimming, Mom would slide into the back seat to sneak in a little more sleep. In the beginning, I wasn't old enough to actually swim with Mike Troy, so I swam with Coach Ken Herron, on the junior development team. The minimum age to be on the senior team, Troy's group, was thirteen. But even the group I swam with was filled with really fast kids like Leslie Mendez, the 11–12 national age group record holder in the 100 fly; Laurie Purdy, who had the fastest 200 medley in the country; and many others. It was intimidating, to be sure, and somehow didn't seem fair. For the past four years I had battled my way up from minnow to shark with CVAA. At the end-of-summer banquet, I'd even been awarded the 11–12 girls' high-point team award. But here I was again, being thrown right back into minnow land. It wasn't that I was slow; it was just that at CNSA the competition was that much better. This was now a familiar theme, and I knew I would need to pay my dues once again before I would grow strong enough to belong in this pond too.

Life at home was getting worse. I began to think that perhaps if I changed my behavior, it would change my father's behavior. I became a chameleon. I learned later that this is a common coping strategy for the child of an alcoholic. First, I tried not talking. After all, silence is golden, right? So I didn't make a peep for days. But that strategy backfired. My silence started an argument between my parents at dinner, and the next thing you knew, the meatloaf was flying, hitting the ceiling. The other kids scattered from the table, but I was too slow and got a sharp slap across the face.

Next, I tried talking all the time. I decided that maybe if I became extra chatty, everyone would notice and like me. I became quite adept at bragging. But that failed as well. I quickly learned that people do not want to be around a braggart.

Finally, I took a page from Mark and Derek's book and I began to misbehave. My brothers were running with the wrong crowd, bailing on classes, and getting into all kinds of trouble. They'd started sniffing the glue they'd used to build their model airplanes years before, and in Chula Vista they graduated to experimenting with a variety of other drugs. While I wasn't interested in doing drugs, I did act out in my own way, morphing from an upstanding A student into the class clown. From the back of the room I would crack funny jokes or whisper snide remarks to make my fellow students laugh. It disappointed my teachers. Naturally, my grades fell, but in an unhealthy way, my confidence grew.

Dad was getting drunk on a regular basis; my brothers were distant, moody, combative, and uncommunicative; and Mom was not being more demonstrably affectionate toward me. In my young, insecure mind, all this had to be my fault. Somehow I must have contributed to this dysfunctional family. If I were a better kid, life in our household would be so much better. My parents would accordingly shower me with love and affection. The fighting would stop. Mark and Derek wouldn't be so angry all the time. Kirsten would stop trying to be the boss of me. Then, like the family in *The Brady Bunch*, we would happily spend time together. But every day when I came home from school or swim practice, things were always the same.

Remember *The Wizard of Oz*? Every year, one of the television networks would broadcast it. It always aired on Sunday night, presumably because it was considered ideal programming for the entire family. Sadly, from the very first time I saw it, I didn't buy into the message "There's no place like home." What if the home you experienced didn't leave you feeling warm and comforted at all? From a very early age I could see that Mom was trying to do the best she could under the circumstances, but I didn't feel safe and I didn't feel secure. Life was fraught, filled with tension and uncertainty. Thankfully, I could disappear into my dreamlike watery world. It had become my home. The water had replaced Night-night. There was nothing to hold on to in any other part of my life. I promised myself that if I was lucky enough to find my way over the rainbow, I'd stay in the Land of Oz forever.

Whenever Father's Day or Dad's birthday would come around, we girls would ask him what he wanted for the occasion, and his pat response was "a little peace and quiet." What he needed a respite from, I never knew. He seemed to have the most uncomplicated life of anyone I knew. His only responsibilities were to go to work, come home, claim his stool, and drink. It wasn't until many years later, when I started to combat my own issues with alcohol, that I realized it was probably the ugly voices in his head he wanted relief from.

CHAPTER 9

Recovery: Zero Hour

T HE NEXT PASSAGE OF MY LIFE plays like a cross between a bad horror flick, where you scream at the screen, "Don't go into the basement, you idiot!" and a disaster film where you watch the world blow up in slow motion. For the moment, however, fast-forward twenty years.

In the parlance of AA, I had become what's referred to as a "shut-in." My roommate had moved out of the house we were renting in Coronado, and now my boyfriend, Dave, a merchant marine, was paying part of the rent. Dad, who lived in the back in a converted garage apartment, was also contributing to the rent. My preoccupation was alcohol. I was using my credit card to fuel my addiction. The only job I still had—lifeguarding—would be coming to an end soon because I had been calling in sick for the past month. I couldn't perform my job anyway. The symptoms of my "illness"—bloodshot eyes, the shakes, and alcohol-infused breath—had become impossible to hide.

On my thirty-first birthday, I managed to go out with my friends Mark and Sandy to the Brigantine, a local bar and restaurant. I didn't want to go, but they talked me into it. Everyone was drinking and laughing and having a good time. Once upon a time, that had been me as well. I had been the quintessential life of the party. But not now. That person had disappeared long ago. Now I felt detached, as if I were from another country or even another world. I took a drink. Nothing happened. I had a second drink. Same result. The alcohol had no effect, none whatsoever. I vanished into the bathroom and did a line of coke, but that didn't do it either. Karlyn, the once energetic and fun party girl, was long gone. She had been replaced by the shell of a human being, consumed by self-loathing and living for one thing only: *that next drink*. But the high was gone. There was no buzz. I had become numb. There was no more "happy place." I went home and, as usual, passed out.

After that night, I didn't leave the house for a month. My world had become one soggy mess of utter despair. If I could just get some sleep, I told myself, I would wake up fresh and be able to sort through everything that was happening. Maybe I could actually get my foot out the door. But I couldn't sleep. All I could do was pass out from drinking.

At this time, Dave was at sea on one of his lengthy cruises. He wrote regularly, as he always did. As each letter arrived, I'd dutifully open it, staple the pages together, and put it with the others. When he was away, he wrote beautiful letters insisting he loved me. But whenever we were together, we couldn't go more than twenty-four hours without being at each other's throats. As for love, what did I know? I was certainly comfortable using Dave. He was, after all, helping me financially, which meant more money could be used to buy my booze. I didn't even feel guilty about it. My mentality, forged years ago, was to take whatever I could get, no matter whom I hurt, including Dave. In fact, I was convinced that the entire world owed me something.

The Pipes DNA is screwed up, plain and simple. That was my thought. Maybe there's just no fighting genetics? Some kids are meant to be brilliant pianists; others, gifted mathematicians. Some, like Mark Spitz or Shane Gould, are meant to be great swimmers. Me, I was meant to be a drunk. There is such a thing as predetermination, isn't there? And Dad? Well, maybe I had had him all wrong all these years. Once you know what you are, what's the point in trying to fight it? I knew what I was and, surprisingly, I was okay with it.

Over the years, Mom, bless her heart, had remained in denial that I had a major problem. Or if she knew, she chose not to address it. She had no idea how low I'd sunk, nor did she realize that her golden child, the one-time swimming prodigy with the can't-miss future, was on the edge of sinking so deep that breaking the surface and breathing again would surely be impossible.

Mom called on April 16, 1993. It was a Thursday.

"How are you doing, Karlyn?"

"I'm sick," I said.

"What's wrong?"

What's wrong? I scoffed to myself. *For starters, I can barely keep my beloved alcohol down anymore. I wrestle the glass, bottle, or jug with shaky hands, finally manage to get some of it down my throat, then immediately find myself racked with nausea. I can't hold a job. I can't be around people. What's wrong?! If you only knew . . .*

"Karlyn?"

"I just, uh, don't feel well," I finally mumbled.

"Well, you've been sick for almost a month now," she said. "You need to go to the doctor."

"I can't."

"You can't, or you won't?" she asked.

"You know I don't have health insurance, Mom."

"I'll pay for your visit to the doctor. I think it's important, Karlyn."

"I don't want to go," I said.

"You *have* to go," she said, in that judgmental tone that reminded me of when I was a teenager trying to get out of swim practice.

"*I don't have to do anything.* Why is everyone always trying to tell me what to do?"

"I'm only trying to help you, Karlyn."

"I don't want your help. Leave me alone!" I shouted, hanging up the phone.

I went to the kitchen and pulled the vodka from the freezer. My hands were shaking, my head was throbbing, and my heart was racing. *How dare she?! I'm thirty-one—how is it she can still make me feel as if I'm letting her down? The only person I'm letting down is me, and I'm an adult. Besides, it's none of her business.* It seemed as if we had always had this turbulent relationship. From day one, she had been more likely to be stoic toward me than soothing. I took several slugs of vodka before I settled down. My body relaxed a bit, but only momentarily. Mom called back.

"You can't be sick for this long, Karlyn," she said. "You need to get checked out. I've made an appointment with Dr. Nichols."

"Andy Nichols?"

"Yes, Andy Nichols," she said. "Your appointment is tomorrow morning at 9:00. I'll be there at 8:30 to pick you up."

"But . . . "

This time it was Mom who hung up.

How humiliating, I thought. Andy Nichols was someone I had swum with at CNSA. He was a national-caliber breaststroker who went on to swim at Stanford and then attended medical school. The trajectory of his life had taken him somewhere up into the stratosphere. The trajectory of mine, meanwhile, had left me somewhere at the bottom of the ocean, scattered like broken pieces of a ship wreck. I reached for the vodka again. *Oh shit! The jig is up. There's no way you're going to be able to lie yourself out of this one.* Andy would take one look at me and see I was a complete fraud. He'd wonder what had happened to the little girl Coach Troy had held in such high regard—the one with the cute smile, a tough-as-nails work ethic, and that rare natural ability everyone admired? *Shit, shit, shit . . . The jig is definitely up.*

The next thing I knew, I was coming to on the kitchen floor after yet another blackout. I had a bump where my head had struck the breakfast bar, and a split lip. Luckily, the cap on the vodka jug lying beside me was still intact, so none of the contents had spilled out. I sat up and started drinking. Within moments, it all went black again.

I came to at 6:00 in the morning and immediately had a drink. Then I passed out again. Mom woke me at 8:30. She thought I was just sick with some virus or such. I *was* sick—just not in the way she thought. I was so drunk I was having a hard time focusing on her face. I knew the first thing I had to do was tell her I was an alcoholic. I'd known it for years, ever since I stumbled across a pamphlet on alcoholism in the locker room at the lifeguard station, but I'd never actually said it to anyone. Now I had to find the strength to confess. To my mother. To the one person I wanted to disappoint least of all, in part because I knew her life had already been filled with so many disappointments.

Mom looked at me and I looked at her. I had no idea what her reaction was going to be. I took a deep breath to brace myself.

"M-Mom, I . . . I think I'm an alcoholic," I said. My words hung in the air.

I had thought the sky was going to open up and a bolt of lightning was going to come cracking down on my head. I deserved it. But Mom just looked at me with compassion and said, "Okay, let's get you to the doctor."

She didn't scream or yell. She didn't cry. She didn't throw her hands up in disgust or shake her head in disapproval. She simply accepted it. She just wanted to get her daughter help. Seeing that, and knowing she really meant it, gave me a tremendous sense of relief.

When we got to the doctor's office, it turned out Andy Nichols wouldn't be seeing me after all. It would instead be one of his colleagues, Dr. Dill. Coronado is a small town, but sometimes it can feel as small as a surfboard. I'd been serving Dr. Dill off and on for years as a waitress at Bula's Pub and Eatery. At some point I had surely been inebriated when I waited on him. As Mom and I waited in the examining room, I knew there was no hiding my condition anymore. As soon as Dr. Dill smelled my breath, took my blood, and checked my urine, it was going to be pretty obvious. On the one hand, I was scared, because I knew everything was about to change and I had no idea what lay ahead; but on the other hand, I was somewhat optimistic, because now that Mom was in the know and on my side, I didn't feel so desperately alone with my litany of problems.

"Dr. Dill, I think I'm an alcoholic," I said quickly when he entered the room.

His response was as nonjudgmental and matter-of-fact as Mom's had been: "Well, let's find you a bed in a rehab, Karlyn."

There was no surprise. No anger. No drama. And no bolt of lightning. When you've been trapped for so long in an addiction—when your world has ground to a halt in all areas not alcohol-related—you don't realize that it's only *your* world that has stopped moving.

Dr. Dill's staff immediately started calling around, and they found a bed at Sharp Cabrillo Hospital in Point Loma. I was told to pack for a few days. Back at my house, as I feigned pulling some things together, Mom went off to the bathroom. Seeing my chance, I made a beeline for the refrigerator. My Smirnoff stash was calling to me. I was determined to have one last drink. "One more for the road" had always been my favorite mantra. *What harm could there be in that? It would only take a second. What difference did it make? I was on my way to rehab.* My body desperately needed it. My psyche desperately needed it. I swung open the door of the freezer and reached for the jug, just as I'd done a thousand times before. But as soon as my hand made contact with the handle and I started to slide the jug out, I heard the bathroom door open. Mom appeared in the corner of my eye. My hand froze. She couldn't see what I was doing—my actions were concealed by the freezer door. I carefully pushed the closed jug back in and slowly closed the door.

CHAPTER 10

Life Without the Elephant

WITH REFLECTION AND SOBRIETY, I can see now that my father's disease affected Mark and Derek most of all. After the move to Chula Vista, and with few positive role models in their lives, they spun totally out of control. Mom and Dad kept getting calls in the middle of the night from the police station. "Your son has been picked up and arrested," the voice on the other end of the line would say. When Derek was sixteen, a police officer wrestled him to the ground and slapped him in handcuffs. Derek was drunk, stoned, or whatever, and he flipped the police officer off. The officer stomped on Derek's hand so hard in retaliation that he broke Derek's wrist. Matters culminated in the summer of 1973 with Derek, as a ward of the court, being shipped off to Rancho Del Campo, a behavioral and substance rehabilitation facility for teen boys, where he stayed for three months.

Mark, meanwhile, would disappear for days without letting anyone know where he was, then suddenly reappear high as a kite. One night when my parents were both out, Mark was tripping on acid and scared the hell out of Kirsten, Kerri, and me. He kept insisting there was someone trying to sneak into the house and get him. We tried to reason with him, but it was no use. I became paranoid myself and spent the whole night watching the hallway for the intruder, but none ever materialized.

That didn't stop Mark from frequently shouting for help and scaring us stiff.

I felt bad for Mark and Derek. They often seemed so directionless. Maybe it was the lack of a father figure that created such a void in their lives. I later experienced the same void. Drugs and alcohol can seem like ways to fill the emptiness and ease the pain, at least temporarily. Both Mark and Derek were extremely bright. Mark's IQ was exceptional, and school was boring for him. With such an active mind he found it hard to stay focused. I remember he used to walk around with a science fiction paperback stuffed in his back pocket. He was always reading. Maybe that was his way of disappearing, to put himself in some faraway futuristic universe? He needed to be challenged academically, but perhaps his teachers felt it was easier to label him a troublemaker and let him slip through the cracks. He dropped out before graduation.

Derek was smart too, but in later years he confessed to me that he has suffered from depression for most of his life. He was so unhappy that he ran away multiple times when we lived in Lompoc. He told me once that over the course of his life he has become addicted to everything and anything he ever tried. He has kept searching for something to numb the pain and fill the gaping hole he has inside.

In 1974, when I was twelve years old, Mom gathered me and my sisters in her bedroom. I figured we were going to talk about the logistics for an upcoming swim meet we'd all signed up for, but instead she announced, "I'm going to get something I've wanted for a very long time."

"A new sewing machine?" I said, only half listening.

"No, a divorce," Mom said.

Kirsten, Kerri, and I all looked at each other for a long moment, and then Kirsten said, "Oh. Okay. Well, what does that mean?"

"It means Daddy's going to move out."

I can't say the news came as a complete surprise to us, as we could all see that the household was in constant chaos. The timing of Mom's decision to get a divorce wasn't accidental: Ga'mee had recently passed away. Mom would be spared her mother's smug "I told you so" about the breakup of her marriage to an unsuitable man.

It was arranged that Dad would take the boys (now sixteen and seventeen), and she'd take us girls. Mark and Derek's behavior had become so uncontrollable and unpredictable that Mom finally realized there was nothing else she could do for them. Dad could at least offer them a place to stay. To this day, however, she carries guilt about the move to Chula Vista. She feels that if the family had stayed in Lompoc, the boys would have been "saved" and would not have had to struggle in life the way they did.

Breaking up the family was a huge financial gamble for my mother. Before the divorce, we lived on a tight budget. Now finances would be even more difficult as Mom would be forced to make do with only one income. We didn't mind making do if it meant life under our roof was less contentious without the boys and less stressful without the "elephant."

My father was given partial custody of us girls, with visitation every other weekend. In keeping with his character and track record, he sometimes forgot he was supposed to pick us up, or he'd show up completely drunk. Once he picked up Kirsten, Kerri, and me to go to our cousin Patti's wedding in Escondido. We piled into his Toyota truck, which he'd customized with a camper shell, and clung to each other, terrified, as the truck swerved to and fro across lanes of freeway traffic. How he didn't get pulled over was beyond me. Secretly, I wished he would be arrested, because then we wouldn't be subjected to his driving anymore. In fact, all I could think of as we finally neared the church was how much more drunk he'd be after the wedding reception and how much more terrifying the ride home would be.

Dad and my brothers moved into a rundown apartment I rarely visited. Dad did make an effort to call each night, though. The phone would ring, and we three Ks would ignore it. None of us wanted to be subjected to his sloppy drunkenness and seemingly insincere attempts to act loving. It was way too late for that.

I couldn't rely on my father for anything, not even something as simple as attending a swim meet. But it was probably just as well. A few years before, when my team was at the L.A. Invitational meet at the historic pool near the Memorial Coliseum, we were eating a picnic lunch on the lawn when Dad drove by on his way to find a parking space. I could see he was having a difficult time making the car go straight. Then I saw him toss a half-full can of beer out of the driver's side window. He didn't think anyone would see it, but we all did. Everyone—from my coaches to my friends and their parents—saw the display. I can still picture the beer can foaming and rolling, still feel my sense of humiliation and shame as I watched it settle to a stop, draining onto the asphalt.

CHAPTER 11

A Desire for Love and a Hunger for Speed

I WAS BLESSED TO HAVE POSITIVE male role models outside my home. My swim coaches at CVAA, Steve Yamamoto and Ken Thiltgen, provided acceptance and support regardless of how fast I swam. At Kellogg Elementary School, I had outstanding male teachers for fourth, fifth, and sixth grades. Mr. Knutson, Mr. Banner, and Mr. Hopkins were not only great motivators, they were caring, approachable, and kind, and I always felt valued regardless of my test scores. It was as if they sensed my troubled heart and went out of their way to make me feel special.

In seventh grade, most of my Kellogg Elementary classmates went to Hilltop Junior High, but due to a school zone change, I went to Castle Park, which was known more for its population of budding gang members than anything else. Here I was, this twelve-year-old tomboy, going to a new school with a brand-new group of classmates. The reception, needless to say, was underwhelming. It was apparent from the first day that it was going to be difficult to fit in. The girls harassed and intimidated me, and the boys called me a dog. Since I had short, distressed "swimmer" hair, buck teeth, and braces, I couldn't disagree with them. I wasn't very attractive. As a matter of fact, I recall looking in a mirror one time and declaring myself downright ugly. *Even Dad thinks so,* I would tell myself. For years he had joked that I had hair like Phyllis Diller, the zany comedian who was so popular at the time. He also used to chide me by saying, "You know, Pumpkin, you have a really yucky voice." In my book, ugly hair and an ugly voice meant ugly inside.

When my braces came off at thirteen, I decided to drop my tomboy look and grow my hair longer. My body started to develop too, which helped with my new look. While I was still feeling like an outsider, physically I was coming into my own. And for the first time in my life, I was attracting male attention.

Kirsten had always been the best swimmer in the family. When she was younger, she was right up there with Jill Sterkel, who would go on to earn four medals in four different Olympic Games. Sterkel made her first U.S. Olympic team when she was fifteen and won gold in Montreal as part of the 4 x 100 free relay. When Kirsten moved into the 13–14 age group, she was still winning right and left, even with her new responsibilities at home. After the divorce, when Mom had to work a second job to make ends meet, Kirsten took it upon herself to help look after me and Kerri. She was determined to protect us from Mark and Derek and their drugged-out friends who often leered at us. Since she didn't want to see us turn out like our brothers, she became something of a disciplinarian.

One day when Kirsten was cooking the traditional pre-meet hamburgers for the three of us, Derek—stoned—wandered into the house. He and Mark had become long-haired hippy types and even more defiant. While they did not live with us anymore, they occasionally came by the house with their equally drugged-out friends in tow. We tried our best to avoid them. As soon as Derek spotted the burgers on the grill, he honed in on them.

"I want one of those," Derek said, reaching toward the stove.

"No," Kirsten said. "These are for the girls."

Derek plucked one of the hot patties off the griddle, and Kirsten grabbed it from him.

"No," she said. "They're for us!"

The two of them started to wrestle, and the burger went flying. Kerri and I were dumbfounded. Derek and Kirsten fell onto the floor, rolling, kicking, and hitting each other. Kirsten was livid. I'd never seen her so angry. Eventually Derek muttered, "Fuck you," got up, and left. Kirsten, huffing hard, retrieved the hamburger and proudly slapped it onto a plate. Kerri eyed it dubiously.

"Well, I'm not gonna eat that," Kerri said.

"Yes, you are," Kirsten said, slamming the plate down in front of Kerri. "I fought hard for that burger and you're going to eat it!"

Nicknamed "Pixie," Kerri was the baby of the family. She was skinny, like me, and she too got cold easily. When we switched to CNSA, she was eleven and wanted to stop swimming. She was very vocal about it. Mom, concerned Kerri would be adrift without the structure of afternoon practices, said, "You can quit swimming, Kerri, as long as you find something else to do after school." That's when Kerri became serious about the performing arts. She'd already been doing chorus and musical theater in school and had recently received well-earned attention for her talents. She had a beautiful voice, could dance well, and loved being on stage in front of people. So while Kirsten and I put our efforts toward gaining attention in the pool, Kerri set her sights on winning acceptance and approval on the stage.

The debate continues: are we who we are as a result of nurture or of nature? Whatever the case, the fact that Mom had not received much affection, love, or support from *her* mom clearly had a profound effect. While she would be the first in line to give us recognition for our accomplishments, words of affection didn't come easily. The best way for her to express her love for us was by cooking healthy dinners, sewing our clothes, doing our laundry, or driving us to swim practice. Her language of love was and still is acts of service, and taking care of us in this way was the equivalent for her of saying, "I love you."

But Kirsten, Kerri, and I sometimes just wanted to be hugged. We wanted to be comforted and reassured that everything would be okay. We wanted to be loved for who we were, not for medals we had won or something we had accomplished. We didn't realize it at the time, but Mom was in survival mode all those years. She was under so much stress, she suffered debilitating migraines. She didn't have time to look at the world through her daughters' eyes. She was struggling just to keep things going. Looking back, I'm sure she could have used the same reassurance we so desperately craved, but there was no one to give it to her.

To get what I needed, the formula was simple: the faster I swam, the more attention I received. Winning led to special treatment. It had a miraculous way of making all of life's problems fade away for the moment. When I won, everyone ignored the fact that I was from a broken family that was just scraping by and had a father who was an irresponsible lush.

I relished the hard work. All day long my head would be filled with the local radio station's Top 40 hits. The pool became something of a juke joint, and while my teammates and I pounded through lengthy sets of 100s or 200s, the rhythm of the music helped motivate me to swim faster and faster. All across the country, I knew, kids just like me were swimming to the same tunes.

When I finally moved up to Coach Mike Troy's senior group, the workouts were harder, but the results I got were almost instantaneous. Any swimmer will tell you that the butterfly is the most physically demanding of all the strokes. It's hard to train and even harder to race. Since Troy's specialty was butterfly, everyone at CNSA trained it . . . a lot. A set of 10 x 100-meter was typical, and 10 x 200 was not uncommon. One time I swam 6,000 meters, almost four miles, in a workout that consisted entirely of fly. Consequently, I became so good at the stroke that at the age of thirteen, when I reached my very first Junior Nationals' time standard, I did it in the 200-meter fly. Later that summer I also qualified in the 400-meter individual medley. Making that cut was important, because Junior Nationals is just one tier below Senior Nationals, and Senior Nationals is one tier below the Olympic Trials. Every meet, from a local regional meet to the Olympics, has cuts, and the faster the cut, the fewer the swimmers who can reach it. I was excited to be moving up, getting faster, and reaching my goals. My first Junior Nationals was in Ithaca, New York. I was one of the youngest competitors there, but I wasn't intimidated. I'd earned my spot and knew I belonged.

I didn't always have that sense of belonging in swimming. At home, Mom was still struggling to make ends meet, and when something like the water heater broke, the situation become even more dire. At CNSA, most of the kids came from upper-middle-class families, and some of my teammates' parents were downright wealthy. Once I went to a slumber party at teammate Krista Kupiec's house in La Jolla, and I remember gazing around at the enormous mansion, tennis and basketball courts, and huge swimming pool, and discovering that there was a whole side of life I wasn't privy to. None of the other girls ever mentioned my family's financial standing, but I had a sinking suspicion that I didn't fit in. When you took away the medium of water, the great equalizer, I felt inferior. All during that slumber party, as my teammates giggled and had fun, I felt as if I were watching from the sidelines.

Troy was a brilliant coach. His swimming pedigree was impeccable. He had swum under the famous "Doc" Counsilman at the University of Indiana, the man whose book *The Science of Swimming* revolutionized the sport. Troy won a gold medal in the 200-meter butterfly at the 1960 Rome Olympics and set the world record for that event six consecutive times. He was one of just a handful of competitive swimmers to have graced the cover of *Sports Illustrated*. Very few great athletes can make

the transition to great coach, but Troy was an exception. He's one of
the biggest reasons why I'm still swimming today. Troy made the sport
interesting and fun. Most importantly, he was a master motivator who
encouraged his swimmers to dream big.

Troy was like a crazy uncle. He was incredibly energetic, sometimes to
the point of mania, but his athletes adored him. One year when Senior
Nationals were on Easter Sunday, he paraded up and down the deck
dressed like the Easter Bunny. His heritage was Irish, and he had been
known to color himself green for St. Patrick's Day and show up at practice
with trays of Shamrock Shakes from McDonald's. In most of the bigger
meets, the top eight swimmers from the morning heats qualify to swim in
the evening finals. The next eight fastest get to swim in a consolation final,
which Troy dubbed the "banana heat." If you made it into the banana heat
and won, Troy would throw you a banana. It'd plop down in the middle
of your lane and bob there like a little yellow buoy. Troy was one of those
larger-than-life coaches, and we all wanted to swim hard for him.

We had an amazing collection of athletes at Coronado. Swimmers
like Mike Stamm, Erin O'Beirne, Cathy Carr, John Topar, and Andy
Nichols, all nationally ranked and experienced in international competitions, came to swim with us because they believed Troy could get them
to the 1976 Olympics. But while Troy kept things playful, there were
also occasional tantrums. He was known to hurl cans of Tab soda, cof-
fee mugs, or even chairs at swimmers he knew weren't putting forth the
effort. He could recognize greatness, and he couldn't stomach watching
it be squandered. His car's license plate spelled out "ATTABOY," one of
his favorite sayings. If you got an "Attaboy!" or "Attagirl!" from Troy in
practice, you knew you had just been recognized for doing something
spectacular. We lived to hear him scream that compliment, because
when he did, you believed anything was possible.

You learn early on that every practice is an opportunity to be your best. It's a chance to get better, stronger, and faster. The competitive swimmer's year is broken down into seasons: fall, winter, and spring are short course seasons; summer is long course. Short course means the competitions are held in 25-yard or 25-meter pools; long course means they're held in 50-meter, Olympic-size pools. We swam long course nearly year-round at CNSA. Most of our training was done at the Coronado Municipal Pool, also referred to as the "muni," but we'd sometimes get water time at the Mike Collins Pool on the Naval Amphibious Base.

From the outside, swimming may appear to be "just swimming," and the length of the pool shouldn't make the least bit of difference. But each course possesses its own unique idiosyncrasies, and it's challenging to perform well in all three. Just as some race car drivers are better suited for NASCAR than they are for Formula 1, some swimmers do better in short course (25-yard and 25-meter) than they do in long course (50-meter).

Everything in the practice pool is organized according to ability, and the coach, in many ways, is like an orchestra conductor. In our senior group, lanes seven and eight would be reserved for the slowest swimmers; lanes four, five, and six for the medium fast; and lanes one, two, and three for the fastest. Troy would adjust his workouts according to skill level, with the faster swimmers getting the most demanding sets.

Lane one swimmers carried prestige and a certain mystique. They ruled the pool. At Coronado Navy, I remember looking over at Olympians like Mike Stamm and Cathy Carr and being intimidated. When they swam back and forth across the pool, they made it look so effortless. What Mike and Cathy did in lane one and what I did in lane eight seemed as far apart as the north and south poles.

Within each lane, the best swimmer always goes first in a set, the next best goes second, and so on. No matter where you fall in the order, you always strive to get stronger so you can move up in the lane. In this sense, swimming is one of the most hierarchical of sports.

It is easy to tell if you are becoming a better swimmer: all you need to do is gauge your performance against those around you. Once you start getting faster than the swimmers ahead of you, you develop a hunger for it. I remember it took me nine months to work my way to the center of the pool. And it took me nearly two more years to get to the other side of the pool. Every day is a test. You might get faster than someone on a kicking set, but they destroy you on a pulling set. You might have the best backstroke in the lane, but be the worst flyer. You need to develop all aspects of your game—every day, all the time.

There are inevitably periods during your training when you feel as if you're stuck. Swimmers swim hundreds of training miles to improve their times by tenths of a second. Big breakthroughs are nice, but as you get older they are the exception and not the rule. Going to a meet and not setting a personal record can be frustrating and is not uncommon. Going through an entire season without setting one can be heartbreaking. It's the nature of the sport. Hard work in the practice pool doesn't guarantee results in the competition pool.

Then there are those training blocks where you feel invincible. You know you've elevated your swimming to a whole new level and you're convinced you can handle anything your coach throws at you. You're one with the water and you can't wait for the next practice to see what else you can do.

A swim coach's job is a delicate balancing act. He wants to challenge you, but not demoralize you. He needs to keep you physically and mentally engaged, which is not as easy as it sounds, especially when you're talking about adolescents who can think of a million other things they'd rather be doing. What Troy did best was to create a recipe that mixed hours of monotonous training with a good share of entertainment. He was a master at it.

It takes years of nurturing to develop a great swimmer. For coaches, it takes looking at the big picture of a swimmer's career while continually taking the little steps needed to get there. It used to be that swimmers, especially females, reached their peak in their mid-teens. For example, Debbie Meyers achieved her greatest success at the age of sixteen, Shirley Babashoff won her first gold medal at fifteen, and Shane Gould won three Olympic titles at the age sixteen and retired from the sport at seventeen.

I remember when I first made it into the fastest lanes. Those swimmers who inhabited the far end of the pool were still godlike to me, but for several months I'd been noticing as I swam a lane or two away that I could almost keep pace with them. Then one day, when we were in the middle of a hard set, I looked over and saw that I was swimming at about the same pace they were. The revelation was eye opening. It was life changing. Suddenly I realized that no matter which lane we swam in, we weren't so different after all.

It was 1976 and I was swimming up a storm. During the school year we were training up to twice a day, Monday through Friday, with an extended session on Saturdays. My body adapted well to the extra workload. Many of my teammates were just as motivated as I was, which was both fun and challenging. We were fearless. When you're young, the pool holds no limits. Anything is possible. We pushed each other in practice and raced hard against each other in meets. Some of our summertime workouts would consist of three hours of freestyle in the morning and two hours of stroke work in the late afternoon. We were racking up 15,000 meters—more than nine miles—a day, week in and week out. That summer at the Junior Olympics, a remarkable seven of the eight swimmers in the finals of the women's 200-meter fly were Coronado Navy swimmers. Our relay combinations, which included me, Laurie, Leslie, Jane Campbell, and Kim Grady, were destroying the 13–14 National Age Group records at every opportunity. We were on fire.

Chapter 12

It Was Easier to Stay Under Water Than Face Reality

MY FATHER WAS THE BAND TEACHER at Chula Vista Junior High School, in the same district as my school, from 1970 to 1982. Sometimes I would meet a kid from his school, and when they found out my last name was Pipes, the question would come up:

"Hey, is your dad the band teacher?"

"Yup. That's my dad," I would say, knowing what was coming.

"I heard he's a drunk."

Showing no emotion, I learned to push my feelings down deep inside. I would try to laugh it off, make a joke of it, but it stung. Even though he no longer lived with us, my father and his alcoholism cast a shadow over my life. I hated it. I didn't want to be near him, and I certainly *never* wanted to be like him.

I will never forget the day Martin, my next door neighbor, confided in me. He carpooled to school with my dad. Martin said Dad would stop off at the same liquor store every morning and buy orange juice and vodka. My father had now taken to drinking during school hours. It'd be orange juice and vodka during the day and beer at night.

Between my schoolwork and my swimming, I was living something of a double life. I suppose it's like that for all kids who are entrenched in serious athletic or other extracurricular pursuits. On the one hand, there was homework, pop quizzes, and reports. There were the lockers that functioned as a place to socialize, the recesses, and the cafeteria that always smelled like mashed potatoes. On the other hand, there was this whole other life. While my bleary-eyed classmates and I were sitting in our first period algebra class watching our teacher scribble out complex formulas on the chalkboard, hardly anyone, including Mr. Fierro, realized I'd already been awake for over four hours. When the bell would ring at the end of the day and we'd all hustle to catch our buses or rides, only a few people knew I was rushing not to get home, but to get to afternoon practice a thirty-minute drive away.

In late summer of 1976, Coach Troy announced to the team that he was putting together a special holiday-season training trip to Asia. It was in large part the Indonesian Swimming Federation's way of thanking us for allowing their swimmers to train with Coronado Navy for the past two years. Only the most dedicated swimmers would be invited. In those days, the best way to get me *really* motivated was to dangle something like that in front of me. Winning races and breaking records wasn't enough; making cuts at Junior or Senior Nationals wasn't enticing. But offer an exotic trip to the other side of the world, and I was in.

Troy explained that twelve of us from the team would be selected and that the choice would be based on attendance and attitude. We had just a few months to prove ourselves. Even though I dreaded the cold muni pool, especially in the early morning, I sucked it up and didn't miss a single practice. When the travel team was announced in mid-November, I was on it.

Of the three weeks we were away, eleven days were spent in Jakarta. We were treated like royalty and stayed at the best hotel in the massive metropolis. Every night we attended private parties. We even met Indonesia's vice president. We trained hard, rain or shine, often with a large crowd of locals watching us from the stands.

One time the pace clock on the side of the pool malfunctioned right in the middle of a challenging set. It's hard to keep track of your times when there's no clock, so it needed to be fixed. Every time Troy jiggled the cord to try to make it work, he'd get an electrical shock. It happened quite a few times and became so comical that the spectators would roar with laughter every time he got zapped. Of course, Troy didn't like getting shocked, or worse yet, getting laughed at, and he began screaming wildly at the mild-mannered Indonesian audience. The folks in the stands quieted down right away, but those of us in the pool just couldn't help ourselves. We burst out laughing so hard it was difficult to go back to work and finish the set.

The team didn't stay just in Jakarta. We traveled to the Indonesian island of Bali, to Hong Kong, to Singapore, and to Bangkok, Thailand. And wherever we traveled, Troy made sure there was a pool available to us so we could continue our practices. We had one workout in Hong Kong where, in spite of the fact that there were twenty swimmers in each lane, Troy issued us the hardest set I could ever imagine. We were given 4 x 400-meter freestyles leaving on a five-minute interval. My personal best at that time was 4:52. It seemed impossible to make just one 400, let alone four with almost no rest. But that day was one of those "on" days for me. Even with the traffic congestion, I hammered out 4:56, 4:55, 4:55, and 4:54. I will never forget that day or that set. It made me believe that hard work really did pay off.

I was fit, fast, and my confidence in my aquatic abilities was growing every day. I started to believe that maybe, just maybe, I could be like Linda Jezek. She had made the 1976 Olympic team and eventually broke a world record in the 200-meter backstroke. I idolized her so much that when she was featured on the cover of *Swimming World* magazine, I tore the cover off, cut out the eyes, and walked around the pool deck with the page held up to my face, saying, "Hi, my name is Linda Jezek." In my book, she was the best.

I aged up in March of 1977 when I turned fifteen, and even though I was now competing against sixteen-, seventeen-, and eighteen-year-olds, I still excelled. I went to short course National Junior Olympics in Dallas that spring and won the 400-yard individual medley (IM). My performance qualified me to compete at USA Senior Nationals the following year and catapulted me over dozens of other girls from all over the country, as well as over my sister and most of my teammates. I also placed fourth in the 200 back, sixth in the 200 IM, and eighth in the 100 back, and our top-notch CNSA relay team won the 400 medley and freestyle relays and placed second in the 800. Everyone was sitting up and taking notice of "those girls from 'Nado," and especially of me. Since I'd overtaken Kirsten in the pool and Kerri was immersed in her performing arts, I was now the one receiving the accolades and drawing all the attention.

Later in the spring of that year, a twenty-one-year old swimmer by the name of Dale Basescu rolled into town from Boulder, Colorado. He was great looking, had the biggest smile I had ever seen, and was something of a free spirit. Kirsten was almost seventeen, and it was obvious she had a crush on the effervescent college boy. When Dale went back to school in the fall, Kirsten ran away to join him. We were all surprised, as none of us had realized just how attached to him she had become. Kirsten also went to Colorado because she wasn't feeling appreciated. She felt that Mom didn't care anyway, so why not go? But things didn't work out with Dale. With nowhere else to turn, she called Mom from a pay phone, and they had a long, emotional conversation. Kirsten came home. That phone call, she later confided to me, was the first time in her life she had really felt loved.

While I was gaining speed and making the qualifying times to go to Senior Nationals, Kirsten was struggling. No matter how hard she trained that summer, her times didn't get better, nor did she make a single cut. Her body wasn't cooperating, and she had no idea why. She was both depressed and frustrated. One day when I came home from the pool, Kirsten greeted me with an odd look on her face. I was surprised she hadn't gone to practice. She had a bag slung over her shoulder, and at first I thought she was going to try to run away again. Then I noticed a gold foil star affixed to the middle of her forehead.

"K-Kirsten?" I said apprehensively.

She didn't saying anything at first and instead handed me a note she'd written that read, "I've just taken ~~20, 25,~~ 30 codeine . . . "

My heart started hammering, and the walls of the house felt as if they were rapidly closing in on me. I could see Mom's empty pill bottle on the kitchen table. I took Kirsten by the shoulders and shook her.

"Kirsten!"

"I used to be a star," she mumbled as she staggered about. "I used to be a star . . . "

I wasn't sure what to do, so I called my brother Mark. A few years previously he had straightened up, enlisted in the army, and become a medic. He was now driving an ambulance and assisting paramedics.

Kirsten wanted to lie down, but I wouldn't let her. I kept prodding her to remain upright. Mark told me they'd be at the house as soon as they could.

"I used to be a star," Kirsten repeated, her words slurred. The sticker fell off.

Thankfully, emergency medical services arrived quickly. I could hear the shrill scream of the siren from several blocks away. I rode in the back with Mark and Kirsten as we sped toward the hospital. When we got to the emergency room, Mom was waiting for us. As they wheeled Kirsten away to pump her stomach, I went through her bag. Inside were a Bible, a collection of poems by Kahlil Gibran, and a swimsuit.

I'd been so focused on my swimming that it never occurred to me how difficult things had been for my big sister. She had that same achy hollowness inside, that same need for outside affirmation that I did. Maybe she had tried to check out because she felt she wasn't a star anymore. Not at home, not at school, not in the pool. I was too young to know how to process this. I felt bad that she felt that way, and I even felt her pain a bit. To cope, I just put my head down and kept swimming. Looking back, it's clear now that there were a lot of similarities between my swimming and my later alcohol addiction. Rather than face reality, it was much easier to keep my head under water.

Kirsten moved to Point Loma to stay with Uncle Bill and Auntie Gracie while she finished high school in hopes that a calmer and more stable environment would prevent future suicide attempts. It was a big commitment for the Spores to take her in, but they provided a safe haven, and as a result Kirsten's mental health improved. She kept swimming, but her heart wasn't in it anymore. No matter how hard she tried, she couldn't get any faster. She also played on the boys' water polo team. When the start whistle blew, she was ferocious. If she couldn't get the results she wanted between the lane lines, she was determined to make up for it on the water polo field and in the classroom.

None of us could have known what was really happening. It turned out that Kirsten, at only seventeen, was in the early stages of multiple sclerosis, and she had already started to lose her mind-muscle connection. Kirsten confided later that she'd begun feeling a strange numbness in her fingers as early as her jaunt to Colorado. She recalled trying to pick up some loose change from a countertop, but her fingers were so numb and uncoordinated that she couldn't grasp the pennies and quarters.

Tragically, her MS progressed more in a year and a half than Ga'mee's did in thirty years. Kirsten was stumbling and losing her balance when she was nineteen, and by the age of twenty-one she was confined to a wheelchair. Even after these setbacks, she still loved being in the water. One summer she traveled to Edinboro, Pennsylvania, and competed in the 29th National Wheelchair Games where she won six events and broke six records. She graduated from San Diego State University with a degree in teaching and met Michael Wolfe, who would eventually become her husband. Michael knew there was a strong possibility she would never walk again. At their wedding it was both heartbreaking and heartwarming to witness his act of love as he scooped up his wife-to-be from her wheelchair and carried her to the altar.

CHAPTER 13

The Moments You Wish
You Could Freeze in Time

T HINGS WERE CHANGING. *I* WAS CHANGING. I was maturing both in height and in femininity, and boys were starting to take notice. The teasing about my appearance stopped almost overnight. I developed surfer-chick good looks and, thanks to the genes passed down from Grandma Pipes, I was lean, tall, and had a bust that filled out a bathing suit quite nicely. Now the boys at my school were bending over backwards to be my friend. I was fifteen, and I reveled in the attention.

It was May 1977 when I got my first real boyfriend. His name was Matt Madruga and he was a swimmer too. He was sixteen, had olive skin with a nice tan, beautiful aquamarine eyes, and he loved to surf. His family lived in Point Loma, and his father was a commercial fisherman.

That first summer of love was heady with emotions, adventure, and experimentation for Matt and me. I loved being around him. It was as if we were both seeing life for the first time through something other than the lenses of our foggy swim goggles. He made me feel special, and it was nice that those feelings weren't based on swimming performance. One night Matt got some rum—kids that age are always resourceful when it comes to getting liquor—and he made us rum-and-Cokes. It made me feel so grown-up, sipping a mixed drink, but I didn't find the taste particularly appealing. It had no effect on me.

Once I discovered boys, and specifically Matt, my entire world turned upside down. Because of my performance in Dallas in the spring, I was selected to go to the first ever Olympic Training Center camp in Colorado Springs. Only the best young swimming prospects in the country were invited, including Melanie Rile, who had won her first national championship when she was only thirteen, and Cynthia "Sippy" Woodhead, who, a year later, would go on to win three gold medals at the World Championships when she was fourteen. It was quite an honor to make the list, and Troy was understandably thrilled that four of his CNSA girls—Laurie, Leslie, Jane, and I—had been selected. No other coach could boast of such a thing. But I turned down the invitation. I said no, and defended my decision with everything I had. My head just wasn't into swimming. It was into Matt and my newfound life outside the pool. Mom hit the roof when I told her I wasn't going. Troy was very disappointed too. No one could understand why I would work so hard to get to that level, only to turn away from it.

I think, in part, I was afraid. I was intimidated by the intense training that would be involved. It was hard enough surviving Troy's hellacious workouts. What would it be like trying to endure the workouts of someone I didn't know, and in thinner air, no less? Training at altitude, we'd all heard, was lung-busting. I was also afraid of not being home. It's strange, in retrospect, given that home had never felt all that hospitable to me. But now home was wherever Matt was, and I was terrified of losing his affection. I felt wanted and needed, and that was exhilarating. I was going to take advantage of this because that emptiness inside, the one I'd been carrying for as long as I could remember, had suddenly started to fill.

There are moments in life you wish you could freeze in time. Are we truly in control of our actions, or is something or someone greater than ourselves in control of them? No one ever sets out to become an alcoholic. My father didn't. He didn't wake up one morning, look out the window at the new day as he stretched his arms wide, and announce to the world, "What a beautiful day! This is a perfect day to become a drunk." Did that summer of my fifteenth year seal my fate, or had it already been determined?

CHAPTER **14**

Recovery: Days 1 and 2

WHILE I DIDN'T EXPERIENCE EVEN the slightest buzz from drinking when I was fifteen and dating my first boyfriend, I was certainly wasted as Mom and I sat in the waiting area of the emergency room at Sharp Cabrillo Hospital in Point Loma. We had arrived at 10:30 or so in the morning, but it took two long hours to be admitted. I was thankful my mom was there to give me support. At one point I turned to her and said, "This is the *emergency* room, right?" She smiled back at me, put a hand on top of mine, and said, "Well, it's a good thing you're not dying."

She couldn't have known it at the time, but my blood work would reveal I *was* dying—I was the walking dead.

I'd like to say that that wait was a good thing for me, that it strengthened my resolve to get through whatever lay ahead, but the truth is I was absolutely terrified. When I was finally admitted and crawled into a bed, I just wanted to sleep. *Maybe, just maybe, they'll give me something to help me finally sleep . . .* Jennifer, a gentle-faced, brunette nurse, took a Polaroid of me. I studied the photo. Even with a split lip, I didn't look half bad.

"Are you feeling okay?" she asked with a comforting smile.

"Yes," I said groggily. "But I'm really thirsty. I feel like I'm burning up."

She disappeared to get me some grape soda. I greedily drank it down.

"Better?" Jennifer asked.

I nodded. But less than five minutes later I was throwing up purple everywhere. My withdrawals had officially started.

Each minute I moved away from my beloved alcohol was another minute I moved further into the personal hell that is detox. I was nauseated and feverish, and I began to convulse. I felt as if I'd wandered into a walk-in refrigerator wearing nothing more than a wet swimsuit. Another nurse covered me with a blanket, but I was still freezing.

My heart was beating so fast that it felt like a fish flopping around in the bottom of a boat. Somehow Jennifer managed to get an IV into my arm so they could run fluids. I needed it, she said, because I was so severely dehydrated. I was also placed on a twenty-four-hour watch. "It's not uncommon in the initial hours of alcohol withdrawal," I overheard Jennifer tell my mother, "to have patients go into cardiac arrest." I heard Mom groan with worry and concern. It must have been pure hell for her to watch her child in such anguish, but she kept a bedside vigil until well after 9:00 p.m. before going home.

The first night was horrible. All I wanted to do was sleep, because sleep meant I could avoid the DTs, but my body never allowed me to drift off too deeply. It was as if every symptom associated with any common illness—a cold, the flu, a "bug," whatever—was thrown together into a huge cauldron and strengthened by a factor of three. I ached all over. My head pounded. My heart raced. I kept trying to vomit, but after the grape soda, there was nothing left to come out. I was still shaking uncontrollably. All the cells in my body were screaming for alcohol, and they were revolting because they were not getting what they wanted. My whole being was begging for alcohol; not for the buzz it could produce, but for the promise of relief from all the painful symptoms. *You need to give me what I need, Karlyn. Just give me what I need and this will all go away . . .*

A team of nurses checked on me every hour on the hour to make sure I was still breathing. Their concern was justified. Death from alcohol withdrawal is far more common than death from heroin withdrawal. I felt as if I were dying. And on a cellular level, I *was*. My potassium level was extremely low, my liver was barely functioning, and I was severely malnourished.

Since I had been drinking around the clock for the past month, I was, in a sense, pickled in vodka. The DUI blood alcohol level in California is .08. For someone my size, that equates to about two 5-ounce glasses of wine. A reading of .40, the equivalent of ten to eleven glasses of wine, usually means the patient is unconscious. At .40, breathing is impaired, the central nervous system is compromised, and the heart is on the verge of complete failure. When I was admitted to the hospital, *a full six hours after my last drink,* my blood alcohol level was .52.

My second day I was told I needed to have a chest x-ray. The nurses tried to coax me out of bed, but I couldn't get up—I was still convulsing too often and too violently. I couldn't stand. I couldn't walk. I couldn't eat. Finally, the nurses found a wheelchair and lined it with blankets. They lifted me out of the bed, put me in the chair, wrapped me up as you would swaddle an infant, and wheeled me down to x-ray. The people I passed in the hall offered sympathetic looks. They had no idea what my illness was, but it was obvious I was very sick. I felt guilty for their concern.

When Mom and her boyfriend, Lloyd, came to visit me that afternoon, I was still shaking and throwing up. At least that's what my body was trying to do. I had experienced dry heaves before, but these were unbelievable. It was as if my body was determined to expel something, anything, even if it was an internal organ. The nurses drew more blood. My blood alcohol level had now dipped to a respectable .34. Horrifyingly, that was a full twenty-four hours after my last drink. I still had the equivalent of eight or nine glasses of wine coursing through my bloodstream.

I begged Mom to do something to help me.

"T-this isn't working, Mom," I said, through trembling lips. "I-I'm not feeling any better. P-please take me home." I knew that if I could just make it home, I could get that one drink that would put an end to this misery.

"I can't do that, Karlyn," Mom said.

"P-please, Mom," I pleaded. "I can't take it anymore."

"No," she said.

"Lloyd?" I said, looking up at him. "P-please . . . ?"

Lloyd, who had become like a father to me, reached down and put a comforting hand on my shoulder. "You're going to be okay, Karlyn, I promise," he said, with concern written all over his gentle face.

I could see that my detox was taking a toll on Mom. She had dark circles under her eyes from lack of sleep, and a line of worry creased her forehead. As she watched me struggle, I'm sure she couldn't help but think back to Dad. He had never once attempted this journey, maybe because he knew how hard it would be. Yet here Mom was, many years later, with a ringside seat to the process—and it was her daughter on the ropes.

Later that afternoon I got a roommate. I couldn't see him because of the drawn curtain separating our beds, but I could sure hear him, especially that night. Whenever I'd finally doze off, I'd be jolted awake by his frantic screams of "No! No! Leave me alone!" To make matters worse, I was having delusions of my own. I kept seeing things—ugly, sneaking things—in the darkness on my side of the room, lurking. It was as if I were in my own personal haunted house, one designed to prey on my darkest fears. As I navigated the scary maze of my delusions, every step took me deeper into the unknown, and around every corner I came face to face with something that terrified me.

Sometime during that second night, I had an epiphany. I realized that the way I was feeling—physically, emotionally, spiritually—could not be worse. There could not possibly be a lower place in the entire world. I had hit true rock bottom. When I came to this conclusion, the odd image of a squashed bug in a gutter popped into my head. The bug was flattened and maimed and hurt, but it wasn't quite dead. It was alive, if just barely. And that bug, even in its sorry state, could look *up*. It may have been moments from expiring, but with one eye it could look up and see that right above it was a curb—a curb that, if reached, offered the promise of something better. And while scaling the height of that curb may have seemed impossible, the potential for scaling it *was* there, because the bug was *still alive*. At that moment, I felt something stirring deep inside me, a feeling I had not felt in a very long time. *Hope.*

Chapter 15

This Isn't My Dream

THE DECISION TO SKIP THE TRAINING CAMP in Colorado Springs when I was fifteen marked a turning point for me. Even though I was coming off the success of my first win at a national-caliber meet, competitive swimming had lost its luster for me. If I could now get the attention I craved outside of the pool, why bother in the pool? Besides, was making an Olympic team really my dream, or was it Troy's or my mother's? Kerri had quit swimming and was now thriving in her passion for theater. And while getting a college scholarship would be nice, I probably wouldn't have to work very hard for one.

A brand-new Karlyn was emerging, and I was really interested in getting to know her. The old Karlyn was so dedicated to swimming that she would race home after school—a mile and a half uphill—to change into her bathing suit and get ready for afternoon practice. The new ninth-grade Karlyn looked for any excuse, would even go to extremes, to get out of practice. I recall one time purposely jamming my index finger so hard it became swollen and black and blue. The school nurse splinted the damaged finger, and I was officially excused from swimming. Those few days of freedom gave me a taste of what it was like to be a normal teenager, not some so-called swimming phenom on her way to stardom.

It's not that I wanted to quit swimming altogether, I just didn't want to do it to such an extreme. Up at 4:20 a.m., traveling thirty minutes to Coronado to swim back and forth in a cold pool for an hour and a half, then back to Chula Vista for school. Repeating the round-trip commute in the afternoon, adding a two-hour swim practice and strength training to the program. Returning home after 7 p.m. and doing it all over again the next day, and the next.

Weekends were easier, with no school and only one long Saturday morning practice. Unless there was a meet. As a member of CNSA's senior team, we traveled all over Southern California to compete against the very best, which meant whole weekends consumed. The plus side was you spent so much time with your swim team that they became your family. It's no wonder that after all these years, my swimming friends, not my school friends, are the relationships I treasure most and that have endured the test of time.

I got my first alcoholic buzz on New Year's Eve that same year. I remember Mom threw a party with a Chinese theme, and everyone was drinking and having a good time in the kitchen creating a delicious Asian meal. Bruce Kinky, a cute swimming friend of mine who was two years older than me, suggested the two of us have some beer in the privacy of the living room. I had tried beer with Matt and knew I didn't like the taste, but I didn't want to come off as a party pooper, so I agreed. Bruce and I were alone with our contraband in the dark room. The beer was as awful as I remembered, but I gulped down the contents of the can anyway.

And then it happened. All of a sudden this warm, fuzzy feeling came over me. I'd never felt anything like it before. Clearly, when I had tried rum with Matt, I hadn't consumed enough to reach this point. Bruce and I drank another beer, and my nose started to get numb, but in a pleasant way. I turned my head, and everything in my peripheral vision blurred. The laughter and conversation in the next room melted away.

I didn't like the taste of beer. What did appeal to me was that marvel-ous feeling of *ahhhhh* . . . Drinking those two beers made everything softer. The hard edges of my world became rounded and smooth. I hadn't experienced such a comforting sensation since I had held my Night-night. When you get a buzz like that, you feel as if everything is going to be okay. You feel funnier, smarter, prettier. You feel . . . *more.* Worry, fear, and insecurities melt away. I finally understood what all the fuss was about. When Bruce and I went back into the other room, I looked around at everyone having a good time and I got it. How could someone not be attracted to what I was feeling? My view of the world, and where I fit in it, suddenly changed. I knew right then and there that alcohol was going to become a very dear friend.

In the fall of 1977, I became a sophomore at Castle Park High School. Back then, the school did not offer a girls' swim team, so I swam on the boys' team. Swim season started at the end of January, and that gave me the perfect opportunity to get out of training. For the next four months I told Troy I was going to high school practices, and I told my high school coach, Mac, I was going to CNSA practices. I wasn't too concerned with putting one over on Mac. Troy was a different story. He and I had a lot of history, and I knew I had to tread carefully. I was getting out of shape, but I didn't mind. All I cared about was hanging out with my new friends, partying every now and then, and doing just enough swimming to get by.

Thankfully, I didn't need to train all that hard to keep up with the boys on my school team. I may have lacked confidence in some areas of my life, but I had grown very sure of my swimming abilities. At one dual meet I swam the 500-yard freestyle, and even though I did the whole thing backstroke, I still lapped everyone else in the pool. At the end of that first season I was named the most valuable swimmer on the Castle Park boys' team. I knew I wasn't swimming anywhere near my potential, but I didn't care. I was popular and associating with kids outside the pool who didn't live the double life I'd been leading. They weren't tethered to such a narrowly focused training regime. Every minute of their day wasn't accounted for before they even woke up. They weren't exhausted all the time. They were "normal" kids, and I envied their freedom.

Most teenagers are defiant to some degree. When you're straddling the border between youth and adulthood, you grow weary of the nonstop parenting. You're sick of life's so-called lessons. Up to this point in my life, I had mostly stayed on the straight and narrow, literally and figuratively. I existed in a confined space defined by two lane lines, and I was guided from one end of the pool to the other by a black line on the bottom. But suddenly I didn't want to live by those restrictions. The orderliness that before had been so appealing and reassuring suddenly made me feel claustrophobic. I wanted out. I wanted to blaze my own path.

My lax habits started to spill over onto my schoolwork. Scarcely a week went by when I didn't ditch school on at least one occasion. I was becoming quite conniving. I even developed a knack for forging Mom's signature. One day it would be *Karlyn has a doctor's appointment on Tuesday*. Another day it would be *Karlyn has a dentist's appointment on Wednesday*. And still another day it would be *Karlyn won't be able to attend class on Friday because of a death in the family*. All my grades, predictably, took a nosedive, but I didn't care. It got so bad that I actually flunked phys ed. That never would have happened before. I, who had always taken pride in being able to do more pull-ups than all the boys in my sixth-grade class, hadn't passed PE.

Meanwhile, Mom was getting more involved with U.S. Masters, a competitive swimming organization for adults. She immersed herself in both the training and the racing opportunities the group afforded. She swam under a charismatic young coach named Ron "Sickie" Marcikic and dutifully attended practice every morning before going to work.

The first U.S. Masters Swimming National Championships, staged in Amarillo, Texas, in 1970, had launched a movement. By 1986, U.S. Masters Swimming, or USMS, registered its twenty-thousandth member, and today that number is over sixty thousand. The growth has been just as impressive worldwide. In 2014 a whopping six thousand swimmers from nearly a hundred countries competed at the 15th FINA (Fédération Internationale de Natation, or International Swimming Federation) World Masters Championships in Montreal, Canada.

Mom was such a proponent of Masters swimming that she got involved with the governing side of the sport too. She and her friend Bill Earley, who helped establish the Coronado Masters Association in 1972, became fixtures on local and national Masters swimming committees. They regularly attended meetings and annual conventions held across the country, and wherever they traveled they were diligent about finding a local Masters team to practice with.

"If I can get up in the morning and swim, Karlyn," she said one night at dinner, when the two of us were alone, "why can't you?" By this time I had turned sixteen and gotten my driver's license, so she had been relieved of her carpooling duties. She assumed that when I left the house in the morning, I was going to swim practice too. Little did she know.

"Maybe I don't want to," I said.

"Maybe I didn't want to drive you to work out every morning for all those years either," she said. "But I did it, didn't I?"

"This isn't my dream, Mom," I said.

"It's not your dream? What the hell is your dream? To win Olympic gold for being the best loafer? You're squandering your God-given talent," she hollered. "There are thousands of kids who would give anything to have the ability you have!"

"Then maybe you should be their mother!" I said, pushing my chair away from the table and storming off to my room.

Rather than continue to butt heads with her or try to explain myself any further, it was easier to become more deceitful. Since I was driving now, Mom had even less control over my whereabouts, and I grabbed every opportunity to explore life outside the pool. She'd gotten me a beat-up, bright green 1962 convertible Volkswagen Bug with a ton of miles on it. The fenders were pushed in and the ragtop was broken, so the roof was permanently open. Mom would come into my room to nudge me awake as usual each morning. And I'd dutifully get all bundled up, ready for practice, and drive away with a tight ball in my stomach because as soon as I reached the Strand in Coronado, I knew I was minutes away from jumping into that hellishly cold pool.

When I did make it to swim practice I worked hard. Maybe it was because the water was so darn cold that if I didn't move fast, I would never warm up. Besides creating body heat, I actually liked training. I enjoyed pushing myself and racing my teammates. So *if* I showed up for practice, for the most part my work ethic was still commendable. The problem was that I could think of hundreds of other activities, sleep included, that I would rather be doing.

At some point I decided it was easier to just get up and *pretend* I was going to practice. I'd get in my little Bug, drive around the corner somewhere, park, climb into the backseat, and go back to sleep. Then I'd wet my hair, come home, and pretend I'd gone to practice. If Mom ever asked, I'd go to great lengths to describe the challenging sets we'd been doing.

I thought I was being pretty clever, lying out of both sides of my mouth, but it eventually caught up to me. CNSA's afternoon practice was from 4:00 to 6:00, and Mom often trained with the Coronado Masters team, whose evening workouts were held Monday, Wednesday, and Friday from 6:00 to 7:30. Like a fool, I started sometimes ditching practice on a Monday, Wednesday, or Friday morning. I'd be in the pool at the end of afternoon workout, and I'd watch Mom come across the deck with her swimsuit and goggles, past Troy. If I saw them speak, my breath would catch because I knew I was busted. Troy, no doubt, would say, "Hi, Adrienne. So where was Karlyn this morning?" And Mom would most surely reply, "Well, she did leave the house . . . " Even before Mom made it home from her practice, I knew I was going to be grounded again.

CHAPTER 16

You Don't Deserve
the Talent You Possess

I STARTED MY FIRST REAL JOB in the summer of 1978 as a pool lifeguard at the historic Hotel del Coronado. Since I was working most afternoons, I had a valid excuse to skip practice. When I did attend, it was mostly to visit and gossip with my teammates Laurie Purdy or Jane Campbell, and to work on my tan.

One of the benefits of being an employee at "The Del" was that we were allowed to order whatever we wanted from the main kitchens for free. Every day I indulged in cheeseburgers, club sandwiches, French fries, milkshakes, and various desserts. Up to this point, I had always been able to eat whatever I wanted without gaining weight. But suddenly, I put on fifteen pounds. I was eating as if I were a hard core swimmer, but I certainly wasn't training like one. That summer I had a crush on a hotel guest about my age. When I expressed an interest in him, he said, "I don't date heavy chicks." Insulted, I initially thought, *What in the heck is he talking about? I'm not heavy!* But then I took a harder look in the mirror and I realized I was. My gazelle-like body had chunked out.

CNSA used to have weigh-ins once a week. I suppose it was a way for Troy to measure our physical development. After one weigh-in, he said, "Karlyn, you're too pretty to be fat." He could see what was happening.

Everyone could see what was happening. It's not as if you could hide it when you're wearing a bathing suit. I knew I had to do something, but I wasn't sure what. I knew one thing I wasn't going to do, though, and that was to start attending more practices.

One of the things Troy was adamant about was helping his swimmers get college scholarships. He had received a free education at Indiana, and he wanted us to enjoy the same perk, to get rewarded for all the sacrifices we'd made during our childhoods to reach a level of proficiency in our sport. He'd mentor us on how to write letters, on what to say and do when we were being recruited. He came down on me pretty hard about my slack training and the fact that I had not even begun one letter to a potential university. But at the end of the day, there wasn't much he could force me to do in or out of the pool.

That fall I contracted mononucleosis. Competitive swimmers are especially susceptible to contracting mono because they're chronically run down. It wasn't exactly a pleasant experience. When the virus first strikes, you feel as if you've been run over by a truck. You get a high fever, your lymph nodes swell up, and you're exhausted all the time.

Getting sick was a blessing in disguise from my point of view. Now I didn't have to go to school *or* practice. For the next three weeks I didn't need to lie to Mom about my whereabouts or worry about going to the pool. I had a valid excuse to be lazy and lounge around the house all day watching soap operas or *Gilligan's Island* reruns. If the weather was good, I would lie out in the sun in the backyard. And, as an added bonus, I lost all the weight I'd put on, so by the end of my convalescence I was right back where I'd started: a lean 117 pounds.

During this time Mom was genuinely concerned about my health and did her best to make sure I had what I needed. But money was still tight and she was working a lot, so I was pretty much left alone during the day. I often wondered what it would be like to have a mom that stayed home all day. Would it feel suffocating, or would I have felt that unconditional love I was seeking?

Throughout my teens, I tended to gravitate toward families that were more stable than mine. My friend Sloan Hubbard, a teammate on CNSA, lived in Coronado. Dick, Sloan's father, was a captain in the navy. I called Sloan's parents Ma and Pa Hubbard. One time in eleventh grade I showed up unexpectedly at their front door after hanging out at the beach all day, saying, "Hey Ma and Pa, would you mind if I took a shower here?" Once I showed up an hour before a school function: "Hey Ma and Pa. I'm going to the homecoming dance and I need to get cleaned up. Oh, and by the way, I told my date to pick me up here. I'll be right back. I just need to get my outfit." They watched, amused, as I grabbed my semi-formal dress from the back of my VW and shook it out. By the time my date arrived, I was spic and span and ready to boogie.

The summer before my senior year, even though I had been named most valuable swimmer for the Castle Park boys' team for the second year in a row, I told Mom I wanted to transfer to Coronado High so I could swim on a girls' team for a change. Most of my friends and the swimmers I knew went to Coronado, I argued, and since I was already working on the island, getting the transfer would simplify my life. At the very least, it would save me an hour of driving every day. What I didn't tell her was that going to Coronado would also facilitate my partying.

The process of filling out the paperwork for an inter-district transfer was a huge project. Anytime an athlete decides to make a transfer, especially to a school only a few cities away, the assumption is it will somehow upset the competitive balance. It can also be perceived as recruiting. I wrote a letter to the California Interscholastic Federation and the State Board of Education presenting my case, explaining that the move was designed to better set me up for college and to further my swimming career. These requests always took forever to get reviewed. In the fall, I reluctantly went back to Castle Park to start my senior year, but three weeks later my application was approved.

Coronado High School, though, was a rude awakening. Their curriculum was much more rigorous than Castle Park's, and I was informed I would have to take several extra classes if I wanted to graduate on time. New school or not, I was still doing as little studying as possible. I was in the mode of creating my own rules. I somehow got it in my head that any rules in place applied to others, but not to me. I felt I deserved special treatment.

In the pool, my lack of focus didn't prevent me from still finding some success. I was swimming faster than people who worked ten times harder than me, and to some degree I felt a bit guilty about it. I could see it in their eyes during practice. I could see it as they hung on to the wall, gasping, between intervals. "Look at her," my fellow CNSA teammate Kay Lundy would say. "She's not even breathing hard. She doesn't even have to work." Part of me wondered, *If I just applied myself, even a little bit, where could I take this thing?* Then a stronger, more aggressive voice would chime in. *Who are you kidding, Karlyn? You're a slacker, and you don't deserve the talent you possess.* It was a daily mental tug-of-war, and the negative side usually won. Besides, I was interested in working less, not more. Who cared what could have been?

The Coronado Islanders girls' team won the San Diego Sectional CIF (California Interscholastic Federation) Championships my senior year. Surprisingly, I placed second in my individual events and, along with Jane Campbell, Kelli Tower, and Terri Scannell, added extra points in the relays. Susie Baxter and Molly Barnum secured the title for us by doing well in both swimming and diving. Winning the title was a pretty big deal because it's always been one of the most competitive conferences in the state. While I did score a lot of points and earned some local acclaim, I knew in my heart that I didn't swim anywhere near my potential because I hadn't put in much training. People like Troy knew damn well what times I should have been posting. As for the others—the ones who weren't as hooked into the sport—I was happy to let them believe whatever they wanted to believe.

CHAPTER 17

Instant Gratification

M Y ADDICTIVE TENDENCIES WERE BEGINNING to rise to the surface. I was unwittingly trying to fill that hollowness inside. I may have suspected the void was there, but I wasn't about to put my life on hold to examine what exactly it was and how it had gotten there. I had morphed into a land animal. A wild horse. The swimming corral had been opened, the fences taken down, and I was galloping free. My plan was to continue galloping through life because that's what wild horses do; they gallop far and wide. Sure, I'd go to college, and maybe one day I'd get my act back together. But that kind of stuff could wait. This roaming about free in unfamiliar terrain was pretty darn fun.

All throughout high school I was flirtatious. I didn't have any serious boyfriends after Matt, but I did date. I had a body that was getting attention, and all the boys wanted to be seen with me. I ate it up. For someone who'd never gotten a second look when I was younger, who'd endured teasing from her father and bullying from classmates, I was now making up for lost time. Some of the guys who wanted to date me were the same ones who'd made fun of my looks when I was younger. I'd go out with them a time or two and then dump them. I enjoyed the sense of control.

Another thing I enjoyed having control over was my eating. I was tall, lean, and blonde. There was no way I was going to jeopardize that look by gaining weight. Years before, I remember Kirsten showing up at a meet after having eaten a huge breakfast and complaining to a coach about the way she was feeling. "I'm really, really full," she moaned. "I don't think I can swim." And the coach had said, "Well, just go into the bathroom and stick a finger down your throat and throw up." That remark stuck with me.

The first time I made myself throw up, I hated it. My face felt as if it was going to explode, my eyes watered, my nose ran, and my stomach hurt. But I couldn't argue with the results. In mere minutes I could go from feeling like the Michelin Man with my belly all stretched out and ready to burst, to feeling like supermodel Cheryl Tiegs with a flat, sexy stomach.

At first I didn't hide my newfound weight-loss strategy and would even brag about it to my friends and teammates. But soon the disgusted looks became too much for me, and I learned to keep it to myself. I didn't know back then that there was a name for what I was doing, but I had just added bulimia to my secret life. It became one of those deep dark parts of me I hoped no one would ever know about. It became a part of my repertoire of deceit. I was also living like a vagabond at this point, bouncing around from place to place to avoid being home as much as possible.

That type of nomadic lifestyle lends itself to a poor diet. I was accountable to no one, and my food choices reflected that. Sometimes on my way to school I'd swing into a donut shop and buy half a dozen of my favorite flavors, retreat to the privacy of my car, and scarf them all down. That was the easy part. The hard part was finding a private place to get rid of them. Once I decided that what I had eaten needed to come back up, I became desperate. I wanted that full feeling *gone*. I would drive around Coronado until I found an unoccupied service station bathroom. I would lock the door, lift up the dirty toilet seat, and get to work. And getting donuts to come up was a *lot* of work. It would take fifteen minutes of jamming my finger down my throat to bring up what had taken only ten minutes to consume.

Afterward, I would take a look in the grimy bathroom mirror and see a puffy, red-faced girl with bloodshot eyes staring back. My heart would be racing, and I always, always, felt a sense of remorse. *Why do I do this to myself?* I would ask. It was unhealthy and a waste of time, energy, and money. But I had no answer. I especially had no answer when I would repeat the same process over and over again, sometimes two or three times a day.

I had started to see that over-consumption also had its consequences with alcohol. A night of heavy drinking left me with a hangover. The cottony mouth, sore eyes, and dull headaches took some getting used to. But with the bulimia came a different kind of consequence. My relationship with food became distorted, and I lost the ability to see it as nourishment. They were odd relationships, the eating and the drinking. The bulimia was a way to gain control, and the drinking was a way to lose it.

I was partying more often now. My friends and I were drinking and doing coke and anything else we could find. I was aligning myself with people who continued to feed my craving for attention, alcohol, and drugs. When you're in the middle of that type of existence, it's as if you're viewing life through a pair of reading glasses. All that matters is what's right in front of you. You're not trying to look into the distance, because it's physically impossible. There's no wide view, no middle view. There's only what's directly in front of you at that particular moment. Your life becomes all about instant gratification.

And the deceit becomes all-consuming. It's one thing to lie to everyone around you. It's another thing altogether to lie to yourself. And that's what I'd started to do, lie to myself. My rational mind would say, *Okay. This isn't good for me. I really need to stop partying and throwing up and dedicate myself to swimming and schoolwork. Yes, that's what I'll do. I sure hope it will give my life some more direction. I'll start tomorrow.*

But then I wouldn't. I had all the best intentions, but I was incapable of following through. I didn't have the strength to fight off the internal monster I had created. And so began the pattern of broken promises I'd make to myself. I learned not to trust myself.

Being labeled a quitter was one of the worst things you could be called in my mind. Dad was a quitter. He quit on his dreams, he quit on his marriage, and he quit on his children. Yet that's exactly what I was doing. Day in and day out, I would quit on myself. *I'm going to stop doing this,* I'd tell myself. *I feel like total crap. Tomorrow I'm going to change.* Then my resolve would disintegrate and I'd go and do it all over again. *I'm going to go to afternoon practice and start to train hard again.* But then I wouldn't do it. The tape that continually looped in my head alternated between devising best intentions and beating myself up because I had no follow-through. *You're a quitter, Karlyn. You're nothing but a useless quitter.*

People who don't have an addictive personality often assume it is a lack of will power that keeps addicts from stopping destructive behaviors. They look at someone whose life is swirling out of control, and they're convinced the solution is easy: "If that type of behavior is not good for you, just stop doing it." If the answer was that simple, as simple as merely flipping a switch, there would be no need for recovery programs.

Your addiction becomes a part of you. It's like a persistent itch on the back of your hand. You can go about your day and throw yourself into other distractions, but that urge to scratch is always there, lurking somewhere just beneath the surface of whatever it is you're doing. When your obsession is at its worst, it takes center stage. It colors everything you say and do. People will argue that some forms of addiction are less dangerous than others. But addiction is addiction, and there are no easy solutions for any form of it. The eight-hundred-pound gorilla of the addiction universe is, and always has been, alcohol addiction. The

World Health Organization reports that there are roughly 140 million alcoholics around the world.* If we were all grouped together in a single territory, we would form the tenth most populous country in the world.

While I was doing everything I could to avoid the pool, all my swimming peers were gearing up for the 1980 Olympic Trials. An elite-level competitive swimmer's career is generally short lived, especially when compared to other sports such as professional baseball or basketball. Most swimmers, once they've reached the height of their abilities, get just one or two cracks at making the Trials and the Olympics. The trick for the coach and the athlete is to time the swimmer's career peak with the Olympic Games' quadrennial scheduling. It's an honor to qualify for the Trials. Reaching that level is even more challenging than qualifying for Senior Nationals.

The Trials that summer were scheduled to be held from July 29th to August 2nd in Irvine, California. Swimmers Sippy Woodhead, Nancy Hogshead, Mary T. Meagher, Jill Sterkel, and superstar Tracy Caulkins from Nashville, Tennessee, were all expected to excel and then roll into the Moscow Olympics later that year to continue America's dominance of the sport. But on March 21st, President Jimmy Carter announced that, because the Soviet Union had failed to withdraw its troops from Afghanistan after being given an ultimatum to do so, the United States would be boycotting the Games. The news was devastating to hundreds of American athletes who had devoted the better part of their lives to the goal of competing in an Olympic Games.

For me, though, news of the boycott was barely a blip on my radar. People who knew I was a swimmer would try to talk to me about it, but I honestly didn't have much of an opinion on the subject. Mine wasn't one of the hearts broken. Of course I felt bad for all the athletes who'd

---

* World Health Organization, *Global Status Report on Alcohol and Health* 2014.

had the rug pulled out from under them, but I was too wrapped up in my own warped life to give the matter much thought. Swimming, to me, was just something to do—or, rather, something *not* to do. It certainly wasn't some love affair. If it had been, I would have made a point of doing more of it.

CHAPTER 18

Down the Rabbit Hole

P RIOR TO MY SENIOR YEAR at Coronado High School, colleges weren't recruiting me. It was partially my fault, because I didn't follow any of Troy's suggestions. The other reason was that I was in an odd situation as a girl swimming on a boys' team. College coaches didn't think to look for my stats in the boys' results. Between my laziness and my lack of exposure, I fell through the cracks. In the late fall of my senior year, after some serious pressure from Mom, I finally took the initiative to write introductory letters to college coaches. Most of my best times had been recorded a few years before, but since I was a versatile swimmer, recruiters took the bait. We sent out letters to about thirty schools all over the country, and, surprisingly, I was offered fifteen full athletic scholarship opportunities.

I checked out the program at UC Santa Barbara with my best friend and CNSA teammate Laurie Purdy, and after meeting the coach and seeing the pool, we spent the rest of the weekend drinking at frat parties. A month later, I took a tour of Nebraska and Colorado, then a few weeks later I traveled to Georgia, Arkansas, and Texas A&M. All paid for by Mom—AIAW (Association for Intercollegiate Athletics for Women) rules did not allow for funding of recruiting trips. For me, it was nothing more than a nonstop party junket.

I was being fawned over everywhere I went, and each school was putting its best foot forward because they knew I could score points for the team if I swam anywhere near to my potential. The typical drill was first to meet the coach face-to-face. They would extol the virtues of their particular institution. Then I was passed off to an upperclassman who had the assignment of showing me a good time. Heavy drinking was always part of the equation. I was being treated like a rock star. And to think I was just a swimmer, an athlete at the bottom of the college athletics food chain. I can only imagine what went on during the men's football or basketball recruiting trips.

While the college coaches and swimmers were on their best behavior, I was not. One of the worst stunts I pulled happened on my visit to the University of Georgia in Athens. Jack Bauerle had recently been appointed head coach, and both the school and the swimming program looked promising. Jack would later go on to become a two-time Olympic coach and lead the Lady Bulldogs to six NCAA championship titles. Sadly, I never had the chance to be coached by Jack as on that trip I completely blew my opportunity for a scholarship by getting so drunk I threw up all over my host's dorm room bed. The next morning when I reported to the pool to swim a 6,000-meter workout, I was nauseated, dehydrated, and had a splitting headache. Jack watched me swim for a short time, then handed me off to an assistant coach to monitor my progress. As soon as Jack left the deck, I was out of the pool, in the showers, and on a shuttle back to the Atlanta airport within thirty minutes. Of course I never heard from Georgia again.

The next stop on the tour was the University of Arkansas in Fayetteville. Sam Freas was the head coach of the men's team and Patty Smith the head coach of the women's team. The men's team was extremely successful. The women's team not at all. But Patty was determined to change that.

Title IX* had been passed in 1972, allowing women more opportunity to compete in college (one of the ten key areas addressed in the legislation), and consequently the school's athletic director had given Patty twelve full scholarships to work with. I toured the small town and the campus, which is set in the Ozark Mountains, and found both to be very picturesque. I learned that the Greek system was popular at Arkansas and, since it was late spring, there was no end to the flow of sorority and fraternity get-togethers.

As a result of the debacle in Georgia, I was hungover when I arrived on campus, but that didn't stop me from drinking the next day. Much to my delight, after meeting with Coach Patty I was handed off to a gorgeous man named Jerry Spencer who would act as my guide. Jerry, a standout sprinter from Sacramento, California, had honed his talents with Sherm Chavoor at the famous Arden Hills Swim Club. He was a little on the shy side, but we hit it off right away. We stayed up all night getting to know each other. As the sun came up, I realized I was caught, hook, line, and sinker. I didn't even need to finish the rest of the recruiting trip. I wanted to go to Arkansas. Since my itinerary was already in place, I checked out Mel Nash at Texas A&M and later on had some discussions with North Carolina State because the coach there was good friends with Troy, but my mind was already made up. I wanted to date Jerry. I was going to become a Razorback.

Jerry and I stayed in touch during the summer. He was training just an hour and a half away in Mission Viejo with Mark Schubert's Nadadores team, so we made a point of seeing each other at meets. I couldn't believe how well things were working out. Arkansas, I became convinced, was going to represent a fresh start for me. I was going to date this cute guy

---

* Also known as "Title 9." A portion of the United States *Education Amendments of 1972*, Public Law No. 92318, 86 Stat. 235 (June 23, 1972), codified at 20 U.S.C. §§ 1681-1688. Signed into law by President Richard Nixon on June 23, 1972. It states "No person in the United States shall, on the basis of sex, be excluded from participation in, be denied the benefits of, or be subjected to discrimination under any education program or activity receiving federal financial assistance."

I'd met by chance, and I was going to dedicate myself to my swimming and get good grades in school. I was going to drink less, and I was going to stop throwing up. I was excited for what this brand-new future held.

After I graduated from high school, I continued the job I had as a beach lifeguard at North Island Naval Air Station. I had started to work for the navy the previous summer. We had a crew of about eight or ten of us working the beach, and nearly all of us were under the legal drinking age. I am not sure whose idea it was, but when it came time to fill out the information card to apply for our military IDs, we all lied about how old we were. That government-issued ID proved to be like Willie Wonka's golden ticket. It allowed us to get into any bar, no questions asked. All summer long our routine was to work the beach during the day and party at night. Some of the guys I worked with were into smoking pot, but I was never really a fan of marijuana. I felt stupid and a bit paranoid when I got stoned. Besides, pot never gave me that warm, fuzzy feeling I was after.

Given the way things had been going with me, I knew deep down that the lifeguard lifestyle wasn't conducive to helping me make good decisions. Yes, I was headed to college on a full athletic scholarship in the fall, so there were solid goals in place, but heck, it was summer! I knew it would be time to buckle down come fall, but in the meantime, my present goals were to get away with skipping practice, spend all day at the beach "working," and drink to excess at night. No matter how you framed it, everything about my life at this point was pretty escapist.

Escape is at the root of any addict's problem. In the beginning, you are sold on a high you want to never end. Once it starts, down the rabbit hole you go. And you're having an absolute ball as you slide along the twisty, winding thrill ride. It's all a great big adventure. You're convinced that since you're the one who initiated the journey, you're in complete control. But then it changes. You stop being the one in control. The high starts controlling you. It becomes the lie. It tells you, *Drink this, take that, and you will be free from all your problems.* The high may mask the pain, but it never takes it away. It's just a temporary fix.

So much of the spiral I found myself in was about self-loathing. Truth be told, I was feeling terrible all the time. I didn't need my mother to point out that I was screwing up my life. I didn't need Troy to tell me. I knew my life was going in the wrong direction. The recording just kept repeating itself over and over in my head: *You're really messing up, Karlyn. Isn't it time to stop?* But the gravitational pull to take the easy way out was calling me, and for the first time in my life I began to feel powerless to stop it.

CHAPTER 19

Eating Disorders Flourished Here

W HEN I ARRIVED AT UNIVERSITY OF ARKANSAS, Coach Patty had twelve women on the team. The nine incoming freshmen arrived early to get acclimated to the campus and our training regimen before classes started. Jerry wouldn't be on campus until two weeks later because he had been invited to compete for the U.S. National team at an international meet held on Maui. At that competition, Jerry swam exceptionally well and placed second in the 50-meter free behind 1976 Olympian and former world record holder Joe Bottom. In the swimming world, Jerry was a rising star, and I secretly hoped some of his shine would rub off on me.

But my resolve to make a brand-new start was shaky from the get-go, especially after my new teammates and I attended the first of many swim-team parties. The alcohol, naturally, was free flowing. And, being away from home for the first time, we all indulged rather liberally. The parties that first week all blended together, and once again I started making poor decisions. A cute freshman on the men's team began to flirt with me, and even though I was known as Jerry's new girlfriend, I enjoyed this guy's attention. Both of us were pretty drunk, and the next thing I knew we were making out in front of everyone. Addiction is a strange thing. It emboldens you to act recklessly, and it lulls you into a mistaken belief that you can get away with your questionable behavior.

When Jerry landed in Fayetteville, he was a changed man. That summer while he was training in Mission Viejo, one of his teammates had died in a car accident. The death shook the entire team. The sprint coach, Al Dorsett, was a devout Christian, and he sat his swimmers down and gave them the fire and brimstone speech. It had a profound impact on Jerry. By the time I saw him again, he'd become a born-again Christian.

Coach Freas, who was also Christian, had an unsettling philosophy that directly impacted the women's team. His unwritten rule for his swimmers was "Go ahead and play around all you want, but don't get too attached to any one woman because she will ruin your swimming and your life. Also, make sure you show up to church every Sunday morning." Of course, his team complied. When Jerry came back to school, he had sworn off partying, he had become celibate, and once he found out I had been unfaithful, he swore off me too.

It was heartbreaking. I'd committed to Arkansas primarily because of my infatuation with this guy, and now he was out of the picture. It was my own fault. I knew I had totally blown it, and that gave me yet another reason to drink.

Things only got worse from there. Not only did the men's and women's teams not practice together, but it was something of a tradition for the men's team to party with us, but not actually date us. It was ironic, to say the least, since it was the members of the men's team who had worked so hard to recruit the swimmers for the women's team.

My best girlfriend freshman year was Maggie Schwindt. Maggie, like Jerry, had swum for Arden Hills. She was a breaststroker with cheerleader good looks, sparkling blue-green eyes, and an irrepressibly positive outlook on life. We'd tool around town in her red Datsun 260Z, going to football games and hunting down all the best parties. Her California license plates read, "GO MAGIE." I know that if not for Maggie, I wouldn't have lasted one month in Fayetteville, let alone a whole year.

It was turning out that Arkansas was not a good fit. I resented that Coach Freas made it clear that he had no respect for the women's team. I was also having a difficult time getting along with Coach Patty. Obviously she was a great recruiter, as she had managed to sign three California women to come to a school in the middle of the Ozark Mountains to join a fledgling team. She was nice enough, but she lacked experience, and compared to what I had done with Troy, her workouts were ill-conceived and boring.

My bulimia, meanwhile, was also in full force. I really wanted Arkansas to be a new leaf when it came to beating my eating disorder. I wasn't too concerned about my drinking since it seemed as if everyone was getting drunk as much as I was. But I did want to stop throwing up, something I'd now been doing almost daily for the past two years. I had no idea how challenging that would be in a college swimming environment.

One of the first things we were ordered to do when we got to campus was report to a lab where our body fat was tested in a water tank. One by one, we climbed into a basket, expelled all the air out of our lungs, and then were completely submerged. Between that and a traditional medical scale, Patty determined what our goal weights were to be. In order to compete at meets, she explained, we would have to have 18 percent body fat or less. I have no idea where that figure came from, but every Friday my teammates and I had a weekly weigh-in. College women, especially freshmen, feel awkward enough about their bodies without having to be subjected to that level of scrutiny. We would all line up in the locker room and the assistant coach would write down the results on a chart. On Thursday and Friday mornings many of us retreated to the sauna to sweat away any extra pounds we'd accumulated during the preceding week.

One day before a dual meet, I came in a little over my goal weight.

Over the past few years, the pounds had gradually crept back on, and I was now up to my pre-mono weight, which varied between 130 and 135 pounds. Even though I was exercising more, my diet was horrible. While I tried to throw it all up, some of it stuck. As a result, my bulimia was causing me to *gain* weight instead of lose it. Patty sent me to the sports medicine lab to be tested with skin calipers. It was humiliating. Since the results showed my body fat was 18.4 percent, I was allowed to compete. Needless to say, eating disorders flourished in this environment.

We had our first away meet on Halloween. The team piled into two vans for the long road trip to Norman, Oklahoma, to compete against the University of Oklahoma (OU). It was an ill-fated adventure from the start. We hit traffic, and one of the vans had engine problems. We were told in advance that we'd get meal money and would stop for lunch en route, so none of us brought cash or food. Because of the delays, though, the trip was taking far longer than planned. By the time we finally reached Norman about eight hours later, none of us had eaten since breakfast, and we were all ravenous. The vans pulled into a Denny's restaurant, and Patty told us we each had seven dollars of credit for food. By this time it was 3:30 or 4:00, and warm-up for the meet started in an hour. We wolfed down pancakes, French fries, sandwiches, and whatever else we could order. The first thing we all did when we reached the pool was hit the bathroom stalls. Nearly half the women on the team intentionally threw up because the meet was ready to start.

Patty had informed us ahead of time that OU would be hosting a Halloween party for us and that we were going to stay overnight in Norman. She also told us that if we swam really well, she'd buy us all the beer we could drink. After the exhausting trip and the wasted food, of course we all swam horribly. Patty was furious. At the end of the meet, she announced, "I'm disgusted with all of you! Forget the party. We're going home right now. And since you guys ate before you swam, we're not stopping for dinner!" Tired, hungry, and deflated, we all piled back into the vans for the long drive back.

Many of the women on the team developed eating disorders. In an attempt to curtail my own bulimia, when I first arrived in Fayetteville I confessed to Maggie. But my plan backfired because once Maggie found out what I was up to, she wanted in on it. We developed a ritual. We'd binge at one of the local eateries, such as Casa Taco or Pizza Hut, or at an all-you-can-eat salad bar, and follow it up taking turns going into the bathroom to throw up. If we binged on campus, we'd sneak off to a dorm other than our own to conceal what we were doing. It was insane behavior. And deep down we were disgusted with ourselves and our addiction to bingeing and purging. But instead of crying about it or seeking professional help, we laughed it off. It was one of the things I did to make it through the day.

Bulimics learn to be very sneaky and can often hide their disorder well, but if you look closely, the telltale signs are there. My face was constantly puffy from the force of the vomiting, I always had gum or mints to cover up my breath, and my teeth were getting stripped of their enamel from all the stomach acid.

I didn't make the connection until later, but the bingeing and purging was a way of numbing my emotions just as alcohol was. I'd try to fill that hollowness inside with comfort foods—foods that were off limits because consuming them would lead to weight gain and embarrassment at the Friday weigh-ins—and then I'd get rid of it all. No matter what I filled my emptiness with, though, whether it was alcohol or food, it was only a temporary fix. So I had no choice but to keep the cycle going. At least that's what my distorted mind believed.

It's challenging enough being a student athlete at a university, and my current lifestyle was making it worse. Since I stayed up late drinking, it was pretty rough trying to get up for a mandatory early morning workout. After practice, I faked going to class so my teammates would think I was pursuing academics just like they were. I'd leave the dorm as if I were going to class, then head for "my" couch in the student union and go right back to sleep. It was the same drill I'd pulled with Mom back home when it came to morning practice.

I don't know how I made it through an entire school year. It was all one great big alcoholic haze. Not surprisingly, by spring I was declared academically ineligible. I actually flunked a course on backpacking, of all things. Backpacking! And here I thought I'd hit bottom when I dropped the ball on PE back in high school. With my scholarship revoked and the swimming now officially gone, I returned home—relieved beyond belief that I'd never have to set foot in Arkansas again.

Mom, of course, was furious. When she was my age, she'd had to work hard to pay for her own books and tuition while attending San Diego State. She couldn't for the life of her understand why I was so willing to throw away a free education. I tried to explain to her how bad everything was—from the uncomfortable dynamics between the men's and women's teams to the unchallenging workouts to the God-awful cafeteria food—but she just looked at me as if I were speaking another language.

CHAPTER 20

The Drinking Permeated Everything

O N RETURNING HOME, I MOVED BACK into my old room with Kerri. We had always gotten along, but we weren't all that close. Our dog-eat-dog family dynamic wasn't conducive to forming tight sibling bonds. Kerri had just graduated from Chula Vista High School's magnet program for the creative and performing arts. A gifted singer and dancer, she had earned a scholarship to attend United States International University to hone her talents. Her life looked like it was on the right path, and I was really proud of her.

I was rehired as a lifeguard at the beach at North Island and slipped right back into my carefree Coronado carousing mode. I wasn't training much because I was working every day and didn't have time. That's the story I told anyone who asked, anyway. A few times a week I'd make an attempt to go to practice, but I just couldn't stick with it. The pool was a symbol of everything I'd worked so hard to achieve and then so carelessly flushed down the toilet.

In late July, Patty called me up out of the blue and said, "I've got good news, Karlyn. We're giving you back your scholarship. If you'll accept it, we're going to redshirt you. You won't be able to compete in any meets for the fall semester, but you'll be able to go to classes and you'll still be

part of the team." She was offering me a second chance. She was giving me an opportunity to make things right. The only catch was that
there would be a new set of rules for me. "You have to commit to coming
to my house every night to study," Patty explained. "I'm going to keep
you there until you're done. You'll train with Sam and the men's team in
the morning, because it's clear you need more of a challenge, and you'll
swim with the women's team at night." I thanked Patty for the offer and
told her I needed to think it over. When I told Mom, she couldn't believe
my good fortune. "They really want you on the team, Karlyn," she said.
"They know how valuable you can be to the program. No one's making
them do this. They could have recruited someone else, but they didn't.
They want *you*."

I didn't have the guts to say no.

As soon as the wheels hit the runway in Fayetteville that fall, I knew
I'd made a mistake. I really, really, *really* didn't want to be there. But I
couldn't tell Mom that. She had always put so much faith in me. Despite
all the grief I'd caused her, and was still causing her, she always believed
in me. I told myself to do it for her. I told myself to just buck up and
make the best of the situation.

So there I was again, starting back up at Arkansas with all the best
intentions. And for a flickering moment everything was actually going
according to plan and I was going to succeed. I was going to classes and
swimming well. Patty had recruited a new woman named Heather Aust,
an all-around great swimmer from Tarrytown, New York, who became
my roommate. Since Heather had a boyfriend, she rarely spent the night
in our dorm room. But she worked hard in the pool. In the morning she,
like me, practiced with the men's team. Heather was faster than me, and
her turns in particular were much quicker than mine, so I knew I had to
work to keep up with her. I always perform better when there's that type
of carrot swinging in front of me. Swimming with the guys and chasing

Heather got me back into shape in no time. Coach Freas, however, never spoke to me. I was cranking out the yardage with his team every morning and swimming really fast, but I don't think he ever acknowledged my presence, let alone my efforts.

Things were looking up, but then that familiar loop began to play in my head. *You're not good enough. You never were. You're just a fraud.* To prove it, as soon as I was done studying at Patty's house, I would go out to the bars. Sometimes some of the women on the team would go with me. If there were no swimmers available, it was always easy to find someone from the dorm to go drink with. I was bouncing from situation to situation, like a hummingbird flitting from one succulent flower to the next. A lot of people were partying. I just found myself doing it a lot more than most.

My choices started to get repetitive, and the results were predictable. *Do I go out and get a six-pack of beer, or do I study for that test I have tomorrow?* More often than not, I'd choose the beer. *Do I go camping with friends for the weekend, or do I work on that project that's due?* I'd go camping, and I'd drink all weekend long. No one ever sat me down and said, "You know what, Karlyn? I think you're drinking way too much. Maybe you should give it a rest tonight." There were no checks in place to slow me down.

I was feeling it all the time. The guilt. *You're doing it again, Karlyn. You're doing it again . . .* It's not as if I would get sick at that time if I didn't have a drink, but I did live for that next buzz. I wanted the feeling that came with it. I wanted to feel happy. I wanted to feel included. I also wanted to forget what a screw-up I was. I wanted to feel numb.

Whenever I was back in San Diego and I'd see Dad and the limited existence he'd carved out for himself, I'd tell myself I was never going to end up like that. Yet here I was becoming a carbon copy of him. I was drinking to forget, exactly like my father did. He'd given up on his dreams. He'd thrown hope away. I had never been able to understand how he could be so incapable of turning his life around. Now I had a sneaking suspicion that I needed help, but I couldn't seem to see a way out. There was no one around to throw me a life preserver, nor did I have the courage to ask. There were, of course, things I could have done to ward off the relentless gravitational pull, but no one ever suggested I explore something like AA or talking to a school counselor. Besides, I liked getting drunk, and changing would require hard work. I was more interested in taking the easy way out.

The drinking permeated everything. When I finally did show up for a class, after not having been there for two weeks, I found myself so far behind that the idea of trying to catch up was overwhelming. My only recourse, I decided, was to stop going to class altogether. *What's the point?* I rationalized. *You're sunk anyway.*

In the end, there were no new beginnings for me that fall. All I'd done was transport my problems to another state again, one where it was harder to conceal my shortcomings. Though I wasn't consciously aware of it, I'd become something of a geographical—just like my father.

I managed to make it to the end of the semester, but the results were horrifying. The grand tally was one D and the rest Fs. Tusk, the enormous hog that served as the university's live mascot, could have taken my classes and done better. My only passing grade was in English, and that had been on my third attempt. My GPA was a whopping 0.36. I don't know how I even managed to get that D. My English teacher must have been a fan of the swim team and given it to me as a favor to Patty. This time when I slunk back to Chula Vista, I knew my tenure at Arkansas was ended. The only thing I succeeded at was failing.

Chapter 21

Was I Driving— or Was My Addiction?

W HEN I GOT BACK TO SOUTHERN CALIFORNIA in December, the plan was for me to go straight into community college, but Mom suggested I take a semester off. In retrospect, that was probably the worst thing I could have done. It was becoming increasingly apparent that I needed some semblance of structure in my life—even though when I did have that structure, I continually deviated from it. For someone like me, leaving things open ended was like putting me in the driver's seat of a car with no brakes and a broken steering wheel.

Even though I had partied hard in Arkansas, I was in good swimming shape when I got home. I did a little training with Mom's Coronado Masters team. It was a good group, especially since it included people like Mom's friend Bill, a former Navy SEAL and local lifeguard, and Dave and Janet Lamott. One of the fastest guys on the team was Lieutenant Mike Keeney, a navy helicopter pilot who was stationed at North Island. I liked going to work out, mostly for the chance to flirt with Mike, but it was a challenge getting myself to attend on a regular basis.

When I wasn't swimming with the CMA (Coronado Masters Association), I tried swimming with CNSA. It was strange being back in the pool with the old team. Troy was long gone by then. He'd moved up to Northern California to coach Walnut Creek Aquabears, east of San Francisco. Bill Steele was the new coach. Bill was good, but he was no Troy. I was one of the fastest swimmers in the pool due to all the hard work I'd put in at Arkansas, but my motivation, not surprisingly, was flagging. I was only nineteen, but I felt ancient compared to the rest of the swimmers, most of whom were in their mid-teens.

I finally decided it was easier to swim with the Masters team. I was dating Mike Keeney by this time, and his being a member helped. He was intensely focused in nearly everything he did, and we enjoyed challenging each other in the water. Sometimes he'd take me to the Officers' Club for a formal occasion. He'd get dressed up in that dashing uniform and he looked so handsome it made me weak in the knees. Throughout the San Diego region there's always been a certain cachet to dating a navy officer, especially after the movie *Top Gun* came out. When I was on Keeney's arm, I felt as if the sparkling aura of his uniform and his determined attitude were rubbing off on me.

Keeney shared a condo on Orange Avenue in Coronado with two other Navy Academy graduates. Just half a block away was a little twelve-table restaurant called Bula's. One of Bula's owners was Steve Lindsey. *Bula* is the Fijian equivalent of *aloha,* so it made sense that the restaurant would have a low-key, beachy feel. When I heard they needed a bartender, I pulled out my trusty government ID, applied for the job, and got it. After a few months, however, Lindsey found out I was underage. Even though he had every right to fire me on the spot, he kept me on as a waitress.

Bula's had a very *Cheers*-like ambiance, complete with an eclectic cast of regulars. Lindsey had done a stint as a waiter at Chart House, a popular restaurant franchise at the time, and he and his partner, Mike Neil, loosely based their menu on Chart House's. Just like Chart House, Bula's had an open-bar kitchen, fresh-baked bread, and an amazing salad bar. It also had an outdoor patio that doubled the restaurant's size in the warm summer months, and it served a huge variety of beers and wines.

Thanks to Keeney's positive influence, I was beginning to get my life back in order. I was in great swimming shape and I had even managed to cut back on my partying. When my shift would end at 10:30 or so at night, the idea of hitting the bars in town just didn't appeal to me. That's not to say I quit drinking; I just toned it down some.

Every spring, the California Department of Parks and Recreation sets about hiring beach lifeguards for the coming summer. The positions are coveted because beach lifeguards earn a lot more money than pool lifeguards. The competition to earn a position is absolutely fierce, with many collegiate swimmers failing to make the cut.

The first step of the hiring process is two tests to prove you're up to the physical challenges of the job. One test is a 1,000-yard ocean swim; the other is a combined 200-yard run, 400-yard swim, and another 200-yard run. The top finishers in the swimming and running tests would qualify for an interview, and those who passed that interview would be selected to attend rigorous training in open-water lifesaving techniques, CPR, and first aid. I sailed through the physical tests and the interview and was tapped to go to Huntington Beach to start my training.

Essentially I was back in school again, but this time I was doing it on my own terms and at one of my favorite places on Earth: the beach. Keeney and I were both happy, because instead of just drifting, I now had something of a plan and I was committed to a direction in life. "It's always important," Keeney would tell me, "to have goals in place."

From the time we started dating, Keeney seemed to take it upon himself to help me straighten out my life. He too had been exposed to alcohol abuse and an impaired parent in childhood, and his way of coping was to strive for excellence in everything he did. The results of his ambitiousness spoke for themselves. He'd really made a life for himself, and he was convinced that with more discipline I could do the same. He wanted me to watch my drinking, which I was on board with. In addition to the lifeguard training I was undertaking, he also wanted me back in school right away, which we both knew would be a good idea. I knew he loved me. But in the back of my mind I had the thought that maybe he was more enamored with the idea of fixing me.

I wasn't so sure I wanted to be anyone's project. Least of all Keeney's. He would continually compare me to Jenny Lamott, a former CNSA teammate of mine. He'd point out how well Jenny was doing in school, how she really had her act together, and how the sky was the limit for her. I'm not sure if he was trying to motivate or inspire me, but the more he brought Jenny up, the more it had the opposite effect on me. I began to feel as if I could never measure up to the person Keeney thought I should be. I also wasn't convinced that I could ever be officer's wife material. *If he only knew the real me he'd dump me in a heartbeat,* I'd tell myself as I lay awake in bed late at night.

I drove up to Huntington State Beach for lifeguard class on the weekends with my friend Chris Barrack, someone I'd known since elementary school. There was a series of written tests for extra credit in the lifeguard training program. We had been briefed in advance that those who scored the highest on these tests would have priority in choosing where to be stationed at the end of training. I copied one of Chris's tests. I didn't even try to disguise my work; I just blatantly copied it. If Keeney had ever found out that I had that side to me, it would have crushed him. I ended up with an overall higher score than Chris, so I got first crack at location. There was only one position open at Silver Strand State Beach in Coronado, and I nabbed it. Chris, meanwhile, was relegated to taking a spot up in North County that was, depending on traffic, a forty-to-sixty-minute commute each way. I felt a little guilty for taking the position that rightfully belonged to Chris, but those feelings didn't last long. I was determined to get what I wanted, no matter who it hurt.

One of the reasons Silver Strand was so appealing to me was because it was where an old flame, Steve Raap (or Raapman, as he was called), had been guarding for the past six seasons. Again, there was that dark side to me—the manipulative side—that Keeney didn't know about. Raapman was more accepting of my faults and let my behavior slide, whereas Keeney was more critical. And as I spent more time with Raapman, I began to realize that my personality, for better or worse, was more aligned with his than with Keeney's. I didn't let him into my darkness—no one had ever been allowed there. But I didn't have to face disappointment from him like I did from Keeney.

When it became clear that Keeney and I were struggling with our relationship, I started drinking more. First I started drinking at Bula's. Just a couple of beers before my shift, or wine I snuck on the job. Being buzzed helped make the time go by faster. I also thought I was a better waitress when I was drinking—more fun, more flirtatious. The big tips I received confirmed what I thought.

When I finally broke up with Keeney, he was devastated. I reassured him that he could find dozens of women who would make a far better officer's wife than I would, but he didn't want to hear it. He was in love and insisted he'd never felt like this before with anyone. When I look back at this and some of the other choices I've made in my life, I wonder if it was me making the decisions, or my addiction.

CHAPTER 22

One Day Closer
to Oblivion

O N THE OUTSIDE, MY LIFE looked pretty good. I was a carefree party girl, a waitress, and a beach lifeguard surrounded by plenty of opportunities to live it up. I loved drinking because it made me feel good. It made me feel happy. It made me forget. But when the high would wear off, I'd know I wasn't happy at all. I was miserable. For the most part though, I kept up such a good facade that no one around me was remotely aware of the emptiness I felt, let alone the acidic feeling of self-loathing that was starting to grow in my gut. In the back of mind I heard a warning. *Watch out Karlyn, you're headed down a dangerous road. Be careful.* But I didn't want to listen. I wanted to have fun. I wanted to feel numb. I wanted to get drunk, no matter what the consequences. After all, you only live once.

Steve Lindsey, the owner of Bula's, was very hands on. He could be a gracious host and conversationalist, but he was also very temperamental. The staff learned to avoid him when he was moody because when the shit hit the fan, more often than not he'd fire the first person he came into contact with, even if it was undeserved. I had my fair share of run-ins with him. Over the next couple of years I probably got fired four or five times. Luckily, I could almost always talk myself back into his good graces, and he'd hire me back.

I doubt Raapman realized I even had an issue with drinking. I may not have been an alcoholic yet, but I was certainly abusing the substance. I was partying more and more, and my entitled view of life was spilling over into my work. I'd taken to ordering food from the restaurant and neglecting to pay for it on occasion. Every once in a while I'd get caught, but not often enough to deter me. I was still having issues with my eating disorder, and working in a restaurant did not help. When it came to my appetite, my internal barometer was completely out of whack. Sometimes I could eat normally for days, but other times if I ate past a certain point of fullness, all bets were off. I'd gorge myself with junk food because I knew I wouldn't be keeping it down anyway. In my twisted mind, binge-ing and purging had become a perfectly reasonable thing to do.

After the first time Lindsey fired me from Bula's, I got a great job working at the Hotel del Coronado again. This time I somehow talked my way into an entry-level management position and became a host-ess in the famed Crown Room restaurant. It was there that I learned a very useful piece of information that completely changed my life. One morning shift, after a hard night of partying, the restaurant supervisor, who was not much older than me, said, "Karlyn, are you hungover?" Paralyzed with fear, I didn't respond. I'd been forewarned that even the tiniest hint of drinking on the job was grounds for termination. "Here," she said. "Let me fix that for you." And she proceeded to make me a Bloody Mary. After I drank it, my hangover went away. All of a sudden the funk in my head cleared, the buzz came back, and I felt absolutely great. My hangover problems were solved.

Up to that point my drinking had been kept in check because there were physical ramifications if I drank too much. But learning this one trick—a drink in the morning would help offset the headache and nau-sea from the night before—was a huge shift for me. I could now put myself in nonstop party mode and never have to suffer through a hang-over again. I didn't last long at The Del in my new management position.

Summer was coming and that meant one thing: time to quit so I could get back to the beach.

The other light-bulb moment I had at this point in my life came from a pamphlet on alcoholism I found in the lifeguard locker room one day at Silver Strand State Beach. There was a check list inside. It was a primer to help determine whether you or someone close to you might have a drinking problem. When I scanned down that list, I remember thinking, *Check, check, check . . .* The pamphlet nearly burned the palms of my hands, so much of what I was reading applied to me. I snapped it shut and quickly put it back where I'd found it. I never looked at it again. If I didn't acknowledge it, it didn't exist.

So I just kept doing what I was doing. I continued to make poor decisions. I continued to hang around places like the late-night restaurant scene that facilitated my drinking. I continued to hang around people like my lifeguard buddies who just wanted to have fun and party.

Sometimes my coworkers and I would head down to Mexico to go dancing, cruise Revolution Boulevard, or just drink on the cheap. Tijuana and Rosarito Beach have always been party hotspots. Mexico was relatively safe back then, and the border crossing was easier. From my home in Chula Vista, I could pop into my VW Bug, drive down, buy a cold six-pack of beer or a liter of tequila and some warm tortillas and be back home in about forty-five minutes. On weekends we would drive to the Rosarito Beach Hotel and dance until the sun came up. I wasn't the only one doing this, as most of us had adopted this ritual back in high school as soon as we got our driver's licenses. Everything was cheaper down there, and we made Mexico our personal playground. The rules were relaxed and the drinking age was never enforced. Needless to say, we crossed the border every chance we could.

After the hiatus suggested by Mom, I enrolled in community college at San Diego Mesa College. The intention was for me to compete on their swim team. I went to a few classes, and I may have actually passed one or two. The majority, though, I flunked. It was Arkansas all over again. I'd find myself falling a little behind, and then a little more, and pretty soon I'd be past the point of no return. I just didn't have the strength to keep up. It happens in long distance swimming competitions too. Someone bolts in front of you, and you tell yourself, *That's okay. Let them get ahead. I'll catch back up to them on the back half.* But their lead continues to build, and try as you might you can't close the distance. And then, just when you're supposed to put the hammer down and make the move you've been building toward, you realize you don't have the energy and you'll never catch that swimmer ahead of you in a million years.

I was telling Mom I was going to school. She had taken an extra job so she could buy me a little red Toyota Tercel adorned with vanity plates that read, "SXY SWMR." She was impressed by how successfully I seemed to be managing my part-time jobs, a full class load, and training. At least that's what she thought. The only thing really full at that point was my beer or wine glass.

Mom was in love. In 1983 she'd fallen head over heels with a fellow Masters swimmer from Del Mar named Lloyd Skramstad who was an interior designer for Foodmaker, Inc., the parent company of Jack in the Box. He was half Filipino and half Norwegian, and his parents had met in the Philippines before the Japanese invasion of World War II. His father survived the infamous Bataan Death March only to die of typhoid in a concentration camp, leaving behind a family of four in Japanese-occupied Manila. Lloyd loved to swim, and after the war he became a nationally ranked competitor. He was so talented that when he left the Philippines at the age of eighteen to join the U.S. Navy, he was asked to compete for the military swim team. He was passionate about both swimming and horticulture, and the backyard of his house was filled with little dish gardens. He had hundreds of them. His hobby suited him well—he was one of the most patient individuals I've ever met. He had been married previously and had three daughters. Lloyd loved swimming as much as Mom did. He loved training and he loved going to meets. They were a perfect match.

Lloyd quickly became the father I had never had. He was supportive, loving, and in his own way, affectionate. He wasn't a big talker, but he was comfortable in his skin and he was a guy you could just sit around with. His love for Mom, and for me, was unconditional. It was very different from anything I'd ever experienced. Lloyd always made sure to tell me how proud he was of me, even when I screwed up. If I got in a fix, he'd loan me money with no questions asked. For the first time in my life, I experienced what it was like to have an actively affectionate and caring father.

Eventually Lloyd even started to introduce me as his daughter. "This is Karlyn. She's my daughter," he'd say with his thick Filipino accent. The look on people's faces was priceless, as the two of us looked nothing alike, especially given my blonde hair. "Oh, this is my *white* daughter," he'd explain, as if momentarily perplexed by their confusion. "My other daughters, they're Filipina and brown like me."

Mom and Lloyd moved in together, into a house in Solana Beach, a coastal town twenty-five miles north of San Diego. I enjoyed driving up there whenever I had free time, and I was relieved the two of them seemed to be happy together. Mom deserved to be happy. It had taken a while, but I was starting to reconcile with her. Instead of resenting her, I began to step back and recognize the sacrifices she'd made for her three Ks. Moving away from the anger I had harbored for so long wasn't easy, and we still got into arguments, particularly when it came to my performance in swimming or school. It's a common mother-daughter dynamic: love and hate, push and pull.

Unfortunately, one result of our repaired relationship was that we began drinking together. Whenever I was up for a visit, Mom, Lloyd, and I would go out to dinner. We'd order a nice bottle of wine and discuss the wonderful bouquet with hints of oak, etc., but I was just playing along. Not once in my entire life did I *ever* drink for taste. I loved the effect of alcohol, but I hated its taste. When I drank with Mom and Lloyd, sometimes we all had so much that we would give each other roadside sobriety tests to see who should drive us home. I liked this turn of events, rationalizing that if Mom couldn't be a mother to me in the traditional sense, at least she could be my drinking buddy.

Mom admitted to me years later that she too used to self-medicate when she was under duress. In particular, when she became a single parent of three and had all those financial worries, she needed something to help her cope with the stress. She was working long hours, and she had to drive to labs all over San Diego County. She was in crisis mode, she said, to save us kids. Things were going poorly with Kirsten, and her "golden child"—me—was misbehaving. And while it may have seemed that Kerri was doing pretty well, she too was exhibiting a wild streak, spending time with friends on crazy jaunts to dance clubs in Mexico.

I lasted all of one semester at San Diego Mesa, and, not surprisingly, I did not compete on their swim team. After that debacle, I enrolled at Southwestern College, another two-year school, this one located in eastern Chula Vista. But I didn't stick around there for very long either. Lindsey rehired me at Bula's and my lifeguarding shifts offered a little bit of stability, but as far as any long-term goals were concerned, I was still struggling.

Next I went to San Diego City College to study calligraphy. Forget curriculums associated with any kind of major, I decided. I was now going to try to get some units by enrolling in lightweight, less challenging classes. I made a commitment to myself that I was going to take a basic calligraphy class and I was going to do it sober. I'd build from there.

And then, once I got back into the flow of school, I'd tackle some core classes. After all, how hard could that be, calligraphy?

As it turned out, it was very hard. Especially for an alcoholic who was in denial about her situation. Two weeks into the semester I walked into a 7-Eleven, bought a cheap bottle of white wine, and drank the whole thing in the parking lot before class. We had a tracing assignment, and I screwed on my best face as I set about doing the work. I took my time, being very deliberate with my pencil strokes. The class was completely silent. Everyone was hunched over their papers. I leaned back to study my progress. It was going well. It was going so well, in fact, that I began to believe I might have found my calling. Maybe I could make a go of all this fancy writing stuff. But when the teacher signaled that time was up and I removed the tracing paper from the letters I'd been copying, I could immediately see what a ridiculously poor job I'd done. My tracing and coordination were so far off base that the teacher must have thought I was suffering from some type of palsy. I ended up dropping that class too.

My effort to reinvigorate my swimming career was as unsuccessful as my educational forays. Day in and day out I would make deals with myself. *Okay, I'm going to make it to practice and I'm going to really dedicate myself. I'm turning over a new leaf. I'm going to go to school, apply myself, and I will reach my potential once and for all.* But part way through the day my resolve would crumble, and I'd be one day further away from the pool or the classroom and one day closer to total oblivion. The loop that played in my head was not all that different from the Top 40 cycle of hits I used to listen to on the radio. One, however, was entertaining, and the other—*Karlyn, you are making poor choices*—was debilitating.

CHAPTER **23**

Where Had the Time Gone?

ALCOHOLICS TEND TO CHOOSE relationships that enable their disease, not heal it. My relationship with Raapman was a classic example of that type of codependency. Neither of us was helping the other in the time-to-grow-up department. We were sharing a rental house in Imperial Beach with two other lifeguards, and it was party central. I was guarding, waiting tables, and avoiding going to school.

I managed to get fired again from Bula's, but luckily one of the regulars took pity on me and hired me on at The Bonita Store Restaurant. If I could just be as nice to myself as others were, I thought, my life would be so much better.

The 1984 Olympic Games in Los Angeles came and went and I barely noticed. I paid only passing attention to the televised coverage of the swimming competitions. I was happy for swimmers like Tracy Caulkins, Nancy Hogshead, and Rowdy Gaines who had hung in there after Jimmy Carter's boycott four years earlier. They were deserving of all the success and accolades they received at the McDonald's Olympic Swim Stadium. More importantly, I knew they could also finally put some closure on their swimming careers—something I was having a difficult time doing because the choices I'd made had left everything in such disarray. *Was I still a swimmer, or was I done too?* I had no idea. I still felt I was a swimmer, and I acted like I was still a swimmer, especially when I was with people who knew nothing about the sport. *But how could I call myself a swimmer if I never swam?*

What struck me most during that summer, as the entire country went Olympics-crazy watching the likes of Caulkins, Mary Lou Retton, and Carl Lewis compete under the backdrop of the vibrant blue Southern California sky, was how quickly the previous four years had slipped by. Caulkins had spent the time in heavy, heavy training. She had poured her heart and soul into one final chance at fulfilling a childhood dream of winning an Olympic gold medal. Each training set, each weightlifting session, and each race at meets big and small was carefully calculated by her and her coach, Randy Reese, to get her to the top of that podium. I, on the other hand, had spent the exact same period muddling through life. I couldn't account for where the time had gone. When I looked back on it, I honestly couldn't distinguish one day from another. Life had become a blur.

In November 1984, Raapman announced, out of the blue, that he was going to fulfill a lifelong dream of cycling around New Zealand. He didn't invite me. It was a peculiar turn of events. He'd planned this whole thing without consulting me. Not that I had the money to join him on such a trip, but that wasn't the point. His decision spoke volumes to how he viewed our relationship. Once he left, I started seeing someone else right away. No way was I waiting around for a guy who took off and left me behind. Then Christmas rolled around and I got a call. He was missing me terribly. He suggested I sell his truck, use the funds to buy a plane ticket, and join him as soon as I could. Even though I was with a new guy, Raapman's offer was too good to pass up. I talked it over with Mom and

Lloyd, and they both said to go for it. "Do it while you still can," Lloyd said. He even offered me a little money for the trip.

Raapman and I toured a big chunk of the country on our bikes. New Zealand was as beautiful as advertised, and there couldn't have been a better way to experience everything the country had to offer. We'd pedal all day and spend nights at campgrounds and youth hostels. Nothing was tightly planned. If we found a place we liked, we'd extend our stay there. We spent time in Otaki, a small town on the North Island, and earned money picking vegetables and fruit. The locals were always friendly and hospitable. If they told us about a little town they thought we should visit, we'd set off on our bikes to check it out. It was an idyllic, carefree existence.

On our way back from New Zealand, I stopped in Hawaii to spend some time on my own. It was on Oahu that I got my first taste of the Hawaiian Islands. Right away, it felt like home. Among other things, Hawaii is the birthplace of one of competitive swimming's most revered figures, Duke Kahanamoku. Duke, who personified a waterman, won medals in the 1912, 1920, and 1924 Olympic Games and helped popularize both competitive swimming and surfing. He also did stints as a lifeguard. His love of all things aquatic led to his inclusion in the 1965 inaugural class of the International Swimming Hall of Fame.

My friend Sloan Hubbard had moved to Hawaii with her family. Her dad, now a navy captain, was stationed at Pearl Harbor. After I landed, I somehow managed to find my way to their house, and I knocked on the Hubbards' door out of the blue, just like I used to back in Coronado. They were kind enough to invite me to stay with them for as long as I liked. No matter how reckless my lifestyle became, I had the sense that there was always a guardian angel looking out for my well-being. She took many different forms, and Dick and Dougie Hubbard were two of those forms.

It was fun spending time with the Hubbards, especially Sloan. She and I toured the island a bit and hung out at the beach catching up, baking in the sun, and, of course, having a beer or two. We even swam a few workouts at the Pearl Harbor pool. Dick and Dougie made sure to include me when they were invited to barbeques and other events. I was still drinking quite a lot, but not so much that I was embarrassing myself. I'd always been able to hide my drunk side pretty well. Not that I ever considered myself a drunk. I was just on vacation in a beautiful place, drinking and having a nice time with some old friends. I was a globe-trotting party girl looking for fun, and my behavior wasn't hurting anybody. At least that's the picture my messed-up psyche had painted.

Ironically, Dick was now going to be the commanding officer of the navy's alcohol and drug rehabilitation center. I was invited to his change of command—a ceremonial transfer of authority from one officer to another, complete with a military band and the symbolic passing of flags. Appropriately, it was a dry affair, and I looked sweet and innocent in a borrowed, conservative Laura Ashley dress. I hadn't been so sweet the night before when I'd liberated a full bottle of Crown Royal scotch from an event we were at. Now while everyone was sitting in rapt attention, listening to somber speeches or inspirational stories of recovery, I couldn't stop thinking about the bottle I had hidden in Sloan's car. It started to signal to me like a lighthouse beacon. I excused myself, saying I needed to use the ladies' room. Instead, I went out to the car and belted back a fair amount of the scotch. It burned going down, but I felt better almost immediately. When I look back, I can see how insane my behavior was, even in these early days. Here I was in the middle of a change of command at an alcohol and drug rehabilitation center, sneaking scotch and having my own little party in the parking lot. Had I been enlisted in the navy, my behavior would have gotten me admitted on the spot. I was one very sick young woman.

Chapter 24

Recovery: Days 3 to 10

S ICK? DEFINITELY. BUT THINGS WERE LOOKING UP. By my third day of recovery, I was seeing signs that I was getting better. I was still having convulsions, but they were diminishing in both frequency and intensity. Though I was still hooked up to an IV, I exulted in moving around under my own power. But the euphoria was short lived. Pretty soon I was shaking again, and I crept right back into bed. I was still having trouble getting any food into myself. "You need to eat, Karlyn," Jennifer said. "You need to get your strength back." But the only thing my stomach could tolerate was Ensure. It tasted chalky, but I could keep it down. It was a start.

I wrote a letter, in shaky handwriting, to my boyfriend, Dave, that day. I told him what I was going through, giving blow-by-blow details. I told him how much I was looking forward to my new life. "It ain't gonna be easy, but neither were Troy's workouts," I wrote. It was the first letter I'd written to Dave in months. But I never sent it. For some reason, I just hung on to it.

Jennifer told me I needed to attend an AA meeting. It was mandatory, an integral part of the protocol.

"But how am I going to do that?" I asked. "Whenever I stand up and try to walk, the room spins and I have an overwhelming urge to puke."

"Who said anything about walking, Karlyn?" Jennifer said with a smile. "This is a five-star resort, remember?"

And the next thing I knew, I was being pushed to my first Alcoholics Anonymous meeting in a wheelchair.

The meeting was held in a conference room, and since it was open to the public, there were about two hundred people in attendance. I met an amputee named Mike. He was a freebase addict. I met my roommate from behind the curtain. His name was Kurt, and he was hooked on heroin. As I watched him fidget and scan the room, I got the sense that Kurt wasn't quite ready to get clean. During the meeting I was still pretty out of it and didn't understand much of what was being said, but it was nice to have a change of scenery. I still felt like crap as I sat there, but at least I was feeling like crap in a different setting.

By the end of Day Three, I finally had enough strength to take a shower. The sensation of warm water flowing over my ravaged body was indescribable. When you've been close to the edge like I had, the smallest luxury can take on monumental proportions.

By Day Four my head was clearer, and I could walk without assistance. As I did laps through the corridor and motored around the nurses' station, I realized I'd turned the corner. I'd endured three full days of living hell, but now I could feel myself getting stronger. I kept going to the meetings. There were three or four a day. Every day.

At some point I finally got up and shared, or told my story. I was nervous as hell, but only for about two seconds. Standing in front of a room full of addicts and alcoholics, I felt an immediate camaraderie. I was surrounded by fellow survivors, all desperately seeking relief from their addictions. I began to feel hopeful that the worst had passed. A tiny kernel of the old Karlyn was beginning to resurface. I continued to exercise a bit and volunteered to help set up the room for meetings. I had the urge to make myself useful, and staying busy helped keep my mind off the uncertainty that lay ahead.

The nurses kept telling me to slow down.

"Easy does it," Jennifer said.

But I didn't want to take it easy. I wanted to get going. I felt as if I'd woken from a coma and had misplaced years of my life that I would never get back. I had no idea what the future had in store for me. I didn't know whether I could still be a lifeguard or whether I'd completely blown that part of my life as I had so many others. I had no idea at the time that my bosses would stick by me. But thankfully, John Waterman, my immediate supervisor and the athletic director at the Naval Amphibious Base, and his boss, John Baker, the head of the Morale, Welfare, and Recreation Department (MWR), had already started the process of ensuring I was placed on disability during my rehabilitation. Looking back on it, I owe an incredible amount to those two men. In my time of need, they stood by me, another manifestation of the guardian angel that protected me throughout those lost years.

On Day Five, I noticed I was still being given a daily dosage of medications. I asked Jennifer what they were.

"V&V," she said. "Vitamins and Valium."

"You're still giving me Valium?" I asked.

"It helps to calm you down."

"I don't need to be calmed down, Jennifer. Here," I said, handing her back the pill. "Take this back and please stop giving it to me. I don't want to be on Valium."

I was terrified I would develop a new addiction. Besides, my head was feeling clearer than it had in years and I didn't want any drug to compromise that.

"You can't do that, Karlyn," she said. "You can't just stop taking your medications."

"Go talk to my doctor about it," I said. "I'm sorry, Jennifer, but I refuse to take any more Valium."

My doctor was consulted, and he agreed that I no longer needed it.

The Big Book,* AA's bible, centers on accepting what is and relinquishing control to a higher power or God. These practices are at the heart of recovery success. But try as I might, I couldn't get it. For the longest time, I couldn't understand what "God" the book was referring to. The only God I knew of was Kirsten's God, and that only because she had become a born-again Christian. Her way of filling that Pipes' void was to embrace religion, and it saved her in more ways than one. I had no issue with the path she'd chosen, and I respected her opinions, but I didn't agree with them. If I was expected to become as devout as my sister, there was no way I was going to succeed at sobriety.

I continued wrestling with the concept of a higher power one morning at breakfast in the cafeteria. God, I knew, meant many different things to many different people. But what did God mean to me? I had no clue. And why would God love someone like me? Deep down I held on to the belief that I was rotten to the core and far beyond saving. This is very typical of the alcoholic personality. But the more I thought about it, the more I realized that when the Big Book refers to God, it's referring to a higher power of *your own understanding*. It could be any entity. It's just not *you*.

I saw a grapefruit sitting on the table. I studied it for a long time. Spontaneously, I decided to make the grapefruit my higher power. Comical, yes, but when I transferred the notion of a higher power from myself to that inanimate object, I finally got it. The important thing to acknowledge, I came to understand, was that *I* wasn't the one in control. There was something greater than myself looking out for me. And the more I used that line of thinking, the more I realized it was consistent with my lifelong feeling that I had a guardian angel keeping tabs on me. Maybe a higher power, maybe even God, had been there all along.

I wouldn't call my revelation a spiritual awakening; it was more of a

---

* Otherwise known as *Alcoholics Anonymous: The Story of How Many Thousands of Men and Women Have Recovered from Alcoholism*, Fourth Edition (New York: Alcoholics Anonymous World Services, Inc., 2001).

release. Acknowledging the fact that there was a higher power eased my guilt. It allowed me to lighten my burden. *Maybe I'm not such a bad person after all. Maybe I don't have to beat myself up for all the poor choices I have made in my life.* It was a breakthrough.

Each patient in the addiction ward wore a wristband, making me feel as if I was under lockdown in a psychiatric ward. But by Day Seven, I was given a pass to leave the hospital and visit a gym across the street. I had lost so much muscle tone over the past several years, and over the past few months in particular, that it felt as if I were living in a different body. I was thrilled to work up a sweat again. It was reassuring to know that even after everything I'd been through, I was still an athlete. Each new day was bringing me new strength, new awareness, and new possibilities.

Another doctor came to see me. I assumed that he, like the others, was there to check my vitals. During my stay I'd become something of an expert on how to read a medical chart, so I started rattling off the numbers, giving him the latest readings for my pulse and blood pressure. He humored me by listening, but it turned out he wasn't all that interested in my blood work. He was a psychologist. He wanted to talk about what was going on in my head, not my veins. Mom had hired him to help me through the recovery process. It cost a lot of money, but she didn't think twice about it. She didn't discuss it with me. She didn't even bring it to my attention. She just did it.

The entire staff at Sharp Cabrillo Hospital had recovery down to a science. They told me that once I was released from treatment it was strongly recommended that I live in a halfway house to minimize the chances of relapsing. They wanted me to be among other recovering alcoholics because doing so would provide me with on-the-scene support. But I couldn't. I told them I needed to go home to take care of my father and my adopted chickens.

"You're going to relapse, Karlyn," Jennifer said. "You have that type of personality. You're already doing too much. You're taking on too much.

You're moving way too fast."

"I can do this, Jennifer," I said.

"It may seem as if you can, but you're still on a pink cloud," she said. "We've been doing this for a long time. We've seen it all before. You're going to come crashing down."

But nothing she said would dissuade me. I was determined to go home, and I did.

Before I entered Sharp Cabrillo Hospital I had been told to pack for two or three days. I was such a wreck, I was there for ten. But the nurses were all amazed at my recovery. They told me they'd seen a lot of people come through over the years and, judging from the way I had looked that first night, they had all been convinced they were going to lose me. They had all thought I was going to die. "We didn't have high hopes that you'd make it," Jennifer said. "Especially after we saw the lab tests."

"That's because you didn't look closely enough at the results," I said.

She studied my face in confusion, not following.

"You didn't see the chlorinated water score," I explained, offering her a smile. "If you had, you would have known that I'm a competitive swimmer. Competitive swimmers learn early on how to endure some pretty hellacious stuff and still survive."

Looking back, I'd like to believe that divine guidance interceded to help save my life. When Mom called Dr. Nichol's office that Thursday, how was it she was able to get me an appointment the very next day? That was something that just didn't happen. Had there been no appointment available that Friday, there's a good chance I wouldn't be here. If the next available slot had been Monday, I would have simply continued to drink the way I was drinking, and I have no doubt that, with a blood alcohol level higher than .52, I would have been dead by the end of the weekend. Mom would have shown up at the house on Monday morning and found my body.

CHAPTER 25

Searching for Something
Beyond the Next Drink

T HE NEED TO TRAVEL—whether for competition, college, or just adventure—was ingrained in me, and so was the habit of homecoming. When I finally got home from the New Zealand adventure with Raapman, I did as I always did: I picked up right where I'd left off. That meant waitressing, lifeguarding, partying, and finding any excuse to avoid going to the pool.

My father, meanwhile, had been retired from teaching now for a few years. He had been given the option to resign from his teaching position when, under the influence, he had gotten up on stage during another junior high school's recital and begun to conduct the band as if they were his own students. In an otherwise unremarkable career, he exited under a cloud of embarrassment and shame. Since he didn't work anymore, he could drink to his heart's content. And that's what he did. He camped out at his small apartment and he drank. His monthly pension and Social Security checks afforded him the ability to drink from morning to night. He didn't have to try to hide it anymore. He'd leave the apartment only if he absolutely had to. Sometimes, out of guilt, I would stop by for a visit. I'd look at him sitting there with the glazed expression he always wore, and I'd remember his response whenever Kirsten, Kerri, and I would ask him what he wanted for Father's Day: "All I want is a little peace and quiet." His wish had finally come true.

But as fate would have it, his perfect retirement didn't last. He had a series of small seizures. My brother Mark called me one day to say Dad was in the hospital, and when I went to see him I nearly didn't recognize him. The ruddy face, the broken capillaries around the nose—those were still the same. It was his temperament that threw me for a loop. The seizures had wiped parts of his brain clean, and some of his long-term memory was gone. He could remember his early years vividly—growing up in Prescott and El Centro—but after that it became hazy. He knew who I was. He remembered Mom and all about his children, but he had completely forgotten just about everything else. In medical lingo, this phenomenon is known as Wernicke-Korsakoff syndrome, commonly called "wet brain." It was eerie. Overnight, Dad became a harmless, child-like individual, completely unaware of his addiction and the destruction it and he had wreaked on his family. He even forgot that he had a drinking problem. In fact, he had no craving for alcohol at all.

My father couldn't care for himself anymore, and in 1984 Kirsten and her family decided to take him in. They'd take over Dad's income and use the money to help pay his expenses. They were living in San Diego at the time, and Kirsten's MS had stabilized to a degree. But still, here she was in a wheelchair with two young kids, and now she was going to become caretaker to our father? But the plan was fine with me. I certainly wasn't jumping up and down waving my hand to volunteer for the assignment.

For Thanksgivings, I had taken to driving up the coast to spend the day with Lloyd and Mom. Lloyd's three daughters would be there, as would a lot of us from the Pipes side of the family. That's Lloyd. He always went out of his way to make sure everyone felt included. He even invited Kirsten and Michael to bring Dad. It was strange, seeing my father in that setting. He would just sit down in a chair in the living room and wait to be summoned to the table. Nothing ever bothered him. There was no anger. His temper seemed to have disappeared completely along with his desire to drink. He was perfectly fine with whatever was happening around him. He appeared as only an empty shell of the bright, dynamic, talented man he had once been.

Eventually Kirsten and Michael moved clear across the country to a small town near Matthews, North Carolina, for Michael's work, and Dad went with them. Mom was pretty upset about the decision. Not because Dad was going with them, but because she was concerned about how the colder weather would affect Kirsten's MS.

Meanwhile, my cravings were getting worse while I was working at Bula's. Whether it was brunch, lunch, or dinner, I'd sneak into the walk-in fridge and drink wine straight from a gallon jug. I'd have one of my coworkers, often a dishwasher, serve as lookout. He'd stand watch near the door while I stood there chugging. The wine helped me get through my shift until I could go back home and drink some more. Once you're hooked into the restaurant scene in Coronado, everyone knows you, and the bartenders are more than happy to pour you some free ones. That allowed me to become quite thrifty. I saved every penny I could. I was working hard that summer to achieve my new goal: a biking adventure in Australia with Raapman.

In the fall of 1985 the California Department of Parks and Recreation announced it would be creating some permanent lifeguard positions. This was big news, because if selected, you'd be able to work year-round as a full-time employee. That not only meant better pay and more job security, but also benefits such as health insurance. Candidates would undergo two rounds of interviews. If you performed well during those, you'd be sent to basic police officer training school in Sylmar. If you passed, you'd eventually become a full-fledged lifeguard peace officer.

Raapman and I both applied. He scored pretty well on the first test. I did too, but I wasn't all that thrilled with the timing of the whole thing. I didn't want to pursue it. My sights were set on Australia, and our departure date was just around the corner.

Shortly after we got back from the first interview, Raapman found out he was to advance to the second round. I was sitting in the room with him when he got the call. He was so excited that he paced around the room while he was on the phone. His second interview, he learned, was scheduled for the following month.

"I'm gonna take this, Karlyn," he said as he hung up.

"What do you mean you're gonna take this?" I said. "We're leaving in a couple of weeks."

"It's something I need to do."

"Hold on a second, Steve," I said, surprised by his newfound ambition. "*We* have plans. We're going to Australia. We've both been working really hard to save up for this trip. Doesn't that count for anything?"

I was devastated. Part of my disappointment arose from the fact that for the first time in a long time I had focused on something and had been successful in achieving it. I had worked my butt off juggling two jobs all summer long and had saved over $5,000. Now Raapman was determined to take that all away from me. That's the way the alcoholic's mind works. It wasn't important that he was pursuing something of his own—something permanent that could pay off for him in the long run. The only thing that mattered to me was how the timing of his interview was going to affect me and my plans.

"Karlyn, this is really important," he said. "I can't just walk away from a great opportunity like this."

"Fine. Do what you need to do, Steve, and I'll do what I need to do."

"What's that supposed to mean?" he said.

"I'm going forward with the trip, just like we planned," I said.

"You're going to go by yourself?"

"Yes."

I was filled with bravado on the outside, but on the inside I was scared to death. I'd never traveled halfway around the world by myself before. I knew I could figure it out, but I was filled with a mixture of excitement and dread as the day drew closer. Once I got to Cairns, Australia, and started moving around a bit, however, I began to feel more and more comfortable with my new sense of freedom. After a few days getting my bearings, I called Raapman and found out he had aced the second interview. I congratulated him, and meant it when I told him I was happy for him.

We spoke again a few days later. The test scores were back. "I guess I wasn't what they were looking for," he said with deep disappointment in his voice. "The good news is that I'll be in Australia in two days." I should have been happy about the turn of events, but I wasn't. Our brief time apart had resulted in a mental shift for me. Part of it may have been that I was still feeling the sting of his willingness to set our plans aside in favor of anything else. But a bigger factor was the measure of confidence I had now gained. I knew I could tackle this adventure without him.

Within a week of Raapman's arrival, we weren't getting along at all. We'd bike some, but then we'd cut that segment of the trip short and ship the bikes up ahead. The magic we'd experienced on our New Zealand trip was replaced by frustration, anger, and resentment. We were camping and riding, just as we'd planned, but there was little to no joy in what we were doing. One week turned into two, two into three, and the situation wasn't improving.

I knew Raapman loved me with his whole heart. But for the life of me, I couldn't return the sentiment in kind. In truth, at twenty-three going on twenty-four, I'm not sure I understood what love meant. How could you understand something if you weren't exposed to it during your childhood? Maybe if I had felt unconditional love and acceptance from my father while I was growing up it would have helped me learn how to love myself, and consequently, the men in my life. But I hadn't had that kind of role model. So instead of accepting Raapman's love for what it was and trusting myself in those emotions, I shut down and built walls to protect myself. And as always, the reel kept playing in my head:

I mean really, how could he possibly love me? I'm unlovable. If he only knew the real me, he wouldn't want to be my friend, let alone my lover.

Our formal parting took place at a Surf Life Saving Club (a volunteer organization for water safety) in Burleigh Heads, an incredibly picturesque town on the south end of Australia's Gold Coast. After an emotional good-bye, Raapman got on his bike and headed south toward Sydney. I can still picture his lonely, hunched figure pedaling down the road. He later told me he was devastated by what happened. It broke his heart. As he rode farther away, he would turn around every so often, hoping I'd be there again right behind him, but I never was.

I stayed on in Australia, determined to continue the solo journey I'd psyched myself up for. In a quaint town called Byron Bay I met a guy named Paul Berry who was vacationing there from Sydney. We hit it off right away. I told him what had happened between Raapman and me and explained I was running low on funds. He asked me if I'd seen Sydney yet, and when I said no he threw my bike in the back of his car and off we went. Paul's sister worked at the North Sydney Olympic Pool and helped me get work. The 50-meter pool, located practically in the shadow of Sydney Harbour Bridge, is spectacular. Many of the great Aussie swimmers, from Dawn Fraser to Murray Rose to Shane Gould, have competed at this historic pool. I found a rental to share in Neutral Bay, a nearby suburb, and settled in. I stayed in Sydney for two months, picking up waitressing jobs, working as a novice coach, and teaching basic swimming skills to kids ages five to eight.

Beer is popular and cheap in Australia, so I now entered a beer-drinking phase. I'd buy a carton and start drinking it as soon as I could. Whatever limits I had placed on myself at home went out the window in Australia. I'd be buzzed as I waited tables. I'd be buzzed as I coached at the pool. I couldn't really train because I was buzzed all the time and it would have been too hard to hide. I was level headed enough to keep my jobs, but just barely. I was saving a little money, but not much.

When my relationship with Paul sputtered out, it was time for me to move on again. I was searching for something—something more than just the next drink—but I had no idea what it was. Wherever I went, I'd meet people and make spur-of-the-moment decisions to spend time with them. I stayed in Canberra for a little bit. Then I went to Melbourne. I was free-floating from place to place. In Adelaide, I jumped onto the Trans-Australian Railway for the long cross-country ride to Perth to visit my friends Joy Petredies, who'd once trained with us at CNSA, and Neil Brooks, a friend I went to school with in Arkansas. Brooksie, as he's more commonly known, was the anchor of the Australian relay team that upset the highly favored Russians at the 1980 Olympics in Moscow. Competitive swimming's popularity is enormous Down Under, and that relay victory had made Brooksie a household name. He was Ian Thorpe before Ian Thorpe.

When I got off the train in Perth, Joy's father was there to pick me up. Brooksie was out of town at the time. Joy's dad took me over to Brooksie's dad's house, and I was invited to stay for a while. Everywhere I went, people introduced me as this phenomenal swimmer from Southern California. Being a swimmer brought panache. It gave me credibility, especially in Australia where everyone is crazy about their swim stars. And even though I was only dipping my toe into a pool every so often, I went along with the charade. Why not, if that's what opened doors for me?

When Brooksie finally got back to Perth, he and I became instant party mates. He was a big man with a big personality, and he liked to drink as much as I did. People recognized him everywhere we went, and we couldn't go to a bar or a restaurant without someone offering to buy us meals and drinks. I was a freewheeling reveler, sponging free food and drink whenever and wherever I could. Excessive drinking tends to impair judgment. Not only was I drifting from city to city and from bar to bar, I was also drifting in and out of causal relationships. It wasn't long before Brooksie and I were fooling around.

CHAPTER 26

Water Reveals the Truth

WHEN I LEFT AUSTRALIA, I flew to Bali to enjoy that island's beaches and nightlife, then traveled over to Java. The plan was to spend time with my friend Dora, an Indonesian swimmer who had boarded at our house years before, but she had no idea I was coming. Jakarta is a huge, sprawling metropolis. It was chaotic and dirty and everywhere I looked there were buses, cars, scooters, pushcarts, and throngs of people all seemingly on top of each other. I hadn't seen or heard from Dora in many years, but when I arrived at the train station I opened the massive phone book and called everyone with her last name. One of them was Johnny Item, Dora's brother. "Hey, Johnny. It's Karlyn Pipes. How are you? I'm good. Actually, I'm at the train station. Could you let your sister know I'm here?" Johnny came to pick me up and took me to Dora's, where I stayed for two weeks.

It's amazing how high-functioning alcoholics can always find ways to manage. Another friend, Toto Dharmadji, had been part of the original Indonesian swim team that had trained with CNSA. He had stayed in the United States, graduated from Coronado High School, and was now also living in Jakarta. Toto was a lot of laughs, and every night he took me out partying, dancing, or to the night markets.

When I first arrived in Bali, I discovered a drink called arrack. Arrack is a lot like moonshine, and it can be as potent as lighter fluid. The best thing about it is that it's really cheap. It was about a dollar for a one-liter (one-quart) bottle, and you don't need to drink much of it to get drunk. The food in Indonesia was inexpensive as well. I could go into a restaurant and spend less than a dollar for an entire meal. I'd eat the food, go into the bathroom, and throw it up. And then I'd go drink some more arrack.

There was a 25-meter pool right across the street from where Dora lived. I could see it from my bedroom window. It beckoned to me, that pool. It glowed like a flare, especially in the morning when I was hungover from the night before. Every day I'd wake up, look out the window, and tell myself, *Today I'm going to go for a swim.* But I'd get distracted. I'd become fixated on having a drink. From the moment I woke, I schemed to get more alcohol. The pull of the bottle was much stronger than the pull of the water. And then, as soon as I finally had that first drink of the day, all my willpower vanished.

On the surface, it appeared I was living the high life, enjoying myself immensely and moving about the globe without a care in the world. What was going on beneath the surface, however, was quite different. The alcoholic mind is similar to that of a person with a split personality. One side of the brain is adept playing the victim and encourages you to wallow in self-pity. *You're a loser, Karlyn. No one really likes you anyway.* All the while the other, more dominant side, possesses a massive ego brimming with self-importance and grandiose illusions. *You are just so wonderful, Karlyn. You're so, so great that even people on the other side of the planet fawn all over you.* That's the thing about drunks. They could be sleeping in a cardboard box, totally down and out, yet they could tell the world they're living like a king in a castle.

Somewhere inside, though, I knew I was being pulled into a watery crevice. My rational side would emerge every so often to warn me of trouble ahead. *You may think this is your path, but how can it possibly be? Are you really so naïve and foolish as to believe that what you're doing is sustainable? You need help, and you're afraid to admit it.* But alcohol has an amazing way of muffling the disturbing voices you don't want to hear.

The contrast between this excursion to Indonesia and my last one was stark. When I'd made the trip with my CNSA elite training group, I was so self-assured. I could take on anything Troy threw at me. The world had seemed vast and full of possibilities. Now here I was only eight years later, incapable of even dipping my toe into a pool, let alone swimming any laps.

I avoided the pool across the street from Dora's house because water reveals the truth. It represented everything I could have been and everything I'd thrown away. Worse, what if my potential wasn't as good as everyone made it out to be? Getting into that pool in Jakarta could reveal only one of two things: I was either a fraud or a complete fuckup. Confronting either revelation was not something I wanted to do. I knew I was a great big lie. This whole jet-setting life I'd created for myself was a lie. My reputation as an Olympic-caliber swimmer was a lie too. I wasn't a talented backstroke swimmer; I was a thief. I wasn't a distance freestyler; I was a cheater. I wasn't a butterfly swimmer; I was a quitter.

Mark Spitz, who won seven gold medals at the 1972 Munich Olympics, said that once he retired he felt as if every day was a day he got to skip practice. Every post-career morning, he explained, was a "woo-hoo" moment. Swimming is such a physically and mentally demanding sport that it's only natural to feel that way. Here I was, ditching practice for months at a time. I thought I was getting away with something. You can try to convince yourself you're okay with it, but the guilt is always there. Even when you're drunk or stoned or high or whatever, the guilt is there. It's deep inside, gnawing at your gut.

CHAPTER 27

It Felt Like Home

W HEN I FINALLY CAME BACK to Southern California, I was flat broke and completely directionless. I didn't even have a car, which made getting around San Diego a nightmare. I moved back into the Chula Vista house that my mom still owned. I called up my friend Mac, who was still lifeguarding at North Island, and he helped get me rehired there. Fortunately there was someone local who also worked on base, and I was able to carpool with him.

Every so often I'd run into Raapman, and I started to pursue him again. I was adept at pushing people away, but I could never tolerate having the tables turned on me. With Raapman, once again, I hungered for a man's approval. I also had abandonment issues. The time our family car broke down by the side of the road and I was terrified I'd never get back to my Night-night, the day my mom threw her belongings into the car and almost drove off, the complete loneliness I felt as I sat naked in my room picking fleas off my body: it's one thing to feel that kind of painful emptiness inside, but to be physically alone as well? That, to me, was untenable.

I once wrote an essay in high school English class about my fear of abandonment. I procrastinated over the assignment for the entire semester. The night before it was due, I finally sat down to write. I didn't even bother typing it. I just put pen to paper and it all came pouring out. Here I was, the star of my high school's boys' swim team, and my father never once came to watch me compete. "I'll come to your meet," he'd say the night before. And in the beginning I got excited when he said that. I wanted to prove to him I'd grown up to be more than just the girl with the yucky voice and the Phyllis Diller hair. I'd go to school the next day filled with anticipation. When it was finally time to swim, I'd put on my team suit and sweats and show up on deck with my teammates. I'd mount the blocks, race hard, and hit the wall first. Everyone would whistle and cheer. Then I'd glance up into the bleachers, hoping my father had seen my performance, but he was never there. Not once. I'd see the faces of other parents, but never my dad's. It happened over and over and over again. Each time, the emptiness inside me grew bigger and bigger. Growing up with an alcoholic father was like growing up in a house without a roof. My dreams and my sense of belonging were doused. In my essay, I wrote about how I began to realize that the only thing I could count on from Dad was that I couldn't count on him. My teacher, Mr. Adair, gave me an A. He could tell my writing had come straight from the void I was describing.

I continued to pursue Raapman, and gradually his resolve weakened. It took a while, but we finally became a couple again by the end of the summer. In the fall of 1986, he told me he was going to move to South Lake Tahoe, in California's Sierra Nevada mountains, to ski and have fun while collecting unemployment. I asked him if I could come along and he said yes. When we got up there, I tried waiting tables, but I got fired for not paying for food I ordered. This was becoming a recurring theme. I'd get a job, but not be able to hold it because of the fallout from my addiction.

My tastes in alcohol had shifted to wine, the cheap stuff in a box that you can find in drugstores. Whenever I could afford it, I'd mix in some vodka. Drugstores are where people buy medicine. They get medications or aspirin or bandages. Initially when I went into drugstores to buy wine, I felt self-conscious. So I'd buy tampons or chewing gum in an attempt to camouflage the wine. Then I realized that other people—people my father's age—were buying liquor by the shopping cart, so I stopped my game playing. I was there to get my medication just like everyone else.

Maggie, my teammate from Arkansas, lived in nearby Sacramento now. We had remained good friends, and to this day our relationship is still strong. Once we were complaining to each other about how out of shape we were getting and how we should be working out more often. We'd be turning twenty-five in the coming months, which meant we would be eligible to swim at the Masters level. (The minimum age has since dropped to eighteen in the United States, though it is still twenty-five internationally.) Maggie mentioned that she was thinking of signing up for the U.S. Masters Swimming National Short Course Championships to be held in Palo Alto at Stanford University. I told her Mom and Lloyd were going to sign up for it. It sounded like fun, and since writing it on the calendar seemed like a great way to stay motivated during the winter, the two of us decided to shoot for it.

I located the pool in South Lake Tahoe and for the first time in years set my sights on doing some regimented training. I'd always had to stay in some kind of decent shape for my annual requalification swim as a state beach lifeguard—at the start of each summer returning guards had to knock off a 1,000-meter ocean swim in twenty minutes. But that was always something I could do with my eyes closed. This, though, was different. I was going to reimmerse myself in the world of interval training and practicing all four strokes, not just freestyle.

The first thing I needed to do was buy a swimsuit. That was a rude awakening. Ever since I had been a teenager, my suits had been free. The new suit set me back a whopping fifty dollars. That was a lot of money at the time, especially for someone who was barely squeaking by. But stepping up to the cash register and making that purchase validated my determination.

There was something about the antiquated, indoor, six-lane 25-yard South Lake Tahoe pool that brought back fond memories from when I first learned to swim in Lompoc. As soon as I stepped through the locker room door onto the pool deck again, it hit me. I was enveloped in the heady aroma of chlorine and wrapped in the warm embrace of humidity. It felt so familiar. It felt like home. *I can do this,* I told myself as I surveyed the facility and watched a few swimmers diligently crossing back and forth. *This is where I'm going to have my new beginning.*

I started swimming three to four times a week and even added weights to my program. Training at altitude was challenging, but I sucked it up and it wasn't long before I saw improvement. It soon became apparent, however, that my newfound dedication did have its limits. I was still drinking. A lot. Still mostly wine, but vodka too. Once in a while Raapman would stumble across a vodka bottle I'd stashed somewhere, but he never connected the dots. Most people close to someone with an addiction usually don't add it all up. Consciously or subconsciously, they choose not to see the signs, or to ignore them if they do. Raapman knew I liked to party. But he had no idea of the extent of my drinking. Like me, he was in denial.

I had no expectations when I went down to Palo Alto to swim at the national championship, so I was surprised when I did pretty well. I placed in the top eight in the 100-yard breaststroke, the 100 backstroke, and the 100 IM. I didn't win anything, but I did post a few respectable times. Maggie did well also. And it was a lot fun. I'd dabbled in Masters swimming before, practicing off and on with the Coronado team, but I'd never really had the full experience until then. The meet was huge, with over 2,500 swimmers. It was competitive, but it was much lower key than I had expected. The overall feeling I had was that people were there to enjoy themselves and seemed genuinely supportive of one another's efforts. I loved the camaraderie and decided I wanted more. I had been back in the water for just over four months, and I began to wonder what would happen if I really trained.

Raapman and I moved back to Coronado for the summer and were both rehired to lifeguard at Silver Strand State Beach. Inspired by what I'd experienced at Stanford, I started to train with more regularity. On my hour-long break I'd drive four miles to Coronado, jump in the muni pool, rush through 2,000 or 2,500 long course meters, then hop back in the car and hustle back to my tower. If I had time, I would squeeze in some Masters workouts after my shift. It wasn't extreme training, especially compared to my CNSA days, but I could tell I was getting into pretty good shape. I set my sights on the Masters National Long Course Championships to be held in Houston, Texas, in August of 1987.

In Texas, I swam even better than I had in Palo Alto. I won the 100- and 200-meter backstrokes in national record times and placed second in the 200 IM, fourth in the 100 fly, and seventh in the 100 breaststroke. June Ford, a swimmer from Oahu, Hawaii, beat me by a second in the 200 IM and claimed the national record for that event. The 400 IM, the last event on my schedule, loomed ahead of both of us. I've always had a love-hate relationship with 400 IM. The event is 100 meters of each stroke. It's long. It's grueling. It's the kind of event that no matter what your fitness level, at some point in the race you feel like stopping. It hurts that bad. Troy used to tell me it was my best event. He said that given the combination of endurance and stroke diversity the race requires, it was right in my sweet spot. I should have been flattered, but I wasn't excited to focus on such a difficult event. The only thing easy about it, as far as I was concerned, was the dive. This may be why, when Michael Phelps announced his comeback in 2014, he was adamant that he would never race 400 IM again.

"You can get her in the 400, Karlyn," said John Tudor, my friend from West Virginia, after he saw June and me race in the 200. "I can tell her weakness is the breaststroke."

"It is?"

"Yes. Here's how you should swim it: let her go on the fly, catch her on the backstroke, pass her on the breaststroke, and then bring it home in the freestyle."

"So I should save some for the breaststroke?" I said, wanting to clarify what my strategy should be.

"Exactly," he said. "That's where she's vulnerable."

I liked the idea of trying to exact a little revenge for my loss in the 200. June and I drew lanes right next to each other. The gun went off and, sure enough, June took off like a bullet in the fly. She was a body length and a half ahead of me as we turned into the backstroke. I slowly reeled her back in and we hit the halfway mark at about the same time. Now it was time to make my move. Midway through the breaststroke leg, I could tell June had gone out too hard the first 100. I still had some left in the tank and I passed her, just as John had said I could. I surged ahead even farther on the freestyle leg. When I hit the wall, John, Mom, Lloyd, Bill Earley, and my fellow teammates were all going nuts. I knew it was a good race, but I didn't understand what all the commotion was about. Then I looked up at the scoreboard and saw I'd swum a 5:12. It was a new FINA Masters world record and as fast as I had ever swum as a teenager.

I found out later that night that John was right in a way: June didn't have a good breaststroke. She had an *exceptional* breaststroke. In fact, she was the national record holder in the breaststroke. But it didn't matter, because she'd inadvertently over-swum the butterfly. That night, fresh off my first-ever world record, I took my partying to new heights.

CHAPTER 28

A High-Maintenance Lifestyle

AFTER MY SUCCESS AT THE MASTERS NATIONALS, wheels started turning in my head. I'd just swum a 5:12 400-meter IM, and the Olympic Trials' standard was 5:07. That seemed very much within reach. I went back to my beach lifeguarding, but I'd had an epiphany: in my twenty-fifth year, *I still had it.* Even with the limited amount of training I'd done, I could still produce solid results in the pool. I decided I was going to go back to college and compete, and I was going to try to qualify for the Olympic Trials. All I needed to do was drop just over five seconds, which, with a little hard work, seemed more than doable. Mom and Lloyd were on board. "I'm so proud of you," Lloyd said. I beamed. Everyone, it seemed, was excited about my newfound enthusiasm and goals. As far as I could tell, only one thing stood in my way: Raapman.

We had been in a rut, neither of us wanting to disrupt the easy familiarity we had with one another. Now, though, I was ready to make the leap. The meet in Texas had invigorated me. It had renewed my enthusiasm for my sport. To make things easier, I decided to go to school out of the area so that Raapman and I wouldn't be near one another and I could focus in earnest.

I moved up the coast to Mission Viejo to swim with Flip Darr, the coach at Saddleback College. Flip was a good coach, but it was September and swimming season for California community colleges did not start until January. That meant I would need to train on my own until then. It became obvious that I wasn't going to maintain my dedication; predictably, I continued to drink. Once again, I'd merely packed my problems into a suitcase and lugged them with me to a new location. I lasted approximately four weeks. I finally decided this whole Saddleback/Trials thing was a dumb idea. Who was I kidding? I had one pretty good race and now I was expecting to snap my fingers and get my long-dormant swimming career back on track? I threw in the towel and went back home. So much for dreams. So much for ambitions. So much for getting excited about anything.

I rented a room in a nice house in Coronado with Dallas Boggs, a navy captain and fellow CMA swimmer. I worked a few more months lifeguarding at Silver Strand State Beach and once again waited tables at Bula's. Lindsey deserved a trophy for giving me so many chances. Luckily the customers loved me. I also slid right back into Coronado's party scene. I'd gotten to the point where I couldn't *not* drink. I avoided Raapman at all costs. It wasn't easy. I'm sure he'd heard from some of our mutual acquaintances that I'd slunk back into town with my tail between my legs, but he didn't try to contact me.

The 1988 Olympic Trials in early March came and went. A twenty-one-year-old by the name of Dara Torres made her second Olympic team. Jill Sterkel also made the team again. Me, I was frittering my life away while still pretending to be something of a swimmer. I promised Mom I'd go with her and Lloyd to Brisbane, Australia, later that summer for the FINA World Masters Championships. But I didn't. I lacked the discipline and never came close to getting in adequate shape to make the meet. I could still talk a good game, but when it came time for execution I was all hot air.

In early summer, I was recruited to take part in the Around the Island Swim, a boat-supported twelve-mile open-water relay that circumnavigated Coronado. It was just one year after my breakthrough meet in Texas, so I was hot property when it came to what I could potentially offer a team. My four teammates, two of whom were Beth Knight and Cathy Neville, were top-notch athletes and had put in a lot of time training for the event. After the initial thirty-minute legs, the rules called for us to wait on the boat and alternate every ten minutes. I showed up to the race extremely hungover, and my swimming performance was pitiful. I swam so poorly that every time I dove into the water I would lose whatever lead we had. Eventually we fell so far behind that we were not competitive at all. I imagined that my teammates were disgusted with me. I had let them down, and we didn't get anywhere close to first place.

My life was turning into a dark, watery mess. It was as if I were being pummeled by the menacing surf the Pacific Ocean likes to deliver during the winter months. Just when I was close enough to the surface to grab a breath of air, another wave would come crashing down, pushing me back toward the bottom. There was no one to blame but myself. I was the one responsible for brewing up the storm that created these inhospitable conditions. Instead of fighting back or trying to rise above, for the next five years I just continued to sink.

I had a new man in my life. Well, technically Murly wasn't new. We had been surf buddies back in the day, and we had both graduated from Coronado High School. We reconnected at a friend's barbecue in the summer of 1988 when I was twenty-six. Romance soon blossomed. When it was time for him to go out to sea as second mate on an oceanographic research vessel, however, things got a little sticky. I hated being alone. So Murly called in some favors and soon I was given a volunteer research assistant position on the ship. I was way under qualified, but it was a great opportunity to see more of the world, and Murly and I could continue our relationship.

I was scheduled to meet the ship in Montevideo, Uruguay, and then we would sail to Argentina, doing research projects along the way. If things went well, there was the potential for future trips. But I turned it down. I gave Murly a made-up excuse about needing to stay focused on my training. While I loved the idea of more world travel, the reality was that I knew I was a full-blown alcoholic and couldn't contemplate a day without drinking. Nor could I possibly stash enough booze on board to keep me happy for the length of time we would be at sea. There was no way I would be able to hide my secret on a relatively small ship. No way, no how. Consequently, I never met the ship, and it wasn't long before our relationship fizzled out. Murly was a great guy, fun to be with, and we shared a lot of history, but I was more interested in my love affair with the bottle than with my boyfriend.

Shortly after that relationship ended, I went back to Hawaii to visit my friend Sloan and her family. I was there for most of the winter of 1988–89, and as usual all Sloan and I did was hang out, drink, and lie in the sun. I came home from that trip saturated with alcohol. I barely passed my requalification test to work another season at the Strand. My days there were numbered. Because of my nightly drinking, I would often show up for work either hungover or still a little bit drunk. The lifestyle of a seasonal beach lifeguard is more carefree and party-oriented than that of a traditional nine-to-five worker, but I was pushing the limits.

It was not long before the head lifeguard, Chuck Chase, and my immediate supervisor, Greg Abbott, were on to me. That summer my work performance was under scrutiny, and consequently I was written up time and again. I was told to get my act together or else. But I couldn't. Eventually I was given the option to either resign or be fired. Even though they had clear evidence that I was unfit to stand duty, I resented both men. I chose to quit, which meant I couldn't collect unemployment, but I could still finagle my way into being hired as a lifeguard elsewhere.

I started working for the navy again at the Naval Amphibious Base in Coronado. My position was in the Athletics Department, which is under MWR (Morale, Welfare, and Recreation). MWR is in charge of all the playing fields, swimming pools, beaches, and clubs on base. In the summer I'd lifeguard at Gator Beach, sharing shifts with my mom's friend and Masters swimmer Bill Earley, who was head guard. I had the urge to confide in Bill, to get his take on what steps I should take to get my life in order. He had been a Navy SEAL. He'd seen his fair share of life. But I resisted. Confiding would mean admitting that I was a screwup. And that I couldn't figure this thing out for myself. And that I'd have to somehow change my behavior, which I was not prepared to do.

The alcohol was affecting everything now. Sometimes my roommate or a coworker would ask, "Have you been drinking, Karlyn?" "Not really," I'd reply. "I just had a glass or two of wine after work." Call it a little white lie. Yes, I'd have a glass or two after work, but that was just a small part of a regimen that was starting earlier and earlier in the day and ending later and later. Sometimes I would drink so much that I'd drive home with a hand over one eye to keep from seeing double. Occasionally I'd get pulled over by the cops, but I had a Police Officers Association sticker on the back of my car, so they'd always let it slide. If the sticker didn't work, I'd drop the names of higher-ups I knew on base, and that would do the trick. Little lies, big lies . . . I knew and used them all. I could recite them in my sleep, I was so adept at spouting them at a moment's notice. My guardian angel was working overtime. She was sweating up a storm and her wings were probably drenched from having to work so hard to keep me out of any real trouble. Miraculously, I was never sexually assaulted while in a drunken stupor. I never got into a car accident or injured another person. I never received a DUI.

I was driving around in a beat-up Toyota Corolla Raapman had given me a few years before. It was so ugly we had christened it The Flea. I had some outstanding parking tickets, but I didn't want to address them. Like everything else, I was hoping the tickets would just go away on their own. The Flea also wasn't registered with the DMV, so I resorted to taking the license plate registration sticker off of someone else's car and sticking it on mine.

It's a high-maintenance lifestyle, drinking. I always had to have alcohol with me, and a big enough purse or bag to stash it in, because I always had to keep enough in my system. If I went to someone's house for dinner and they weren't serving alcohol, I had to make sure I brought my own. If I went out with friends, I drank plenty before and after so it didn't look like I was drinking to excess while we were together. The fear of getting found out or busted for something I was surely doing wrong permeated almost every waking hour. I became paranoid and regularly changed liquor stores so that no one clerk would see the amount of alcohol I was buying. It's a tricky thing, feeding your addiction while trying to keep up appearances.

Even with the walls closing in on me, I still had a knack for piecing things together. Or so I thought. Lindsey finally fired me from Bula's for good. I begged and begged to come back, but this time he wouldn't bend. As a result, I found myself bouncing from one restaurant to another. I'd get a waitressing job at one place, but within a short period of time I'd start calling in sick or just not show up at all, and I'd be let go. I'd immediately find my way into a new situation, but nothing lasted longer than a month or two. Coronado is a small town, and there weren't that many restaurants. Pretty soon my reputation got around, and no one would hire me.

I was coaching Masters swimming and giving swimming lessons. The navy sent me some SEAL candidates for swim instruction. For a while I also worked as a manager at the Central Wine and Cheese, a deli located next to Bula's, and bartended at the Coronado Cays Yacht club and picked up a few shifts at Danny's Pub. My life was a mishmash of whatever jobs would keep me afloat and facilitate my drinking. I was still functioning, but only barely. Whenever one of the many plates I was spinning would fall and break, another plate would come along to take its place.

My bartending experience came in handy when I started working both at the Officers' Club and at private parties and weddings. Being around liquor in a setting like that is an alcoholic's wildest dream. Before every party, I'd have to stock my bar. Unsupervised, I'd go into the liquor closet and pull out the different bottles I would need for the event. Little did anyone know that I was absolutely the last person who should have been put in charge of a task like that. I'd take a nearly full bottle of vodka and log it as only half full because I knew that by the end of the night, that was how much I would drink.

I'd sometimes work at Green Acres, a bar in the Bachelor Officers Quarters. As the gal in charge, I had full run of the place. That meant even more free alcohol. I really worked it well. I could drink and get paid at the same time. Since I was cute and flirtatious, I could get away with all the deceit. As long as I chewed minty gum and kept a safe enough distance from people so that they couldn't smell my breath, nobody would know I'd been drinking.

One evening I was bartending at a small private party for an army general. Everyone was drinking and having a great time, including me, though of course my drinking was surreptitious. A heavyset man walked up to my little bar and said, "I'd like to have a . . . " He suddenly stopped and moved away. I was drunk, but not so drunk that I didn't notice the peculiarity of his behavior. I left my station and followed him at a distance. He had gone into a dark corner behind some serving trays. "Are you okay?" I asked. He looked at me, and I could tell that, no, he wasn't okay. His eyes looked ready to erupt. I went behind him and started abdominal thrusts. Apparently he had inhaled a grape, whole, and it had lodged in his windpipe. When I did the thrusts, I did them with so much force that not only did the grape come out, so did his false teeth! They went flying across the floor. After catching our breaths, we located his teeth, and he went right back to the party. He didn't say a word to anyone. Maybe he was ashamed about his false teeth, or about choking in the first place. He gave me a nice tip, but that was it.

Later, after the party had wrapped up, the general's wife came up to me, told me the guests had loved me, and gave me a big tip.

"I enjoyed it too," I said. "Everything was great, except for the guy who almost choked to death."

The hostess gave me a puzzled look, and I told her what had happened. She related the story to someone else, and eventually it reached the commanding officer of the base. The CO's assistant came down to discuss the incident with me, and the navy researched the details. They contacted the man I had helped, and he confirmed I'd saved his life. As a way of honoring me for my actions the navy held a Karlyn Pipes Day on the base. The huge marquee at the entrance announced the fact to everyone who drove past. It was strange. My day-to-day life was in absolute disarray. I had a secret life filled with lying, stealing, and drinking to oblivion. Yet here I was being honored for exemplary actions on the job. It's strange sometimes how life works.

CHAPTER 29

Taking Care of Daddy

AYS TURNED TO MONTHS, months turned to years, and the next thing I knew I was approaching my thirtieth birthday. One day in late 1991 I got a desperate call from Kirsten. While she was still confined to a wheelchair, her MS had been stable for many years. But the stress of taking care of her growing family and our dad had started to cause vision problems for her. Dad had been treated for prostate cancer, but now his health was rapidly deteriorating. She had hit her limit.

"The kids don't need to be exposed to this," Kirsten said.

"Has his memory gotten that bad?" I asked.

"It's not that. It's his incontinence," she said. "He's making a mess all over the house, including in the tub and on the kids' bath toys. It's your turn, Karlyn."

"W-what do you mean?" I said.

"You're going to be taking care of Daddy now."

"Me? Kirsten, I'm sharing a tiny apartment with a roommate and struggling to make ends meet. I don't have any room for him."

"Well, figure it out," she said. "You can use his pension to help pay for his food and rent."

Joe Kernan, a swimmer and Naval Academy classmate of Keeney's, owned a house in Coronado on Palm Avenue. Oddly, it was right next door to Susie Baxter's house where I had sought refuge during my high school years. Joe's tenants had given notice and I knew he was looking for new ones. The place wasn't spacious by any stretch of the imagination (two bedrooms, one bath), but there was a separate garage apartment for my father. My roommate and I moved into the house, and Dad moved into the apartment. Sometimes you can only laugh at the way life plays out. My father's alcoholism had wreaked havoc on my entire family. I personally had worked very hard to bury the need for any emotional attachment to this man. But now here I was, full-blown in my disease, and I'd suddenly become his caretaker.

I hadn't spent much time with my father for over twenty years, and I was stunned by how severely his alcoholism had affected his memory. While he hadn't had a drink in almost ten years, his brain was fried. When he read a newspaper and got to the bottom of the page, he couldn't remember anything from the upper sections, so he would begin again. All day long he would read the same page over and over, never remembering a single fact. He also had no recollection of the screaming matches he used to have with my mother and brothers. He didn't remember teasing me. He didn't remember all the broken promises he'd made. He was just this pleasant, absent-minded old man who would obediently do whatever was asked of him.

Once he was settled in, Dad's greatest preoccupation became dumpster diving. He would pick up trash all over town. He'd get up in the morning and go for a walk, cruising the streets and alleys of affluent Coronado. I reasoned that since he was a product of the Depression, he and his siblings had probably never been given anything other than hand-me-downs, so in his mind he was foraging for useful items. Whatever the cause of his behavior, it was what it was. Sometimes I'd be driving down the street and would see him digging through someone's garbage can. Watching him reminded me of the embarrassment I had felt when I was a kid and my classmates would joke about the drunk music teacher. Now whenever I saw my father carting around his latest find, I'd stifle my discomfort by telling myself, *Well, that's my dad.*

Joe's prior tenants had been keeping chickens, and they left them behind. There was a little coop in the back of the house with four laying hens. I fed them leftover food or grain every morning, and sometimes when I was really inebriated I would have long conversations with them. I didn't find it the least bit odd that in the process of becoming the caretaker for my father, I'd also become a chicken farmer. Add it to my curriculum vitae. Who knew chickens were even allowed on Coronado Island?

The same year Dad moved in, I started seeing a local guy named Dave. He was a smart, handsome, six-foot-four, two-hundred-pound man with dark hair and blue eyes, and our physical attraction to one another was immediate. He was a bit unsettled when it came to employment, and he worked sometimes as a car mechanic, sometimes as an IT guy, and eventually became a merchant marine. He'd be out at sea for months at a time, but whenever he came back, we were together. Dave liked to get wasted as much as I did. Cooped up and away from civilization for so long, as soon as he reached shore he would make up for lost time on the party scene.

I never tried to stop drinking. I wasn't the typical alcoholic who says, "I can control it," "I'm only going to drink beer," or "I'm only going to drink between the hours of x and y." I felt guilty about what I was doing, yes. But I never took any measures to try to stop the madness.

One day Dave came back from one of his big trips with his pockets bulging with money.

"I'd like to get you something," he said. "What can I get for you, Karlyn?"

I thought about it for a long moment.

"I haven't been to a dentist in six years. Can we please go to the dentist?"

"Anything you want," he said.

Most women, when offered such a chance to spoil themselves, would ask for jewelry or a vacation, but I didn't have the luxury to choose something frivolous. My addiction was robbing me of those choices.

So Dave paid for my dental work. My teeth were a mess from all the years of throwing up, and my front ones needed expensive porcelain veneers. It wasn't cheap, but it was Dave's gift to me. That's the drinking way of life. Personal care, the ability to show up for work on time, to pay parking tickets, to pay bills—it all gets pushed aside in favor of the next glass. You're not making good choices and you're not choosing healthy relationships. Every decision you make, in the end, has to do with trying to maintain an utterly unsustainable lifestyle.

On one occasion I was able to make it through an entire day without alcohol. Dave suggested I try it. I had told him I was concerned—maybe I was drinking too much. "If you're worried about it, Karlyn, just don't drink for a day. If you can make it through an entire day, then you probably don't have a problem." Well, it wasn't easy, but I made it. I spent the entire day obsessing about getting a drink. To try to take my mind off the craving, I went to three movies. It helped the day go by faster. I had a fitful night of sleep, and the next morning the first thing I did was reach for a bottle. Since Dave partied as much as anyone I'd ever met, he probably wasn't the best guy to be doling out substance abuse wisdom. And even though, according to Dave's theory, I should have felt relieved that I had in fact made it through an entire day without touching booze, I didn't feel relieved at all.

Dave had his own set of issues. He felt that everyone in his life had left him. His mom had left him. His dad had left him. All of his previous girl-friends had left him. He was broken in so many ways, and his addictions, I knew, were a byproduct of that. I decided early on that I wasn't going to be the next in a long string of people to abandon him. I knew what his psychic pain felt like. I knew because I had it too. Whereas others might see only Dave's problems, I saw his potential. He was a talented mechanical engineer and he knew computers. I respected and appreciated his gifts. But our relationship began to get combative. Instead of working with one another to overcome our insecurities, we started to take them out on each other.

At some point my roommate moved out, and Dave started paying half the rent. That should have been a good thing—a sign that our relationship was maturing. It wasn't. Dave's addiction to marijuana rivaled mine to alcohol. He got to where he couldn't live without it. And he wouldn't let anything get in the way of feeding his addiction. When he and his crewmates needed to undergo drug testing, he'd buy urine from one of his friends and pass it off as his own.

When he wasn't high, Dave was a nice, likable guy. But when he smoked or drank, his dark, angry side would come out, and he'd get verbally abusive toward me. Whenever he was out at sea, he would write me long, passionate letters professing his undying love. At first I found them very romantic. But when he returned home and went on one of his alcohol or drug binges, he would have rages that absolutely terrified me.

It was obvious we both had serious addiction issues, but Dave felt a bit superior because at least he had a steady job. Me? I was totally directionless. One day he posed a question.

"Karlyn, what are you passionate about?" he asked with mild curiosity.

"What do you mean?" I said with a blank expression. I didn't understand the question. He dropped the subject, and it never came up again.

Dave never physically abused me, but he did subject me to mental and emotional abuse. My self-esteem was so low that I put up with it. I was like a little girl again, desperate for whatever scraps of attention I could get. And then there was that loyalty issue. I didn't want to abandon Dave when I knew he needed my help. I was convinced I would be the one who would ease his pain. I wanted to fix him. I wanted to help him realize his potential. Unbeknownst to me, I had fallen into codependency.

It was easier for me to help Dave than to help myself. It was *always* easier for me to help anyone other than myself. That's what a good codependent does. An alcoholic is addicted to drinking, a drug addict is addicted to drugs, and a codependent is addicted to fixing people. We invest time and energy in helping others instead of ourselves. When it came to listening to my girlfriends complain about their relationships, I was the sounding board, the one who doled out beautiful words of wisdom. And yet my own life was in tatters. I was a closet alcoholic taking care of my alcoholic father and loving a substance-abusing boyfriend with an unpredictable temper. And I had the answers? Even my mother could see what was going on and was concerned.

Maybe Mom saw the parallels between Dave and my father. Neither one had a history of physical violence, but both had tempers that revealed volatile and unpredictable natures. Add drugs or alcohol and you have a very scary situation for any parent to watch. Mom confided to Lloyd that she was afraid for my well being. In fact she had a nightmare where she received a call in the middle of the night to go down to the county morgue to identify my body. Perhaps "concerned" is putting it lightly.

I was primarily a wine drinker now, and I drank it straight from the box. Franzia was the cheapest buzz I could find. I'd buy quite a few boxes at a time, telling any cashier who appeared curious that I was throwing a big party for a bunch of close friends. At home, I wouldn't even bother with a glass. I'd just lift up the box, put the spigot in my mouth, and chug twenty or thirty gulps. *Glug glug glug.* I would take as many gulps as I could on one breath. When I was in Arkansas, we'd do no-breathers at the end of practice to help build our stamina. "Four 25-yard freestyles on the thirty seconds with no breath," Coach Freas would call out. "On the top. First group, ready . . . go!" The objective was to simulate the stress our bodies would be feeling at the end of a race so that we would learn how to deal with the discomfort. Now I was doing no-breathers in front of the fridge. *Glug glug glug.* When I was finished with the boxes, I'd store the empties in my closet because I was too embarrassed to put them in the dumpster outside.

One fateful day, Dave introduced the concept of his-and-hers shot glasses. We'd wake up in the morning and the first thing we'd do was each have a shot of vodka in our matching glasses. I was now so deep into my disease that it didn't even occur to me at the time that vodka was the exact liquor Dad used to pick up with orange juice on his way to school. Once Dave brought straight vodka into the equation, wine simply didn't do it for me anymore. Franzia's alcohol-by-volume percentage was 12–13 percent. Vodka was closer to 40 percent. Wine would help me maintain a buzz, but it wasn't enough to *get* me the buzz. And I needed to be buzzed—all the time. No two ways about it: if I didn't drink, I'd start shaking.

Ah, the lunacy that defines your existence when you're a practicing alcoholic. Each step, each action, each thought, revolves around one thing: getting that next drink. I was drinking in the morning. I was drinking all day long. I was delivering sandwiches to the local bars and getting shots as tips. I was stealing the miniature bottles of alcohol from the deli where I worked. I always had a stash with me. In my car, in my handbag, in my duffle bag. At a movie, at a restaurant, on a date. I carried it with me wherever I went.

Incredibly, I was still swimming a few days a week. Not in the pool, mind you, but out in San Diego Bay. Lindsey had closed Bula's a few years back and had opened a new restaurant called the Bay Beach Cafe at the Coronado Ferry Landing. For old times' sake, Lindsey and I would occasionally go out for lunch or have a drink together, though he never offered to rehire me. His new place was right on the water, and from his barstool he had an expansive view of the bay. I would bop on down, high as a kite, and check in.

"Hey Steve, I'm going for a swim," I would tell him. "If I'm not back in about forty-five minutes, send out the navy to look for me."

With that, I would dive into the murky water and stroke away to a nearby aircraft carrier anchored offshore. To anyone else this might have seemed like insane behavior: I was drunk, swimming alone in open water, and dodging massive container ships and naval vessels. To me, however, it made perfect sense. If I swam down at the muni pool, anyone within fifteen feet of me would smell my breath and know I had been drinking. Swimming in the bay solved my problem. I could drink as much as I wanted and still get in some kind of workout. Besides, I had Lindsey as a "lifeguard" if I needed any help.

Other than the sporadic open-water sessions, the only training I was doing was lifting a glass of vodka to my mouth and drinking it down. I was a regular at a number of the bars in Coronado like The Brigantine and McP's Irish Pub, slurring my words but still talking a good game. Whenever I wanted to get someone to buy me a drink, I'd say, "I'm a world-record holder." Oh man, did I capitalize on that. People who knew me would introduce me with "Karlyn is a champion swimmer." I was still resting on laurels I had frittered away years ago. I was thirty. By 1992, I was so far gone that there wasn't a shred of fifteen-year-old Karlyn inside me, let alone the Masters swimmer who had set a world record just five years prior. What was left was an empty, hollowed-out, broken-down shell of a human being. I was a hopeless, helpless alcoholic.

It wasn't as if I didn't believe I deserved what was happening to me. I wasn't trying to blame anyone else for the mess I'd created. I had made those choices. I was the one who had had the potential and the seemingly limitless opportunities, and I was the one who had thrown them away. The whole sequence of events, from my teen years forward, was a series of poor decisions based on either men or alcohol or both. Those choices had led me to this place. They're what had led to this direction-less life of mine. Go to school, get a degree, and settle down, *or* become a beach lifeguard, bartender, and waitress. It was one or the other; the two couldn't coexist. I knew it. In my soul, I knew it. And I kept choosing the easier one—the one where I didn't have to perform. On the path I opted for, nothing was expected of me.

The life-of-the-party girl no longer looked so lively. In the morning when I came to, every cell in my body needed booze. The problem was, in addition to dealing with DTs, I now also had to contend with nonstop nausea. I would grab my "Hers" glass and with unstable hands fill it with vodka. Sometimes my hand would be shaking so much that the rim of the glass would rattle loudly and forcefully against my newly veneered front teeth, threatening breakage. I didn't care. I needed that drink more than I needed nice teeth.

Once the drink went down, the next step was to keep it down. I would be so nauseated that simply looking at the bathroom would make me feel like throwing up the vodka I had just chugged. If that happened—and it happened a lot—I was back to square one. I had to have a drink and I had to keep it down, plain and simple. Some mornings it took three attempts before one drink would stay in my stomach. And while the alcohol momentarily calmed my jangled nerves, it also washed away any hope that this day would be different from any other.

I was perfectly okay with being a washed-out drunken flunky. What was the point of hopes and dreams anyway? At least I tried to convince myself of that. In my mind, I wasn't really hurting anyone else, so how bad could it be? If I was the only one who had to deal with the conse-quences of my actions and if I was okay with it, then where was the problem? That's the addle-brained rationale. The clear mind would step back and, upon reflection, recognize that I was giving up just as my father had done. It would point out that the notion that his drinking had affected no one but himself was tragic at best. But mostly just absurd. The problem was, I no longer possessed a clear mind.

I began using money from my credit card to pay rent. Not surprisingly, the debt started to pile up. All the plates I'd been spinning were now dropping. One after another after another they'd hit the floor and break, and I was so exhausted that I just didn't have the energy to put new ones back up. It used to be that whenever I'd get fired from one job I'd immediately find another. I was lucky that way; I was the cute little swimmer girl. But now I was a full-blown alcoholic. There was no denying it. I knew I needed to get sober, but in order to get sober I needed to go to rehab. I needed to go somewhere to medically detox. But I didn't have money and I didn't have health insurance. This barrier seemed as insurmountable to me as Mount Everest. I couldn't for the life of me figure out how to get the help I knew I needed.

So the madness just continued. Dave went back out to sea, and I was again left alone to fend for myself. 1992 came and went, but besides my new love affair with vodka, I can hardly recall a thing about that whole year. Alcoholism can be very isolating as it progresses. I started having old boyfriends or friends deliver alcohol to my house because I was too messed up to go get it myself. When I was forced to go out and get vodka and Gatorade I was scared someone would see the state I was in. Dad was still out roaming the alleys. I was ensuring he was fed, but he was mostly on his own because I was immersed in my own situation. I had finally relinquished control to my addiction. One might think that there would be some sort of peace and acceptance in this, but there was none. I was afraid to die, but I had no idea how to live.

And then, miraculously, the phone rang, and it was my mother calling.

My mom Adrienne Spore (front right) as a San Diego State majorette at 19

My father Howard Pipes at 24 looking pretty handsome with his trombone

Mom and Dad's wedding in 1955

Sharing my Night-night with Kerri and Daddy

Mark, myself, Kirsten, Kerri, and Derek fit perfectly in the back of our VW bus.

Kindergarten school picture, age 5

My first bike at age 6 in 1968 in Lompoc, California

Age 10 in 1972 in full tomboy mode. I took it as a compliment when people thought I was a boy.

Swimming for the Lompoc Marlins was a family affair. I loved going to practice and swim meets wearing my new Dolfin team suit.

Top swimmers in the open 100-meter backstroke at a 1974 swim meet in Chula Vista, from left: me, Connie Humphrey, Teri McKeever, Jenny Lamott, Kirsten Pipes, Mary Ann Keshka, Patty Martinez, Elena Leonard

On our way to Indonesia in December of 1977 when I was just shy of 14. When Mike Troy wasn't kicking our butts in the pool, he was actually quite fun to be around.

At age 17 with Mike Smith, Laurie Purdy, and Jenny Lamott catching some rays in La Jolla in 1979

Heading out to a frat party during my freshman year at the University of Arkansas with my best friend Maggie Schwindt. 1980

When I was with Raapman, we would head to Baja, Mexico, drink a lot of beer, and lay out in the sun. The drinking and throwing up always made my face look puffy. Age 20, 1982

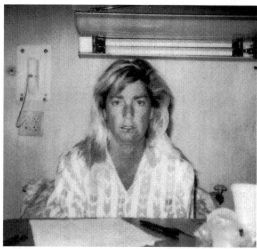

Fast forward to April 17, 1993, at Sharp Cabrillo Hospital. My picture was taken right after I was admitted. Even though I had a split lip, I thought this picture of me was pretty good.

August 17, 1993. The day I met my future husband Eric Neilsen (left), shown here with my lifeguard buddy Darryl Jett. I am swimming in my first Master's meet in Mission Viejo, just four months sober.

Celebrating one year of dating Eric by going to my mom's house in La Bufadora, Mexico. No beer, no tequila, no drinking . . . no problem!

My surrogate dad Lloyd Skramstad and Mom walking me down the aisle on my wedding day, September 16, 1995.

Jack Babashoff

Jack Babashoff

Our Gator Beach wedding reception in Coronado began with the bride and groom testing the water, then offered a half-mile open-water race for our guests. The swim was sponsored by Speedo.

Groomsmen Alan Voisard and
Mark Anderson assist Eric in the
pre-race briefing. About 150 guests
participated in the event wearing
our "Eric and Karlyn's Wedding
and Rough Water Swim" caps
donated by Paradowski's Swim
and Sport.

Jack Babashoff

In 1997 at the age of 35 I
accepted a full athletic scholarship to swim for Pat Skehan at
Cal State Bakersfield (CSUB).
It was one of the best decisions
of my life. I enjoyed the school,
the team, and the town.

Eric Neilsen

Teamwork! Joining my CSUB teammates Cory Snow, Amy Hurst, and
Charli Shearard on the podium after
winning the final event of the meet,
the 400-yard freestyle relay. The win
secured the CSUB women's team
a second place overall finish at the
NCAA DIV II Championships in
Canton, Ohio, March 1998.

Eric Neilsen

I was honored to grace the cover of SWIM Magazine for the second time in 1998.

Eric Neilsen

Demonstrating a streamline body position at an Aquatic Edge Faster Freestyle clinic. I inherited my teaching talent from my dad.

Eric and Mom always helped out at my Girl Scout events, as did many of my Masters' swimming friends.

In 2004 we moved to
Kona, Hawaii. I love the
warm, clear water and
swimming with turtles,
dolphins, and manta rays.

Charlotte Brynn

In 2005 I joined coach Harry Canales and the Kona Dolphin Swim Team.
Since I did not have kids of my own, training with these speedsters helped
to fill that void. From left: Jacque, Bhillie, Malia, Dane, me, Nick, Marissa,
JP, Megan, Jade, Emily, and Joshua.

I love to swim and I love to
race! However, now it's about
having fun instead of breaking records.

Kees-Jan van Overbeeke

*In the summer of 2012 I acciden-
tally became the Sicilian Regional
Champion for Aquathlon (run/
swim/run). Who knew?*

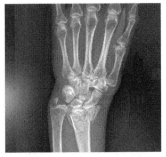

*My shattered wrist in May
of 2013. I'm grateful that it
healed and so did my heart.*

Grant Miller

*I was able to swim with
a broken wrist thanks to
Tabi King of DJO Global,
who fitted me with an
EXOS waterproof cast.*

*The start of a new era—triathlon! In
2013, Bike Works of Kona gave me a cool
new tri-kit and I was off and running.
Swimming and biking, too!*

*Mom's 80th birthday
party and family reunion
in Coronado, June 2014.
From left: Mom, Mark, me,
Kirsten, Kerri, and Derek.*

*In July of 2014, Mom set new U.S. Masters
National record for the 80–84 age group
in Lake Placid, NY. She completed a 2-mile
cable swim in 65 degree water in 1 hour 19
minutes, a whopping 23 minutes off the previous best. Her mantra for the chilly swim:
"I am one tough BROAD! I can do this!"*

*Mom and I at the enshrinement
ceremony to be inducted into the
International Swimming Hall of
Fame in June of 2015. This was
one of the most amazing experiences of our lives.*

CHAPTER 30

Recovery: Day 11 and Beyond

R ELIEF. I FELT RELIEF WHEN I ADMITTED to Mom I had a problem. I felt even more relief when I told Dr. Dill I was an alcoholic. But the real relief—the relief that allowed me to see daylight where before there had been only darkness—started once I finally got through the detox process. I realized I didn't have to endure that miserable lifestyle anymore. The AA Program has a popular saying: "Are you sick and tired of being sick and tired?" I certainly was. While I had knocked the huge monkey called alcohol off my back, I was also left with an enormous gap in my daily routine. So much of my energy, so many hours in my day, had been devoted to being an alcoholic. Now I was going back home, back to the scene of the crime, back to a life I had no idea how to live.

The Program cautions alcoholics about triggers, especially during the early days of sobriety. You are susceptible to relapsing when you emerge, Rip van Winkle–like, from your drug- or alcohol-induced comatose existence, because you are completely unfamiliar with the world around you. It's like the stark change of scenery in *The Wizard of Oz* from black-and-white Kansas to Technicolor Oz. If you want to have any hope of surviving, you have to acknowledge that your existence as you once knew it is over. You have crossed a threshold. There was the alcohol life, and now there is the non-alcohol life. You may have changed—you may have made the commitment to sobriety—but how do you reconcile your new needs and wants with the old environment you call home?

The most common triggers, we're warned, are people, places, and things. In a perfect world, a recovering alcoholic could wipe the slate clean and start anew. But the world is an imperfect place. I was going back to an empty house. I was going back to my dad, yes, but he certainly was in no shape to offer much in the way of encouragement. On the one hand, the empty house was a good thing because it gave me some room to breathe. On the other hand, I didn't have a support system in place. Dave was scheduled to arrive back in port in less than two weeks, but what kind of emotional backing could I expect from him? How would our relationship, which was dysfunctional to begin with, survive the huge change that had occurred while he was away?

The important thing was that, for the first time in years, I had *hope*. My swimming comeback at age twenty-five had actually escalated my drinking. In retrospect, breaking a world record in Houston turned out to be a terrible thing for me because it merely reinforced in my head that I was a quitter. It is difficult for alcoholics to accept success—it scares us. We don't feel worthy of the accolades and we are sure we can't live up to the image. *Look at what you could have been, Karlyn. Have a little peek at all the talent you squandered . . .* And once that recording started to play again in my head, it all went to hell. And why did I drink? For my entire drinking career my motivation was always "drink not to think." My failings, my shortcomings, everything I gave up or sabotaged—I wanted to shut it all out. As much as I had tried to distance myself from my father and his alcoholism, I had in many ways unwittingly become a carbon copy of him. Just as he couldn't deal with the acclaim for his school bands, I couldn't come to grips with the success I found in the pool. It was easier to succeed at failure.

Early in my sobriety, I realized I had been granted a gift—the precious gift of life. I needed to prize it like nothing I'd ever had before. I've never been one to do things halfway. It's in my nature, as it is with so many alcoholics, to be all or nothing. So I was ready to dive into this sobriety thing headfirst. I was going to approach my recovery with the same fortitude, commitment, and narrow focus I'd exhibited when Troy had announced the requirements for making the training trip to Asia. It excited me. It gave me direction. Sticking with sobriety represented the first time in a long time I had had a specific goal in front of me and the criteria for achieving that goal. But I knew this goal was enormously more important than posting a fast time or breaking a record. It was life or death. Succeed, and the Program promised me a life I could never in my wildest dreams have imagined. Fail, and I knew, at my core, that I would die. It was a no-brainer. With stakes this high and the clearest mind in over sixteen years, I chose *life*.

The Program encourages the newly sober to attend ninety meetings in ninety days. If you can commit to that, they suggest, it's a great way to jump-start your recovery. I used the wall calendar in the kitchen to chart my progress. The Alano Club in Coronado had six meetings a day, with the first at 7:00 a.m. Since my sleep patterns were out of whack anyway, it wasn't difficult to commit to that early morning meeting. But that wasn't enough for me. I wanted to get the principles of the program as quickly as possible, so I started to go to two and sometimes three meetings a day. During those first three months, I went to a whopping 142 meetings. I was like the kid who arrived in the room even before the teacher and sat in the front row of the class.

That first weekend out of rehab, my brother Derek took me to a retreat for recovering addicts and alcoholics at Lake Henshaw. Hundreds of enthusiastic, happy, *sober* people arrived, filling up the entire campground. Derek, whom I'd sometimes partied with in the past, had now

been sober for about three years. I found myself in this strangely comforting environment where I was surrounded by people who'd all been
through a lot of the same things I'd been through. Being among them
filled me with promise. It reinforced the hope I had of a brand-new life
ahead of me.

There was a small, kidney-shaped pool at the campground. It couldn't
have been more than twelve yards across. I slipped into the water and
floated, weightless. It was cathartic. I felt so good. I realized how much
I missed the water. I swam a few easy laps. It was as if everything I'd ever
craved from alcohol, all those feelings and sensations I'd yearned for,
were there for me in that pool's blue surface. It felt like home, that pool.
It was deeply healing, both physically and emotionally.

The entire weekend was memorable. I was learning about the
Twelve Steps. I had so many questions. There was so much I wanted
to know from the other members of this new tribe of mine. How did
I get a sponsor? What could I expect when I got back home? Did anyone ever fully recover? What did the Fourth Step, the one about moral
inventory, really mean? I wanted to hustle through those Twelve Steps
right away so I could get settled into a non-alcoholic life. As with my
swimming when I was young, I was driven to attain the goal of "perfect"
sobriety.

"How am I doing so far, Derek?" I asked on the drive back home.

"You're a newbie, Karlyn. You're really green. You're squirrely."

"Squirrely?" I questioned.

"Yeah," Derek said with a smile. "Settle down."

"But I want to be known as the person who got through all the steps
the fastest," I said.

Derek laughed. "It doesn't work that way, Sis," he said. "This isn't
some swimming cut you're trying to nail by the end of the summer. Take
a deep breath. It's a life-long haul."

After the retreat, I went to see my boss at the Navy Amphibious Base at Coronado. John couldn't get over the change in me. "You look terrific, Karlyn," he said. I'd been lifeguarding at NAB from 1989 to 1993, and in all those years he had never seen a healthy Karlyn. John explained that they'd keep me on disability for the time being and would eventually work me back into the schedule.

"Here's the thing," he said. "Once we bring you back in, we won't tolerate any unexcused absences. We have the right to drug- or alcohol-test you at any point in time. If you fail a test, you're out. Basically, you've used up all of your mulligans. Do you understand?"

I nodded. "I really appreciate your belief in me, John."

"If you mean that, now is your chance to prove it," he said. "Show everyone I know that I'm not making a huge mistake by doing this."

There are two 50-meter pools at NAB. We used to refer to one, the Navy SEAL combat training tank, as the George Worthington Baths. George, a Naval Academy graduate and UDT (Underwater Demolition Team)/ SEAL who had risen to the rank of rear admiral, was someone I'd known for years from the Coronado Masters team. I walked onto the pool deck for the first time since I'd been reinstituted, and there was Admiral George, as gorgeous, tan, and fit in his sixties as ever.

"Hi, Karlyn," he said.

"Hey, Admiral George."

"Going to get in a few laps?" he asked.

"That's the plan," I said.

"Well, it's a beautiful day. Have a nice swim."

"You too," I said.

I stood there on the pool deck for a long time. The water looked inviting, but I couldn't get in. It was one thing to have been in that little pool at Lake Henshaw, but it was another thing altogether to be confronted with the prospect of diving into a 50-meter competition pool. I watched

George ease into the water. He swam across with grace and confidence, as if he hadn't a care in the world. I moved closer to the edge to follow suit, but I still couldn't do it. I couldn't coax myself into the water. This wasn't the typical dread a swimmer experiences before that initial first dive. It was different. I felt oddly disappointed. I wanted to get in, didn't I? The pool, I was hoping, would be a place I could easily go back to. It held so much promise, unlike so many other things in my toxic lifestyle.

As I stood there watching Admiral George continue to stroke back and forth, the water called out to me. She whispered, *It's okay, Karlyn. Come on in. You'll be fine.* But not even her reassurances moved me. I was still paralyzed.

What exactly is holding you back? The answer came to me almost immediately: it was the idea of who I used to be. It was the thought of what I could and should have been. Even though I felt like a completely new person, the tape inside my head—the one I'd tried so valiantly to silence with my drinking—was still looping. *All that wasted potential . . . All that squandered natural ability . . . The skipped practices . . . The races not swum . . . The lies.* Fear and guilt swirled around me.

The new Karlyn had to put a different tape on. The sober, clear-headed Karlyn wanted to be heard above that noise. *That's the past; this is the now.* I began to have a heart-to-heart conversation with myself as I stood on that pool deck.

What is it you want to do this very moment, Karlyn?

I want to swim.

Are you sure?

Yes, I'm positive.

Okay, but we need to lay out a few ground rules first. In order for you to reconcile what's happened, we need to put things in perspective. If you never again swim faster than two minutes in the 100-meter freestyle, are you going to be okay with that?

Yes.

If you never win another race, never set another record, if nobody

ever compliments or praises you for your swimming ability—can you live
with that?

Yes.

Are you SURE?

I took a deep breath.

Yes. Yes, I am.

And with that I took another deep breath and dove in. I kept my hands and arms together tight in front of my head in a streamlined position and glided underwater as far as I could. And that sense of coming home—that elation I had first felt in that little kidney-shaped campground pool—was magnified tenfold at the George Worthington Baths. That first trip across the pool was euphoric, because I realized I had finally come to a place where I could let go of my swimming past. The old Karlyn wasn't invited to this next phase of my life. For my survival and sanity, I had to jettison her, like a sailor doing a burial at sea. The new Karlyn was okay with that.

I wanted to swim because of what swimming did for me at its most basic level: it made me feel good. Sure, I was good at it. I always had been. But more importantly, the water made me feel good about *myself*. I trusted her to take care of me. I'd found my way home. Even after everything I'd been through—my descent into the abyss of addiction—the water was still my best friend. And I never, ever, wanted to deny myself that friendship again.

CHAPTER 31

A Natural High

T HAT FIRST DAY I WAS SO OUT OF SHAPE I could barely swim 400 meters. I was beat afterward, complete toast as they say, but in a good way. I went back the next day and knocked off 600 meters. The next I managed to do a whopping 800. When I was younger, that distance would have been nothing more than a warm-up for me. But that was then. Now I was relearning how to swim. I was starting out slow and teaching myself how to be an athlete again.

My sobriety was a crash course on relearning *everything*. I had to teach myself how to eat again. Because of my bulimia, my nutritional habits were atrocious. I had to relearn normal sleep patterns, how to structure a day, and even how to properly communicate with people. Since I hadn't really spoken to anybody for years *sober*, my social skills were rusty.

The Program was invaluable. I was surrounded by people who had been there. When I first came into "the rooms," as any AA meeting is known, I had nothing to lose and everything to gain. The Program is aptly called a fellowship because attending meetings creates an inspiring solidarity. In the rooms, you can share your insecurities and laugh about your foibles. How do you dance, if you've never been sober on a dance floor? Is it possible to attend a wedding and forgo the champagne toast gracefully? How can you get through the stresses associated with a Thanksgiving Day meal if you can't keep draining your wine glass? How do you get intimate with someone when you're not completely wasted? No one at the meetings was there to judge. It was all about commiserating with and supporting one another.

I was on such a natural high it was scary. I kept hearing from everyone in the Program, including my sponsor, Donna, that I needed to slow down. "Be careful, Karlyn. You're on a pink cloud," she said, making reference to the euphoric feeling the newly sober often experience. "And remember *HALT*. Try not to get too *hungry*, *angry*, *lonely*, or *tired*, because that's when we make bad decisions." I took the advice to heart. Besides Donna and the fellowship, I still had this feeling that someone or something was guiding me. Maybe it was that mysterious guardian angel of mine again? Was she the one who was insisting that swimming was a very good thing for me?

Exercise, I discovered, sped up my recovery. It not only helped cleanse me of any residual alcohol left after detox, but it also helped repair the damage I'd done to my heart, lungs, and other organs. Instead of sitting at home watching television, I would go for a run. I even signed up for a 5k. Between the swimming, which was becoming a daily ritual, the running, and all those meetings, I was getting into pretty decent mental and physical shape.

Dave came back when I was two and a half weeks sober. We had a long talk, and he was perfectly fine with my sobriety. He even *sounded* supportive. Within a day or so, however, he was right back in his gotta-make-up-for-lost-time party mode. One afternoon as we drove to Solana Beach to visit Mom and Lloyd, Dave lit up a joint in the car. I cracked open the window, but the smoke still filled the interior. *Okay, he's either not taking my sobriety seriously, he doesn't care about my sobriety, or he just can't help himself,* I thought. Whichever way, I realized, it was problematic. The unspoken message was clear: "Knock yourself out, Karlyn, but don't try to put it on me because I don't want any part of it."

Fortunately I had no desire to drink (and pot had never been my drug of choice). Even during those horrific initial days of rehab, I didn't actually need alcohol. I wanted a drink, yes, but it was only because I knew having one would stop me from being sick. And once I left the hospital I reasoned I had too much to lose to drink again. I wanted to live. I was one of the lucky ones. I felt blessed and immensely grateful that the obsession had been removed for me. Many people still have the longing for alcohol, even years into recovery.

We'd been through a lot together, Dave and I. He contributed to the rent. He was helpful when it came to taking care of Dad and doing handyman things. But if he was content to light up joints around me and drink to excess regardless of how it might affect me, I knew that being around him would be the end of my abstinence. The Program was right: sobriety is a selfish act, in that it is ours and ours alone. We cannot expect all others to nurture it or even to understand it.

Early sobriety is tenuous at best. To help with motivation, whether you are newly sober or an old-timer, the Program has a reward system. At meetings you are presented with different colored chips, each color representing a different sobriety milestone. A silver, or "desire," chip, for instance, represents one day of sobriety; a red chip is thirty days; a blue chip, six months; and so on. A bronze chip represents one full year of sobriety. That's a big one. But the person who has the longest sobriety, we're taught, is not the person who's accumulated the most chips or who's made it through the most years. It's the person who gets up in the morning the earliest and goes to bed the latest, sober. That's the truth behind the Program's "one day at a time" mantra. Sometimes it's making it through not even one day at a time, but just one hour or even one minute. When you're having a really crappy day and life brings you to your knees, you're sometimes trying to survive just one moment at a time.

My gut was telling me I had to distance myself from Dave. His habits were becoming dangerous to my resolve. Maybe that's why I never sent him the letter I had written while I was in the hospital. Maybe I foresaw that we would reach this crossroads, that ours was a classic dead-end relationship.

One day, after Dave came home drunk, I finally told him it wasn't working out. We argued, and it got ugly fast. No matter how much he tried to tell me he could change, I refused to budge. I kept telling him to pack his stuff and move out. He eventually relented. He found his own place, a small apartment not far away, but he kept coming around to visit. He kept telling me he loved me and couldn't live without me.

I didn't understand it at the time, but my codependent personality was still rearing its ugly head. I was also afraid to be alone, afraid to face this new life of sobriety on my own. I began to wonder if maybe it could work between the two of us. Just like a drug addict or an alcoholic, when you grow up deploying codependent behaviors to survive, letting go of your "projects" can be just as hard as putting down a drink or a joint. After all, maybe Dave could change, and I could be the one to help him. We would both be sober and happy and supportive of one another. But then I'd remember Dad's issues. *You cannot help someone who doesn't want to be helped.* It took years for my mother to finally come to terms with that. Was I really prepared to go down that same dead-end street with Dave?

A few days after he moved out, I came home from work to find Dave at the house waiting for me. He was drinking a beer and shooting the breeze with Dad. My father always liked having Dave around. As I put my things away and settled in, I reminded myself that this was one of the red flags I'd been warned about in meetings. Dave was all three of the people-place-thing triggers wrapped into one. In lifeguard-speak, he was the deadly rip current not visible to the naked eye. After we finished dinner, I again told him to leave me alone. "If you truly love me, Dave, you'll give me the space I need to figure this all out." Thankfully, he granted me my wish, and our relationship finally came to an end.

CHAPTER **32**

Life on Life's Terms

W HEN THE BIG BOOK WAS PUBLISHED in 1939, few could have
imagined the worldwide impact it would have. The whole
notion of the Twelve Steps as a course of action for recovery was ground-
breaking—especially the First Step, in which the addict admits that
he or she is powerless over his or her addiction. The book details the
personal experiences of not just the Program's founders, Bill W. and
Dr. Bob, but also of many others who have suffered from alcoholism.
It's these anecdotes that elevate the material from dry and sometimes
preachy to resonate and compelling. When reading the case studies,
you're immediately struck by the resilience of the human spirit. So many
of the anonymous individuals were dealt losing hands in life. Some were
emotionally and physically traumatized before even leaving the cradle.
Reading their accounts is heart wrenching. And yet, thanks in large part
to the Program and its principles, these people managed to persevere.
To survive. The Program offered them light, hope, and a blueprint for a
new life.

The concept is simple. Bill W. and Dr. Bob found that the illusive
ingredient to staying sober is to work with another alcoholic. Plain and
simple—it's one drunk helping another drunk not pick up that next
drink. No other method, no other treatment works as well. It was, and

still is, magical in its simplicity and effectiveness.

Many aspects of the Program have become part of our common language, and many of its sayings and axioms are all too familiar. "Hello, my name is Joe, and I'm an alcoholic" has been done to death by standup comedians; it barely qualifies as an amusing punch line anymore. But the mere fact that the Program is so well known demonstrates the reach it has had into the world's collective consciousness. I'm not sure what Bill W. had in mind when he sat down to describe his Twelve Steps, but over thirty million copies of the Big Book have been printed to date, and in 1999 the addict-turned-author was named one of *Time* magazine's 100 Most Important People of the Century.

Even though I was feeling better, I was struggling to feel comfortable in my new skin. I wasn't quite sure what my new skin was, to tell the truth. I collected my three-month chip, but I still felt as if I were walking on ground that could open up and swallow me whole at any moment. *Was sobriety something I could keep up? Would I wake up tomorrow morning and suddenly have the urge to drink?* I had no idea. I was on a road that I had never navigated before, and it was fraught with dangerous curves and life-threatening cliffs. I did my best to stay the course and control only what I could: my attitude. Gratefully, I realized that under the heavy layers of my hard-knock life, I was a genuinely positive person. Given the uncertainty that lay ahead, my positive outlook was indeed a blessing.

The Program teaches us that, as survivors, we have only today. The gifts that come our way—in particular, our new sober lifestyle—are based on gratitude, surrender, and a willingness to do something different than what we've done before. It's about accepting our flaws and the mistakes we've made and learning to be at peace with them. It's about getting out of our own way. AA has been described as an action-based program of recovery. The definition of insanity recited many times in the rooms as "doing the same thing over and over and expecting different results" reinforces that we need to always be ready to change our course of action to keep our sobriety. There is no finite. There is no end game. There's no mastering the process, earning a world record time, and being done with it. Sobriety, as my brother Derek had pointed out, is a lifelong process.

I continued to go to as many meetings as I could. At some point, attending them was no longer about drinking or not drinking. It became much more. I needed to figure out the reasons behind why I drank. Drinking is just the symptom, not the disease. The actual disease was my "stinking thinking."

Sitting in the rooms began to shed light on how I could "live life on life's terms." Now that I wasn't burying myself in a substance to deaden reality, how would I stand up to that reality? In the past, if I had a rough day—if I got into an argument with my boyfriend or got fired from Bula's—having that first drink was like releasing air from a tire. The pressure I felt inside would build and build, but once I took that first sip—*pssssss* . . . I could immediately feel myself begin to relax. But what happens when the outlet you've relied on is no longer available?

Life on life's terms. It sounds easy enough, but it turned out to be very challenging. At the age of thirty-one I was trying to figure out how to be a sober woman. Everything the alcoholic learns from a sober perspective is learned in baby steps. Life isn't always fluffy and soft. It has edges—sometimes very jagged edges. But we must learn to negotiate our way through life without taking the easy way out by getting drunk. We need to embrace the waves of uncertainty and in letting go learn to make peace with the rough waters.

Some alcoholics can't get past the unfairness of it all. They flip through a magazine and are confronted with ads depicting beautiful, youthful men and women hanging out in edgy bars or at trendy cocktail parties or nightclubs. They turn on the TV to watch a ballgame and see a nonstop barrage of commercials reminding them that drinking beer is one of America's favorite pastimes. Drink. Drink and have fun. Drink and be *more. Why can't I be having a good time too?* some wonder. *Maybe if I can just teach myself how to drink in moderation, "like a gentleman," I can be part of the in crowd too.* But there's the rub. For the alcoholic, the Big Book reminds us, there is no such thing as drinking "like a gentleman." If you give an alcoholic a bottomless bottle of whiskey, they will want another one—just in case! One drink is one too many, and a bottomless bottle is never enough. My mind can convince me that this line of thinking is perfectly rational. I realized that the sooner I came to grips with the fact that I never had and never will have a "normal" relationship with alcohol, the better chance I would have of staying sober.

While the meetings were very structured, the formats and topics changed depending on the venue. Sometimes there were readings. Someone would read a selection from the Big Book or other "conference approved" literature, and we'd all express how it related to our own situations. Other times it would be a speakers meeting, where one person from the fellowship was preselected to get up and share their "experience, strength, and hope" with the audience. We also had group shares, going around the room and giving everyone an opportunity to speak. I always enjoyed "stick" meetings. A can containing wooden craft sticks with a slogan or a reference to the Big Book written on each would be passed around the room. Everyone would take a stick, read the topic on it, and then share based on that topic. I never failed to pull a stick that had spot-on significance to something going on in my life right then. It was uncanny. The Program is like that. Whenever I found myself feeling stuck, a sign from my Higher Power would appear to move me forward. Of course, a huge part of every meeting is about positive reinforcement from the fellowship. We're all in this together, and we can get through it together.

Meetings teach you to listen. If you choose to or are selected to speak, it is expected that you will limit yourself to a few minutes. Longer than that and it's likely that you are wandering into an unwanted "drunka-logue." Unless you're congratulating someone on a milestone, you don't address people directly. One person has the floor, and everyone else simply listens. And that's where the nuggets come from—the listening. Someone will raise his or her hand to speak and even though he or she is from a completely different walk of life from you—different age, dif-ferent nationality, different everything—as soon as they start to speak, you realize how much you have in common. The story they're telling is *your* story.

It isn't always easy to sit in the rooms. Sometimes your ego gets the best of you, and your self-centeredness from your drinking days comes out. There are still times when I sit through an entire evening and find myself not connecting with anything anyone says. But then it happens, a spark. A speaker will say something that resonates with me, and I'll have a priceless moment of clarity. We call them "God shots." One little God shot makes your whole day, and sometimes your whole week.

I've attended AA meetings all over the world. I've been to meetings conducted in Spanish and other foreign languages. Sometimes I can't understand a single word being said. But I don't have to. Sitting in a room with a bunch of other former drunks is continually one of the most amazing experiences I can have, because we've all walked the same path. We've all hit rock bottom, and now our butts are in these chairs in the name of good health, sanity, and solidarity. Each and every one of us is a miracle, and the inspiration that gives me is inexpressible.

If someone breaks their sobriety, they disappear from the rooms. We say they have gone "back out." You may not see them at meetings any-more, but their absence is felt. And when someone who has relapsed finds the wherewithal to rejoin the group, to come and sit and share again, they are welcomed back with open arms, to people eager to hear their story. Everyone else in the room genuinely wants to hear the experiences of these folks, sometimes affectionately called "retreads." Their experiences are something the rest of us need to hear. We're not there to judge. We're there to share, listen, and learn. It's one thing to be on a successful sobriety trajectory; it's another thing altogether to be retreading. Those who ventured back to the dark side and return to tell about it have valuable lessons to share.

There's no shame in returning after a relapse. Everyone is welcomed back and even thanked profusely for being there. It's the newcomer or the returnee who helps those with time in the program stay sober. It's a stark reminder to all of us of the danger that is "out there" when a drink is picked up. Someone who has slipped may feel personal shame and guilt. But the group continues to offer encouragement and support. "Keep coming back." "Willingness is the key." "It works if you work it."

What if I were to relapse? Would I have the courage to stand up in the room and announce, "Hi, my name is Karlyn, and I have one day sober."?

CHAPTER 33

Seek Progress, Not Perfection

I STARTED COMING TO TERMS with my mom while I was in rehab. What I realized as I started transitioning into a sober lifestyle was that I couldn't keep holding on to my deep-seated resentment. I needed to move forward. It became clear to me during my stay at Sharp Cabrillo that my mom truly wanted to help me, and in that regard I was very lucky. In rehab and through some counseling, I figured out that while it was too late for young Karlyn to have Mom as a nurturing mother, it certainly wasn't too late for grown-up Karlyn to have her as a friend. So that's what I did. I began to view her as a very good, very reliable friend.

Unlike Dave, Mom and Lloyd were very mindful of their behavior during my early months of recovery. Whenever I'd drive up to visit them for the weekend, they made a point of removing all alcohol from the house and abstaining while I was there. They even cut back on their own drinking in general. We all needed to go through an acclimation period and get to know one another without alcohol in the equation. Lloyd had never seen me when I wasn't a party animal. It felt good to know they were both making an effort to help me maintain my sobriety. And the more time we spent together, the more we realized how much we liked each other's company even without the enhancement of alcohol.

Whenever I went to swim-team parties during my "lost years," as I started to refer to them, I always drank. Whenever there was a Coronado Masters board meeting, I always attended, not because I was particularly interested in the organizational side of our team, but because there was always free booze available. At the time, I was under the assumption that everyone else was putting it away as much as I was. It is common for alcoholics to have this misconception; it's one of the arguments they make to themselves to defend their indulgence. In my mind, everyone else was at the party for the alcohol too. It wasn't until I attended my first party sober that I began to realize how few people actually drank and that hardly anyone drank to get drunk. It was a revelation, especially as swimmers are notorious for being big partiers. But it was refreshing to see that the people I was going to be around—the ones I would be surrounding myself with as I immersed myself deeper and deeper into Masters swimming—were just not that into drinking.

In the earliest days of my sobriety, Donna, my sponsor, shared a visual exercise with me that had a profound effect. "Take a glass of beer, wine, vodka, or anything with alcohol in it, and set it on a table next to a glass of poison," she said. "Look at those glasses and come to the understanding that no matter which one you pick up, the end result will be exactly the same. Drinking from either glass is going to kill you."

Alcohol addiction, I was taught, is an incredibly powerful, insidious disease, and it never lies dormant. While you're in meetings and in recovery, the disease isn't sliding off somewhere into the background. Not only is it keeping pace with you, it's getting stronger. If you drop down to do ten pushups, it'll drop down to do twenty. If you go to a meeting because you desperately need the positive reinforcement, your addiction is there as soon as you go out the door, waiting to welcome you back.

Alcoholism is a formidable adversary. As the Big Book says, it's "cunning, baffling, and powerful," and the moment you think you have it licked, it will crush you. As soon as you relax, alcoholism will get the upper hand. You have no idea what moves are up its sleeve. But when you can step back and really understand that a glass of wine is equivalent to a glass of poison, you begin to appreciate the seriousness of the battle.

Another profound shift in my way of thinking was to recognize that I needed to get my ego in check, big time. In the Program, "ego" stands for "Edging God Out." Alcoholics are notorious for over-sized egos, and I was no exception. Ever since I was young, I had felt that I deserved special treatment, that the world owed me something. But that type of thinking doesn't fly in the sober world. I had to accept the fact that not only could I not drink with abandon; I couldn't drink at all. It could kill me. It doesn't matter that everyone else in the world can have alcohol— I can't.

Thanks to the Program, I was also getting my eating disorder under control. Since I was now training regularly and feeling strong both in and out of the water, I began to be able to look at food as fuel rather than as escape. I became accountable for what I ate, and I learned to make better food choices. I wasn't perfect, but I was making progress. The Program says "seek progress, not perfection," so that's what I did. Like alcoholism, bulimia is a disease that flourishes in secrecy.*

I started swimming more regularly with Coronado Masters. Mom was on the team, as were a number of other friends whom now I considered almost family—Admiral George, Bill Earley, Mike Keeney, the Lamotts, Fritz Homans, Larry Cartwright, Hilary Thompson, Phil Garn, Scott and Marcy Huball, and Pete Toennies. So many of them had watched

---

* For more on the experience of bulimia, read Caroline Adams Miller's book *My Name Is Caroline.* In 1988, Miller, a Harvard swimmer, had the guts to write and publish a memoir of her struggle with bulimia, the first book of its kind. The work is a personal account of her "descent into bulimia, leading up to a final victorious triumph over the addiction" with the help of a twelve-step program. Bravo, Caroline, for publicly sharing your struggles and your story of recovery, and for shedding light on this dark and ugly disease.

me drift off course, and now they were watching me slowly swim back to shore. Much like the fellowship's acceptance of retreads, the Masters team was nonjudgmental about my past. That's one of the many great attributes of the Masters organization: it accepts all comers. And it's been my experience of competitive swimmers in general that they are always supportive of one another, and forgiving as well.

It had been only a few months since rehab, but I could feel myself getting stronger and fitter. Between lifeguarding at the Naval Amphibious Base, training, and AA meetings, I had more than enough to keep me busy. Mom, Lloyd, some of our teammates, and I signed up for the 1993 Southern Pacific Masters Association (SPMA) Long Course Meters Regional Championships, which were scheduled to be held in Mission Viejo in August. I was only four months sober, but I was getting the itch to compete again. It's one thing to believe you're in good shape based on what you've been able to do in practice; it's another thing altogether to step up on the blocks and see what kind of form you're really in. Vicki Davidson, daughter of NFL great Ben Davidson, was also registered for the meet, and we were in the same age group. My first event was the 200-meter backstroke. Before the race, Vicki's coach, Chuck Hay, warned me, "She's tough, Karlyn. She's really going to be strong on that second half." I was more than ready to accept the challenge.

The gun went off, and immediately I felt I was back in my element. Vicky and I were even at the 50, and then I began to build a slight lead. I extended that lead after the first 100. Going into the second half of the race, I remembered what Chuck had said, and I continued to put distance between us, charging hard to the wall. Vicki swam well, but I managed to beat her by a few body lengths. When I looked up at the clock, I was blown away to see I'd swum a 2:30—equivalent to my lifetime best when I was a teenager. I had also broken the San Diego Imperial (SI) Masters Swimming record, no easy feat given the number of fast swimmers who have competed in that region over the years. The most important thing, though, was that I was having fun.

While in the warm-up pool before the race, I had noticed a guy I had seen the week before at an open-water event hosted by Coronado Masters. We started talking, and I found out his name was Eric Neilsen. He was both a swimmer and a coach from the Center for Sports Medicine, a facility in Clairemont, a suburb in northern San Diego. I found him to be boyishly cute and a little shy.

As is the case with just about everything else, the Program has suggested guidelines when it comes to dating. They recommend avoiding it for your first year of sobriety. Conventional wisdom holds that you need to get your own life in order before you think about getting involved in anyone else's. It made sense to me, and I was not looking for anything from Eric. I simply enjoyed the moment.

The next day at the meet Eric and I talked more in between events. In addition to coaching at the Center, he also did aquatic rehabilitation therapy. He'd graduated from Cal Poly in 1990 with a degree in industrial technology, but when he moved to San Diego he realized his true passion was athletic performance. He lived in Ocean Beach, and I considered him very date-worthy. I mentioned to him that I needed a ride back home to Coronado, and he quickly offered to take me.

The rest of the meet was wonderful, with me swimming well in all my events and getting to know Eric better. On the drive back to Coronado, I kept wondering whether getting into a relationship was something I should do. The Big Book, I knew, cautioned against it. But the excitement of being attracted to someone and having them, in turn, be attracted to me—without any alcohol involved!—was simply too irresistible to pass up. Besides, Eric appeared to be a really nice guy. Normal, even.

CHAPTER **34**

Attitude Is
the Mind's Paintbrush

E RIC WOULD SOMETIMES COME TO VISIT me at my lifeguard tower, and we enjoyed some lovely conversations. When he asked me out on our first official date, I was up front about my past. I'm not sure if I was trying to warn him off or test his level of interest, but he insisted he was completely fine with it. I told him about the drinking and the recreational drugs I'd done, about the poor choices in my relationships. I even told him about the bulimia. He just shrugged. Nothing, I would soon learn, ever seemed to faze him. And that's Eric, the man I fell head over heels for. He would come to teach me so much about taking things in stride. I'd never before felt such acceptance in a romantic relationship.

For decades picturesque La Jolla Cove has played host to one of the most popular open-water swim competitions around. In September of 1993, the group that puts on the La Jolla Rough Water Swim added a three-mile race they dubbed the Gatorman. Despite my aversion to cold water, I signed up. The water in the cove that day *was* cold, about 59 degrees. Pools, in contrast, are generally heated to around 80 degrees.

I swam hard from the get-go and surprised myself by winning the women's race. The water was crystal clear, and we all enjoyed cruising over kelp beds, bat rays, perch, garibaldi, and leopard sharks. Hitting the beach first was confirmation that my swimming fitness was growing. One of the other competitors remarked after the race that I took off so fast from the start that she thought I had a plane to catch. In some ways I did. I was approaching my swimming as if I were an impatient traveler eager to see as much of the world as I could after having been grounded for much too long.

Even with my lifeguarding at the pool and the beach, I was struggling to make ends meet. I could always go back to bartending or waitressing to bump up my income, but that, I knew, would be tempting fate. I needed to keep my distance from the life I'd worked so hard to extricate myself from. Fortunately, I no longer had to worry about spending money on alcohol. It's unbelievable how expensive a substance addiction can be.

One day John Waterman called me into his office. In the past, whenever someone of authority called me in for a meeting, I would be petrified because it usually meant I'd been caught screwing something up. Now, though, I had no reason to go slinking in there because my work habits, from what I could tell, had been exemplary. That was yet another revelation of sobriety—not having to live a life of fear.

"How's everything going, Karlyn?" he said.

"Great, John."

"Are you happy working here?"

"Yes."

"Good," he said. "We're happy with you working here, too. We have an opening for a recreation aide with MWR, and John Baker and I really think you should consider it. It's in Building 162, where the gym is. It's a full-time job, five days a week. The bad news is that it's a low-ranking

GS-3 (government service) job and the pay is only about $15,000 a year. But the good news is the position offers benefits, including health insurance and a retirement plan."

I accepted it with thanks. John said I could think on it, but I knew I didn't have to.

"I really appreciate everything you and JB (John Baker) have done for me. I'd love to continue working with you in whatever capacity you see fit." I left John's office with a great sense of satisfaction. Being offered this position was further evidence that I was indeed getting more grounded and heading in the right direction.

My new job was far from glamorous. I was responsible for checking in gym visitors, washing towels, and issuing gear like balls and bats, socks and jocks. But I took the job seriously.

I wanted to repay my two Johns—Waterman and Baker—for having so much faith in me. They took a chance on an ex-drunk, and I was determined not to let them down. I worked every day from 7:30 a.m. to 4:00 p.m. I also started to train a bit more seriously. Working in Building 162 had its advantages. I had a 50-meter pool literally down the hall, a gym across the parking lot, and the beach was close enough that I could go for a run on my lunch hour. These were extra benefits that helped to make up for the small salary.

It's remarkable how tidy my life became once I stopped chasing the bottle. The drama melted away, and it became easier to focus on the day-to-day business of life. When you're sober, showing up to work on time, executing your job duties, being honest, and staying true to your word become easier. For the first time I could remember, I began to take pride in my accountability and performance.

Part of getting my life back in order, I knew, would be to face another one of my demons: going back to school. Southwestern Community College was offering general education classes on base, and I enrolled in a history course to get my feet wet. I studied during the lull at work between loads of laundry and the morning and afternoon rushes. I easily passed the class and looked into taking more. I was moving forward again, bit by bit. I didn't stop to think about where I'd been. I only focused on where I was going.

I enrolled in more community college classes, some of which were even held at my alma mater, Coronado High School. I consistently earned top marks in every class I took. Years before I couldn't tolerate sitting in a classroom and never really cared what grade I got. Now I was excited to learn, excited by the challenge. It wasn't the material that had changed, it was me. "Attitude," the saying goes, "is the mind's paintbrush. It can color any situation." Having a new outlook, I was discovering, was making all the difference in the world.

Because I was technically a recreation major, MWR paid for my classes. Years later, John Baker went from MWR director of NAB, a very small base, to being the worldwide Fleet and Family Readiness Program Director, Navy Installations Command (CNIC). He was responsible for the navy's entire quality of life program on seventy-two installations and 285 navy ships, with a budget of $2.5 billion. His rating was equal to that of a one-star admiral. But JB never forgot about me. When I was in Washington, D.C., to teach a Faster Freestyle clinic, he took time out of his busy schedule to meet me for a swim. JB, in his youth, had been a top-notch swimmer from the Seattle area who could break a minute in the 100-yard breaststroke. That was a seriously fast time for the mid-1970s, and any swimmer knows that dipping under the 60-second barrier for that distance in any stroke is still a milestone. JB understood the sport and could appreciate everything I'd accomplished in the pool. He could also see just how far my life had progressed. I, in turn, wanted to acknowledge his contribution to my recovery.

"I didn't do anything, Karlyn," he insisted. "You did it all, and I'm just so proud of you."

"You guys, my two Johns, believed in me before I believed in myself. I will forever be grateful for that," I said with misty eyes. "Thank you for taking a chance on me."

CHAPTER 35

Working My Way Into
a "Do-Over"

C OMPETITIVE SWIMMERS OFTEN DEVELOP a love-hate relationship
with their sport. The year-round training is strenuous, tedious,
and can become all-consuming, eating up every spare minute of the
day. Over 99 percent of a competitive swimmer's time in the pool is
devoted to training. Less than 1 percent is spent actually racing. So what
could possibly be the motivation? Money and fame are usually reserved
for more high-profile sports such as golf or tennis. What keeps swimmers coming back is the exhilaration of racing and competing against
one another. It's that 1 percent that keeps the desire burning day to day
and year to year.

Racing is about forcing yourself out of your comfort zone. It's about
submerging yourself in a swirling witch's brew of nerves and confidence and self-doubt and adrenaline and dread and anticipation. It's
an insistence on stepping up on the blocks and testing oneself. Those
who compete understand how trials evoke heightened awareness, self-
growth, and wisdom. Each race, each training session, and even each
stroke is an opportunity to do something different, do it over, do it better. The Program is a lot like that. One moment, one minute, one day is
a second chance to restart your life and do it better. Both swimming and

sobriety require you to step outside your comfort zone, have faith, let go, wait, and see what happens next.

In November 1993 I swam in my second meet since getting sober, and I again did well. More importantly, I was really having fun. A few weeks later, I was scheduled to compete in a 25-meter meet in Carlsbad. I was looking forward to the competition, especially since I hadn't done much short course racing. On the first day of the meet, just six months sober, I broke the world record in the 200-meter backstroke for my age group (30–34). Six years after I'd broken my first world record in Houston, I was breaking my second. The personal backdrop to the two records couldn't have been more different. For the first one I was in a tailspin headed for a near-fatal crash landing. With the second, I had just launched into my new life. One month later Mom, Lloyd, and I traveled to the Southern Pacific Short Course Meters Regional Championships in Cerritos where I broke four more world records, a few of which had been long standing.

It occurred to me that I was working my way into a "do-over." How few of us ever get a second chance at life? If it hadn't been for that call from my mother on that fateful day when I hit my rock bottom; if it hadn't been for my ability to embrace sobriety and the Program with open arms; if it hadn't been for swimming, I wouldn't be getting this chance. I was so very blessed to be the recipient of this amazing do-over, and I was not going to waste a second of it. Swimming was no longer something I *had* to do; it was something I *wanted* to do. I was paying my own membership dues, getting myself to practice on time, and pushing myself as hard as I could during workouts. It was all coming from within me.

In addition to swimming with Coronado Masters a few nights a week, I started practicing with Eric's team up in Clairemont. His group was great, and the fast lane was loaded with talent, including 1976 Olympic silver medalist Jack Babashoff, head coach Alan Voisard, and the tenacious Dianne Gleason. She, like me, could hold her own against any male swimmer. Darrell Jett, a lifeguard buddy from Silver Strand, and Colin Chinn rounded out the lane. Training with fast swimmers, it's been proven time and again, makes you swim faster, and this was certainly the case at the Center. We were all feeding off one another to become fitter, faster, and stronger, and Eric enjoyed coaching such a motivated group of athletes. Whenever swimmers see enthusiasm and excitement coming from a coach, it makes them want to raise their level of performance even higher.

The racing was easy. I've always been competitive, and I've always enjoyed going up against other swimmers. But every time I got up on the blocks, it wasn't really about racing the people next to me. It was about proving to myself that I did, in fact, have follow-through. *That I wasn't a quitter.* Competitive swimming is very black and white. You either swim or you don't. Few things outside the pool are that clear. When the starter says, "Swimmers, take your mark," you're there to prove your mettle. You're making a commitment to push yourself to the best of your abilities. How well you place in the race is almost beside the point. For me the records I was breaking were just icing on the cake. At the end of the day, it was my willingness to try that mattered most. I was suiting up for life and everything it had to offer.

I kept getting faster. By spring of the next year, less than a year into my sobriety, I went to the SPMA Short Course Yards Regional Championships in Mission Viejo. At the age of thirty-two, I broke a minute in the 100-yard fly for the first time in my life. In freestyle, butterfly, backstroke, breaststroke—straight across the board—I was swimming times comparable to or faster than my personal lifetime bests. It was exhilarating. Every time I hit the wall and looked up at the scoreboard to see my time, it was like Christmas. I treated each race like a treasured gift.

During my lost years, hours would melt into days, and sometimes I had a difficult time distinguishing one week from the next. Time is elusive when you're under the thumb of addiction. You're so focused on the all-consuming obsession of getting that next fix that the hands on the clock become an afterthought. Before you know it, you're into a new month, and then a new year, and then yet another new year. I was so focused on surviving that I hadn't been living life. It was as if I had been a detached bystander, my back turned on the parade that was marching past on the street behind me.

But now I'd gotten a handle on the clock. That's another treasured aspect of swimming, the time component. Once I was back in the pool, my focus became about minutes, seconds, and miniscule portions of a second. Competitive swimmers undertake months of hard training to shave off just a few precious tenths of a second on race day. One slight adjustment on a turn, for example, can reap huge benefits. It can become the difference between hitting a qualifying standard or falling short, between breaking or not breaking a record. Sometimes you hit the wall and look up at the scoreboard to see that you reached your goal by a mere one-one-hundredth of a second. That precious moment leaves you beaming for days, weeks. Where else in life does something like that happen?

And I couldn't wait to go to practice. I began to wonder every day just how fast could I swim? Exactly what were my limits? All through work or classes, I'd be chomping at the bit, ready to get back to the pool to test myself some more. At the Center we were blessed to have twenty-seven organized practices per week to choose from. Besides Eric, we had other great coaches like Alan Voisard, the head coach, and Dale Shimato. Every workout had a different vibe and a different cast of characters, and the coach on deck would modify the workout and pace according to the swimmers present. Since I was also swimming with Coronado Masters and training long course meters, going to the Center was a great opportunity to train short course yards.

The best evening to swim was Wednesday. I'm not sure why, but you could always count on a posse of fast swimmers showing up ready to rumble. Eric would announce a warm-up set, and we'd all dive into the water like giddy age-groupers. Once we loosened up, he would give us the main event. Eric was brilliant at writing workouts. He was creative and flexible, adjusting his sets as needed. He loved challenging us, and we loved being challenged. My lane mates and I would beat each other up, encouraging one another to keep digging a little bit deeper and to hang in there as hitting the intervals grew more difficult. Afterward we'd all sit in the Jacuzzi and congratulate each other on our efforts, and then go out to eat. No way was I even thinking about drinking when I had all this invigorating training and positive reinforcement keeping me engaged. All my senses rose to the surface when I was in the water. Heck, I was having amazing fun just *being alive.*

CHAPTER **36**

My First "Birthday"

A YEAR OF SOBRIETY IS A HUGE MILESTONE. It's your symbolic first "birthday." Everyone in the Program has been given a chance at their very own do-over, so we count the years starting from that first day you put the bottle down. Reaching the year mark is a significant accomplishment, and it's even celebrated with a cake. Those who have been in the rooms with you, your family and friends, anyone in the Program—all are invited to mark this special day. While my "belly button" birthday is March 18th, my sobriety birthday is April 17, 1993.

As I progressed in recovery after my one-year anniversary, I attended more women-only meetings and saw how prevalent depression is for so many of us in recovery. Listening to other women's stories gave me perspective. When it came to my own recovery, I was lucky I had had swimming to throw myself into. It was helping me to redefine myself. In fact, I'm convinced that for sobriety, there's no substitute for a physically active lifestyle. Not only does it provide an activity to fill the void left by avoiding situations that trigger the desire to drink, but it aids in stimulating the chemicals necessary for a healthy mental outlook as well.

I had my own bouts of depression when I first got sober, mainly associated with the guilt I felt about everything I'd given up, both in school and in the pool, and for letting Mom down. But what made me feel the worst was realizing how many people I'd hurt along the way. In listening to other women's accounts, I learned that their lives, like mine, had been burdened with an exhausting heaviness. They had felt the same void and had spent the same inordinate amount of time trying to fill it with drink or a drug. Their journeys were made all the more difficult by that persistent dark cloud of clinical depression that enveloped them.

I had been wrong about so many things during my lost years. When I was in the depths of my darkness, I was under the misguided belief that the only person I could rely on to scratch the match to light the candle to help me find a way out was me. I had stubbornly clung to the jaded mindset of that naked little girl, alone in her bedroom, determined to rid the house of fleas all by herself. I never asked for help, in part because I didn't believe I could trust anyone to give it. It's precisely that type of thinking that keeps addicts in their addiction.

The reality was that my life began to get better only when I put faith in someone, or something, other than myself. When I started to believe that my Higher Power had a plan for me and that all I needed to do was trust. I was fortunate to have significant support right from the beginning. Mom and Lloyd, Jennifer and the other nurses at Sharp Cabrillo, my fellow rehabbers, and of course Eric, who had my back from the moment we became a couple—they all gave me the support I needed in the beginning of my sobriety. Even my swimming improvements were a collaborative effort. I couldn't have achieved them without my coaches and lane mates. There is strength in numbers indeed.

Eric didn't drink very much or very often. He's what people in the Program refer to as a "normie." Like a lot of people, he went through some periods where he probably drank more often than he should have, but it was never an obsession with him, and it was certainly never an addiction. From what I could see, no one in his family seemed to be afflicted with the disease. His extended family was involved in the wine business. Eric's mom, Janet, was a social drinker who enjoyed throwing parties and loved good wine and the occasional mixed drink, but not once did I see her overindulge or get drunk.

Eric grew up in Alamo, California, and he and his younger sister, Diane, had a happy childhood. He idolized his father, Bob, and was crushed when he unexpectedly left the family when Eric was just thirteen. When Bob moved out, Janet went back to work to support the family, driving forty-five miles each way to a job in San Jose. To ease the burden and provide some emotional stability, Eric's widowed grandmother moved in to help take care of the two kids.

Consequently, much of Eric's teen years were marked by the absence of a father figure. After his father left, Eric didn't see him for an entire year. For someone entering the confusing years of puberty, that must have been traumatic. He eventually reestablished contact with his father, but the relationship was always awkward. When I came into the picture, I was taken aback by the superficiality of their relationship. Phone calls were rare, and what little time they did spend together was far from intimate. Fortunately, I felt very much at home and comfortable around the rest of Eric's family. When we went up to Northern California to introduce me to his mother, Eric and I decided we didn't need to tell her about my alcoholism straight away.

"She'll be fine with it, Karlyn, but we don't need to put it out there right off the bat," Eric said.

"But isn't she going to suspect something?" I said.

"No. Don't be silly," he said. "Drinking has never really been a big thing in my family."

As soon as we got to the house and after Eric made the introductions, one of the first things Janet said to me was, "I was just about to make a highball, Karlyn. Would you like to join me?"

"No, thanks, Janet," I managed. "I'm, uh, okay. I'm good. But thank you for offering."

Eric and I howled about it afterwards.

One of the most informative things I observed as I moved into the world of sobriety was other people's behavior around alcohol. The more alcohol people consume, for example, the louder they tend to become. There's also a typical cycle to the process that you aren't aware of when you're the one drinking. First things become more cheerful and happy. Then they start to get loud and boisterous. Next, matters become sloppy. Finally, the mood may get a little bit angry or sorrowful. As someone who was now sober, it was interesting to see, through the actions of others, just how ugly and obnoxious I had been. And I had been totally oblivious. At the time I had thought, as I was making myself the center of attention, that I was funny and interesting. Viewing it from the vantage point of my new-found sobriety, I couldn't help but cringe and feel a sense of shame.

Weightlessness. I was feeling it in the water, yes, but more importantly I was feeling it in my life. It was such a huge burden off my shoulders, not having to deal with the high maintenance addiction lifestyle. I was so light and grateful and happy for that. Nothing, from what I could see in my new sober life, could top that. Sometimes I'd just have to pinch myself. All I had to do was take one ingredient—alcohol—out of my life, and I received so much in return. I was getting back my sport, my health, my mental clarity, my zest for life. I was opening the door to a healthy relationship for the first time ever. That seemed like a pretty darn good deal. Where else in life can you find a deal like that?

The new Karlyn, I was learning, was happy by nature just about all the time. A lot of that happiness was because I'd rediscovered hope, something I hadn't had in years. In my case, I had had to detox physically first and get the booze out of my system. A bigger task was to retrain my brain to stop the stinking thinking and learn how to let go of the self-doubt and self-pity that had plagued me for years. It took a lot of work and mental reprogramming, but once I started to believe there was hope for a better future, that hope opened up possibilities I never could have imagined.

CHAPTER 37

Just Grateful to Be
on the Blocks

I T'S OFTEN SAID THAT MASTERS SWIMMING gives retired swimmers an opportunity to address unfinished business, another version of a do-over. So many gifted athletes from around the world never reach their goals and dreams, which often were the Olympic Games. Even the handful who do make it to the Olympics may be disappointed with how they fared there. Maybe they didn't qualify for the finals of their event, or maybe they didn't earn a medal, or maybe the silver or bronze medal they did earn wasn't the one they had been chasing all those years. Competitive swimmers devote the better part of their childhoods to attaining a career-defining moment, and once that moment has passed, their lives can be filled with a tremendous sense of emptiness or even failure. Masters swimming allows competitive swimmers to not only continue in the sport, but to do so on their own terms.

To be sure, not everyone who's affiliated with U.S. Masters Swimming chooses to race. The vast majority of members, in fact, are more interested in swimming's health and fitness benefits and the day-to-day camaraderie of training and practice than in actual competition. But those who do compete know they'd better bring their best stuff to the blocks. As more and more former USA National Swim Team members and Olympians have joined the Masters ranks, the level of competition has grown exponentially more challenging. The U.S. Masters and FINA record books are now generously sprinkled with the names of famous competitive swimmers who originally made their mark at the Olympic Games, including Rowdy Gaines, Jim Montgomery, Dara Torres, Sheila Taormina, Janet Evans, and Matt Biondi. More recently, swimmers like Misty Hyman, Cullen Jones, and Darien Townsend are adding U.S. Masters Nationals to their schedules, lending both credibility and competitiveness to the meets. Some of these swimming greats will attend something similar to a World Cup event one weekend, racing the fastest swimmers on the planet, and then attend a Masters meet with the same gusto and drive the next weekend. Owning a Masters world or national record is an honor and an accomplishment, regardless of age or experience.

The 1994 FINA Masters World Championships were held in Montreal, Canada. I was just a year sober, but I really wanted to go. It was a costly proposition, so Mom suggested I put together a little campaign to solicit donations from our swimming family and friends. Those in our inner circle knew the behind-the-scenes story of what I'd been through, and they were more than happy to support the effort. The Hubbards chipped in. So did the Purdys and Bill Earley and many more from Coronado Masters. We raised the necessary funds for me to make the trip, and I wound up having a stellar meet. I became a world champion by winning gold in every race I swam, and I set new Masters world records in five events. All of a sudden, I was on the map. People wanted to know who the heck Karlyn Pipes was and where she'd come from. In my 400 IM, I swam a 5:07, which was a lifetime best by five seconds and much faster than the time I'd swum as a twenty-five-year-old in Houston. It was also the equivalent of the Olympic Trials time standard I had set out to achieve on my ill-fated move to Mission Viejo back in 1987. Now the

Trials cut was a much faster 4:59, but I was still extremely happy with my performance and the effort I had made to swim so well.

I arrived back home to a request from the *San Diego Union-Tribune* for an interview. When the journalist, Josie Karp, started asking questions, I spilled my whole story. She was floored. Later, when I spoke to my sponsor, Donna, she reminded me about the Program's tradition of anonymity. AA has always placed principles over personalities, and that humility forms the basis for the Program's twelfth tenet, or tradition. In fact, the true identity of Bill W., cofounder of the Program, wasn't even revealed until after his death. After thinking it over, I called Josie back.

"Josie, I'm sorry, but please pull the plug on the story," I told her. "You should probably do it on somebody else."

"I'd rather not do that, Karlyn," she said.

"I never should have told you so much about my background," I said. "If this story comes out and I relapse, it's going to reflect poorly on the Program. And that's the last thing I want to do."

"I see your point," Josie said. "How about if I rewrite the story?"

"You'd do that?"

"In a heartbeat. I don't want to get scooped on this thing. Tell you what, Karlyn—I'll even give you final approval of the content."

Josie was kind enough to do a complete rewrite, and I was on the front page of the sports section. It included a huge, full-color shot of me doing butterfly, and the corresponding article was titled "Faster than ever at 32, Pipes dreaming again." I read the story carefully a few times, petrified that Josie might have gone back on her promise. But the only allusion to my alcoholism was a sentence I absolutely loved: "Less than a year and a half ago, the fastest thing about Pipes was her lifestyle." That was it. I was elated, and I called Josie up to tell her so. That experience helped shape the way I would handle the press going forward. Many times I would share my story off the record. Whenever I spoke on the record, I would often include sayings or phrases that people familiar with the Program would clue in to and be able to connect the dots from.

After the article came out, I immediately took a copy to Sharp Cabrillo Hospital. Jennifer and the other nurses were thrilled. They confided to me that they had been very worried I was going to relapse, especially given how gung-ho I had been to start assimilating into the "real world." When it comes to recovery, they explained, it's almost always the tortoise that fares best. Luckily, this hare had had lane lines to keep her on the straight and narrow.

When I first got sober and I was that squashed bug in the gutter gazing up at the seemingly insurmountable curb, I knew I had a gift in hand. And now I was getting this enormous do-over. Once I started moving in that direction, it unearthed a determined Karlyn who had been buried for too long. It was the Karlyn who wanted to succeed. The Karlyn who wanted to win.

With that awareness came a tremendous sense of gratitude. I'd get on the blocks before a race and I'd just be thankful. I'd be thankful for Eric and the love he and I shared, thankful for the water, and thankful for Masters swimming. I've met so many dynamic individuals and developed so many invaluable relationships because of my association with Masters, including my friendships with people like Phil Whitten, Gary Quinn, Jane Asher, David Radcliffe, and many more. Without Masters, I would be an anonymous lap swimmer at an anonymous pool. U.S. Masters Swimming provided me with an environment in which to engage, thrive, and succeed. It allowed me to regain my self-confidence and self-esteem, and it added a richness to my life that simply hadn't been there before.

The next set of races came around in December, and I continued to improve my times and break records. The swimsuit manufacturer TYR started giving me free suits, a great little perk. Getting free stuff always brought back memories of Mom rewarding my sisters and me for dropping our times. It also reminded me of the day I learned that Olympians were the recipients of a lot of cool swag. Maybe the best way to motivate me was to simply swing a freebie or two in front of my eyes!

It's a little strange knowing that you've done something better or faster than anyone else in the world. You feel as if you've scaled some sort of peak. You are deemed the best, at that moment in time, in that particular stroke and distance. It's heady stuff. Records, however, as the saying goes, are meant to be broken. Today there are fourteen-year-old boys who can swim as fast as Mark Spitz swam at the 1972 Olympics. It's just the nature of the beast. Part of the evolution can be attributed to better training methods, both in and out of the water, and better techniques, in particular the emphasis now being placed on underwater streamlining off the walls.

As an athlete, though, you can't help but grow somewhat attached to your records and accomplishments. They become part of you, of your identity. I decided I wanted to try to throw down some performances that would stand the test of time. Janet Evans set multiple world and Olympic records in distance freestyle that, astonishingly, stood for nearly twenty years. Eric and I began to wonder if it would be possible for me to establish that type of legacy in Masters swimming as well.

The deeper I got into my second swimming career, the more I realized how much I loved the sensation of simply being in the water. Not just in swimming pools, but in any body of water. Ever since I found the courage to cross Lake Sequoia all those years ago, the open water has always been a magical place for me. When I was a beach lifeguard, I used to gaze out at the Pacific Ocean stretching into the horizon and feel both strength and serenity. The idea of being out in the middle of open water with nothing to hold on to might be terrifying to some, but for me it's comforting. I love slipping into a liquid world without walls, lane lines, or starting blocks. It is my way of communing with nature.

Happily, my comeback coincided with the explosive growth of

open-water swimming competitions. By 1994, races were popping up in rivers, lakes, and oceans all over the world. Part of the attraction, I think, is the sense of freedom offered by wide-open spaces. Since most competitive swimmers have honed their skills in a low-sensory state crossing back and forth in a nondescript, four-walled bathtub, it seems natural that many would eventually yearn for a different kind of swimming experience. In races such as the La Jolla Gatorman, concepts such as time and space are shifted. Swimming becomes about much more than simply pace clocks and stopwatches. Don't get me wrong. There's still the competitive aspect—swimmers are trying to get from Point A to Point B the fastest—but in the open water, a spiritual aspect enters into the swim as well. How can you not feel connected to nature and the cosmos when you're swimming over schools of fish and alongside turtles, dolphins, and sometimes even a shark or two?

After my success at the inaugural Gatorman, I went back to the La Jolla Rough Water Swim the following year and raised the stakes even higher. I became the first swimmer to win what is now called the Daily Double, capturing first place in both the 1- and 3-mile races for the women's division within the span of just a few hours. It's a feat I managed to duplicate a few years later. I also won the USMS 5K Open Water National Championship on Catalina Island and the Coronado Annual July 4th Rough Water Swim on multiple occasions. I was the overall winner and course record holder for the Base-to-Base swim, regularly competing against the best Navy SEALs the military had to offer. I was blessed to call Coronado home, because throughout the summer there seemed to be no end of inspiring open-water swims within easy driving distance up and down the coast.

Eric and I were becoming a formidable team. He was devising amazing workouts to make me fitter and faster, and I was going to meets and tearing it up. More importantly, we were getting along really well away from the pool. It was so refreshing to finally be in a relationship that was good for me. I trusted Eric with my heart, and he rewarded that trust with his love.

It wasn't long before Eric, with his love of nicknames, started referring to me as Spider. The name came to him when he noticed that in freestyle my arms looked as if I were crawling across the water like a spider. It stuck. In addition to swimming, we enjoyed long hikes through the Laguna and Palomar Mountains, and we used our time together to talk about our hopes and aspirations. We encouraged one another to dream big.

"Where do you see yourself in five years?" I asked him one day.

"With you," he said. "I want to be with you in five years, and ten years and twenty years and beyond. Do you see yourself with me?"

"Yeah."

"And what do you see yourself doing?"

"I want to do things that have never been done before in the pool," I said.

"Well, I want to be the coach who guides you to do things that have never been done before in the pool," he said with a laugh.

"I also want to be married and have kids," I said.

Eric looked at me and smiled. "I want that too, Spider."

When he said that—and I could see he meant it—it was difficult to contain my emotions. It was the first time anyone had said that to me.

Since everything was coming together for us, Eric and I also started kicking around the idea of me going back to school full time. Part of me was still pinching myself, wondering how this really nice guy could love someone as damaged as me. Eric wrote me love letters and romantic notes, and he'd often come by work to drop off flowers. It was flattering. On the inside, though, I was still wrestling with low self-esteem. It was the same with my swimming. On the outside, there was public Karlyn, who was breaking records every time she got in the water and earning a tremendous amount of attention and acclaim. That Karlyn had healthy self-esteem and a good-sized ego. But inside, there was still private Karlyn, whose self-esteem and sense of self-worth had not quite caught up with what the public saw. Consequently, public Karlyn often felt like a bit of an imposter.

The Program's milestone chips are nice to hold in your hand, but they represent only one small part of the struggle. So much of my recovery was becoming about coming to grips with self-acceptance. It was about trying to get past the layers of self-loathing accumulated over the course of my addiction. Even though I had turned a very big corner by getting sober, I was still having a difficult time forgiving myself for all the harm I'd caused and the damage I'd done. With Mom, it was guilt over not appreciating her gifts to me when I was growing up. She sacrificed an enormous amount on my behalf. And there was the scholarship opportunity I walked away from—twice. For any parent, a scholarship for their child is a huge thing. It's not just being able to tell someone, "My daughter's on an athletic scholarship." It's validation of the path you helped your child pursue. It's a financial reward, too. It's a reward for all the sacrifices made hauling a child back and forth from the pool and spending long weekends at swim meets. How could I have treated a free college education so cavalierly? I tossed it away as if it were an empty beer can.

The other thing I was still trying to resolve was my connection with a higher power. I still felt a hollowness inside, and I had no idea where it came from. Was it my ultimate lack of self-acceptance? The Program was helping me reconcile pre-sobriety Karlyn with post-sobriety Karlyn, but it wasn't as easy as changing the page on a calendar. I could turn away from alcohol and not look back, but it wasn't as easy to do that with the wreckage of my past. The ugliness I felt inside ran deep and made me wonder why God would ever want to love someone as broken as me.

CHAPTER 38

Racing with the Kids

R ATHER THAN DWELL TOO LONG on my concerns about a higher
power, I found it easier to hop in the pool and swim. In my watery
world, doubts about my worthiness were conveniently washed away.
While I was still making it to meetings three or four times a week, I was
spending the bulk of my free time training and preparing for the next
competition. Back when I swam for Troy at CNSA, I was usually the last
person in the water and the first person out. Now that I was swimming
for myself, I was often the first in the water and almost always the last
out. I swam as often as I could, for as long as I could, and as hard and fast
as my body would allow. I was tenacious and dedicated. How things had
changed from when I was young!

Racing was rekindling a passion in me that had been dormant for far
too long. In my first swimming career, Troy would tell us what meets
to attend and which events to sign up for. We became specialists early
on, swimming the same races over and over. It made sense, since the
idea was to maximize our ability in our best events. As a Masters swimmer, though, I was able to swim anything that appealed to me. Instead
of having to sign up for the 200-meter fly, I could sign up for the 50.
Instead of having to face that dreaded 400 IM each and every meet,
I could swim the always-fun 100 IM.

Everything about competition, from the pre-meet preparation to the post-race warm-down, made me feel alive. In the moments leading up to a race, my body would feel as if it were on fire. It would tingle in anticipation. Once the gun went off, my performance became my entire focus. It became about keeping my excitement in check and monitoring my energy level for the task at hand. The world shrunk to what was going on inside the pool, inside my lane, and inside my head.

When I was younger, the only way I knew to measure my self-worth was to compare myself to others. I wouldn't just try to be the best swimmer at meets; I'd try to be the best one in practice. I wanted to be the best during kicking sets, pulling sets, and main sets. If I was faster than someone that meant I was better than they were. It's a twisted value system, and I used it as a strategy to feed my low self-esteem. With Masters swimming, though, the rules changed. I was measuring myself against myself. It was about chasing the clock and trying to improve. Yes, if someone was beside me during a race my competitive instinct would kick in and I'd want to touch the wall first, but mostly it was about me and the clock.

By late 1994, Eric and I had begun to wonder just how far we could take this do-over thing. I was still swimming lifetime bests and dropping my times like crazy. Could I qualify for Senior Nationals again after being away from the sport for so long? What about the 1996 Olympic Trials? How rewarding it would be to make the Trials! And what about competing in college? Was that realistic for someone in her mid-thirties?

We realized that, in order to raise the level of my game still higher, I would need to start training with even faster swimmers—elite level kids, to be exact. Jon Larson had taken over head coaching duties at my old team, CNSA, and one weekend I drove up to an age group meet in Poway with the sole intention of meeting him. I hadn't been to an age group meet in years. Seeing all the young kids hanging out and racing brought back a lot of memories—of Kirsten and me when we were younger, of all my old teammates and the hours we'd spent with one another during practice and at weekend-long swim meets. Back then I was too young to realize it, but those were some of the best years of my life.

I spotted Jon across the deck and moved up to introduce myself.

"Hey, Jon. My name's Karlyn Pipes," I said, poking out my right hand. "I swam for Mike Troy and CNSA back in the late '70s. Now I'm a Masters swimmer, and I'd like to start swimming with you."

Jon, his eyes partially concealed by the dark lenses of his sunglasses, gave me the once over. He offered me a weak smile as we shook hands. I'm sure he could tell right away that the two of us were roughly the same age.

"I currently go a 2:08 in the 200-yard backstroke," I said. "What I'm really interested in is dropping that time down to a 2:02 so that I can make Senior Nationals, and then I'd like to try to qualify for the Olympic Trials."

He nodded without saying anything. Jon had been around the block when it came to swimming and had some decent personal and professional credentials. He swam collegiately for four years, the last two at powerhouse Alabama. He had been an undergraduate assistant to Alabama coach Don Gambril and did a two-year internship with famed Olympic coach Mark Schubert. I am sure, however, that in all his years of coaching, he had never encountered anything like this before. Skepticism was written all over his face.

"Since I work at NAB in Coronado," I continued, "I thought it would be convenient for me to jump in with your senior group in the afternoon."

"My senior group?"

"Yeah."

"Sure, uh, Karen . . ."

"Karlyn," I said.

"Right. *Karlyn*," Jon said, correcting himself. "Well, I appreciate your ambition, and I'd love to help you reach your goals."

"You would?"

"Sure," he said. "Tell you what. Why don't you show up for afternoon practice on Monday? We start at 4:00."

"Perfect," I said. "I'll see you then."

I walked away, pleased as punch about the way things had gone.

Monday rolled around, and it was a bright, sunny day. Since I didn't get off work until 4:15, I was a little late. Jon, I could tell, was surprised to see me. While he was trying to wrap his head around exactly how to introduce this thirty-something woman to his swimmers, I stared at the pool. It was exactly as I'd left it when I walked away from Troy's workouts for the last time. Even the lane lines looked the same, as if they'd never been upgraded.

There were probably twelve kids in Jon's senior group, and the fastest ones were strong, lanky teenage boys. Jon pointed to a lane and told me to go ahead and jump in. Jon's a distance type of coach. In a distance coach's mind, the more they can pile on the better. After I did an abbreviated warm-up to get loose, Jon had us do a kick set and a pull set. All the boys were teasing one another and getting ready for what was coming up next—a 3,200-meter distance set of 800s on a challenging interval. There were two lanes that were all going to tackle it together. I started cautiously at the back, but by the time we were halfway through, I had passed every boy ahead of me and was leading the lane. I was averaging 1:13 per 100 meters and swimming as fast as the set of 400s I'd done in Hong Kong back when I was fifteen. Maybe even faster. I glanced up at Jon in between repeats and flashed him a quick, breathless smile. He looked at me in disbelief, shook his head, and muttered to himself, "My workouts will never be the same . . . "

Jon later told me he thought I was completely off my rocker when I approached him in Poway. He told me he figured he'd never see me again, and for sure didn't think I had the tenacity to show up at his workout. Turns out, I surprised him both in and out of the water. Thanks to Jon, I had yet another opportunity to train, and I had a feeling this turn of events would take me to a whole new level. I began to swim with CNSA on a regular basis, and we all thrived. The kids on the team became my rabbits, my pursuit of them urging me on to greater efforts, and I became theirs. We were teammates in every sense of the word, regardless of our difference in age. Of course ego factored into the equation, as there was no way those teenage boys—or girls—were ever going to let some lady as old as their moms outperform them without a fight.

I was amazed by just how strong I was becoming. Sobriety had given me back my pre-drinking musculature and cardiovascular system. I regained my power and stamina of old. I was also eating better than ever, and was grateful that with all the work I was doing in the Program, the desire to binge and purge had drained away like my desire to drink had. I was also grateful that my mental faculties had come back. I was very fortunate that all the years of heavy substance abuse hadn't permanently fried my brain.

Patti Waterman, my boss John's wife, was the swim coach at Palomar College. Palomar is located in San Marcos, about an hour's drive north of Coronado. Years before, when I lived in Chula Vista, I used to baby-sit Patti's niece Tami Bruce, who would later go on to win seven NCAA (National Collegiate Athletic Association) national swim titles at the University of Florida and qualify for the 1988 Olympic team. One day I joked to Patti, "If you get your husband to let me off work a little early, I'll come swim for you at Palomar." At first Patti laughed it off, but after she thought about it for a bit, she ran my college eligibility to see where my status stood. She discovered that I did, in fact, have two full years of community college eligibility. While I would need to keep my job at NAB, she could arrange to help me get the courses I needed to begin competing at the collegiate level again.

Because I had dropped out of University of Arkansas, I was now considered a "4-2-4." I'd gone to a four-year school, and now I was transferring to a two-year school. Once that happened, I would need to graduate from the two-year school before I could be eligible to go back to a four-year school. It didn't matter to me what hoops I needed to jump through. I just wanted to keep moving toward a degree and, if possible, figure out a way to compete collegiately.

It took patience and a lot of work, but the following year I swam for Patti at Palomar. One night a week, I'd make the commute with John up to San Marcos and spend three hours in the math lab. Between that course and the other general education classes I took at NAB or online, we managed to cobble together the twelve units I needed to be eligible to compete in the spring. The logistics were a little crazy, but we made it work. Since I was working in the recreation field, I also managed to get work experience credits, since recreation was my declared major at the time. It wasn't lost on me the lengths I was going to for both school and swimming. It was a far cry from the days when neither one meant a thing to me. I was so appreciative of everything I was being able to make happen for myself.

I didn't mind the work I needed to do to keep swimming fast, just as I didn't mind the studying required to maintain a high grade point average. Everything I was doing was a personal challenge. *Can I measure up? Can I continue with this roll I'm on?* It was all about me challenging myself to be the very best I could be.

Swimming at Palomar was a blast. I couldn't have asked for a better experience or a more positive environment in which to thrive. I loved being back on a real campus and going to school. I loved swimming with either Patti or Coach Scott Lawson whenever I had the opportunity. My age didn't matter, and both the young women and the young men on the teams were open and accepting. Some even came to me for advice. The irony of me doling out advice to someone younger was not lost on me, but my experience, both in and out of the pool, was not without value. It was so much fun to be a part of the team and be traveling to dual meets, conferences, and state championships. I felt like I truly belonged. I was so grateful for the chance to do this over, to do this right. I often had to pinch myself and take a moment to acknowledge that it was not long ago that I had been a helpless, hopeless alcoholic drowning in vodka.

Palomar College had a solid women's team. After the first year, I looked up every school record and formulated a plan for how to break each one. These are the types of challenges that keep the competitive athlete engaged. One by one, I started knocking down the records. Breaststroke has never been my strong suit, but I was in such good shape that I broke those records too. I lowered my times to a 0:51 in the 100-yard free, a 1:51 in the 200-yard free, and a 4:56 in the 500-yard free. I eventually came within a whisker of fulfilling my goal of getting every record. The only one that eluded me was Tracy Lincoln's super fast 10:20 in the 1,000-yard free. I believe that record still stands today. Along the way, I also racked up four national and five California Community College records and was named Pacific Coast Athletic Conference Swimmer of the Year twice. Academically, I made the dean's list every semester and managed to graduate with a 4.0 GPA. Years later, in 2012, I was inducted into Palomar College's Hall of Fame as part of the inaugural class. Patti, who'd been so instrumental in getting my collegiate academic and swimming careers back on track, gave my introductory remarks and accepted the award on my behalf.

CHAPTER 39

From Recovery to Rediscovery

E RIC WAS ALWAYS A NUMBERS GUY, and he was fascinated by the science behind coaching. When he first met Hal Goforth, an exercise physiologist for the navy, it was a match made in heaven. Hal, a pioneer in the field, had done it all. He had worked extensively with Navy SEALs and was among the first to research both the recovery benefits of consuming protein after hard training sessions and the positive effects of caffeine on racing performance. Hal himself was a runner and ran his first Boston Marathon in 1975. A legend of sorts in the long-distance running community, he's run over thirty Boston Marathons since that debut and clocked a sub-3:00-hour time at the age of sixty.

When Eric started running, Hal took him under his wing. He would write up Eric's training program and do a lot of the long runs with him. Pretty soon Eric got fast enough to qualify for the Boston Marathon. He improved so much that it was not long before he too ran under 3:00 hours. Hal often referred to Eric as his lab rat. The two of them spent hours talking about exercise physiology and optimal training methodologies. Coaching an elite athlete to greatness isn't as simple as pushing him or her to exhaustion day in and day out. Achieving peak performance is a delicate process of give and take and of learning how to tap into different energy levels at the right time. Eric, naturally, used what he was absorbing from Hal and others in his own coaching at the Center for Sports Medicine and to help me become the very best swimmer I could be.

On the home front, my father was in failing health. The prostate cancer that had been in remission came back in 1995, and the doctors informed us there wasn't much more that could be done for him. Fortunately, he wasn't in pain.

I'd like to think that toward the end of his life I gave my father the peace and quiet he had always wanted. I took care of his needs and made sure he had plenty to eat, even if it wasn't very healthy. He became enamored with instant oatmeal, so we'd buy six boxes at a time. When he developed a craving for microwaveable barbecue sandwiches, I would take him shopping and fill the cart with them. His favorite meal, however, was a Banquet TV dinner. We bought those too.

I did everything I could to make sure his life was as uncomplicated as possible. He had the freedom to walk whenever he wanted and to collect whatever he found along the way. His apartment was filled with an odd assortment of finds—photo albums, a riding crop, locked locks with no keys—and I didn't hassle him about bringing junk home. It occurred to me only later, after he had passed away, that perhaps his foraging was a manifestation of every addict's search to fill that emptiness inside. Since he'd lost his craving to drink, he couldn't fill it with alcohol, so instead he was filling it with whatever items he would find during his daily wanderings. He took what others had thrown away and gave it a home. In an odd way, we managed to have a decent relationship, and sometimes we even talked about the past.

"Would you like to go to an AA meeting with me, Daddy?" I once asked him, months after I returned home from rehab.

"Oh, no," he said softly. "I'm good."

"Did you ever go to AA?"

"Oh, no," he said. "No. I didn't need AA at all."

"Did you used to drink a lot?"

"Oh, I used to have a beer or two every once in a while," he said.

I could have been incensed at his amnesia or berated and bullied him into at least some kind of explanation for his behavior. But what was the point? He didn't remember. The Program taught me that holding on to resentments hurts only me, not the other person. *Live and let live* is one of the Program's primary tenets. So that's what I did with my dad.

I'm happy I was given the opportunity to spend that time with him. True, he had never been the father I wanted or needed. But what I discovered was that it didn't do either of us any good for me to hang on to his failings. While it was not possible for me to erase the memories of my childhood experience, I was certainly capable of forgiving him. Once I did, I felt a tremendous sense of peace and release.

I realized the end was near when I walked into my father's apartment and spied him bracing himself against a countertop as he tried to cross the small room. He couldn't walk on his own anymore. Eric and I took him to the hospital, and we learned the cancer had spread to his spine. The doctors and nurses were surprised he wasn't in more pain, but his alcoholism had apparently dulled his pain sensors. He hadn't had a drink in a long time, but the damage he'd done to his body had been that long lasting. He went from the hospital to a nursing home, and then back to the hospital a final time. In April 1995, he quietly passed away.

For a long time I thought that the only things I had inherited from my dad were his blue eyes, his dimples, and the gene for alcoholism. But before alcohol washed away his hopes and dreams, my dad had been an exceptional teacher who knew intuitively what approach or what words to use bring out the best in his students. It wasn't until years later, when

I began teaching, that I realized my father had passed on this amazing gift to me as well.

The only way to make Nationals was to make the cut, or the time standard. It was that way when I was thirteen and trying to qualify for my first Junior Nationals, and it was that way twenty years later when I was aiming for Senior Nationals in the midst of my do-over. It makes no difference whether you achieve the standard by five seconds or by three-hundredths of a second. Once you make it, you're eligible to participate in one of the most prestigious swimming competitions in the United States. The standards themselves, however, change from year to year. They keep getting faster, which means that you, as a swimmer, are aiming at a constantly moving target.

On May 18th, Eric and I went to the Masters Short Course National Championships in Fort Lauderdale, Florida, and I managed to again better my time in the 200-yard backstroke. I was now down to a 2:02.26, the target I had discussed with Coach Jon when he and I first met, but now I needed to go even faster. To qualify for Senior Nationals, I had to swim 2:01.79 in the 200-yard or 2:20.79 in the 200-meter. From the short course championships we jumped straight into the Alamo Challenge, a USA Swimming (USAS)–hosted long course meters meet which was conveniently held at the same facility a week later.

By this time I had become an equal-opportunity swimmer. On any given day, I was competing against college students, fellow Masters swimmers, or girls young enough to be my daughters. It was entertaining, to say the least. I again missed the time standard in the 200-meter backstroke at the Alamo meet, but I nailed it in the 200 IM. Eric and I were ecstatic. I immediately called Mom and Lloyd to tell them the good news. The best part was that since the 1995 National Championships were scheduled to be in Pasadena, Mom and Lloyd would be able to come and watch me swim. Eric's mother, Janet, would also be there. Once I'd made one cut and the pressure was off, I wound up making two more cuts in the following weeks, in the 400 IM and the elusive 200 backstroke.

The Rose Bowl Aquatics Center, a beautiful outdoor facility built in 1990, is located just south of the iconic Rose Bowl stadium. All the top swimmers in the country converged there for the National Championships. At thirty-three, I was the oldest competitor. All my peers from my age group days had long since retired. Even the legendary sprinter Tom Jager, who at the age of thirty-two seemed prehistoric compared to the other swimmers, was younger than me.

Sometimes you only realize how much you've missed something after you get it back. My entire recovery, it seems, was about rediscovery. As I sat in the bleachers watching wave after wave of the best swimmers in the country mount the blocks during the morning preliminary heats, I soaked in the scene. Whether it's a low-key competition or a highly charged, well-attended championship, there's a certain rhythm and flow to a swim meet—a unique ambiance that only swimmers fully appreciate.

One of the first things you notice is the nervous energy of the swimmers as they stand behind the blocks readying themselves for the task ahead. They stretch limbs and fidget with goggle straps, caps, and swimsuits. Some take deep, chest-filling breaths. Others hop up and down, slap their chests or legs, or do jumping jacks to stimulate blood flow and elevate their heart rates. Their bodies, I know from experience, are alive with anticipation.

When the last swimmer in the preceding heat touches the wall, the swimmers in the next heat move forward as if they're actors in a theater production making an entrance. The starter, dressed in white, blows a whistle—a series of two short chirps—to notify the upcoming field of swimmers to prepare to race. The swimmers who have just completed their event wearily hoist themselves from the water. Once the pool is empty, the starter blows a longer blast, signaling it's time for the incoming heat of athletes to mount the blocks. Everything goes silent. If it is an outdoor venue, the scene is particularly arresting. The water, translucent pale blue and alluring beneath a bright summer sky, is still. The air shimmers, as if a storm were ready to erupt. The starter calls the swimmers to their marks, and then, at the sound of the horn, everything explodes into life again—from the turbulence on the surface to the shadows intricately dancing on the bottom of the pool to the onlookers who cheer wildly for their favorites. Even the lane lines and backstroke flags suddenly seem more vivid.

There is a musical quality to it all. There's the sound of the rhythmic splashes as swimmers' arms stroke their way across the pool, the authoritative voice of the PA announcer who introduces the competitors one lane at a time, the chorus of one- and two-syllable cheers from the spectators hollering "Go!" or "Hup!" and the high-pitched, bird-like whistles of the coaches as they attempt to spur on their swimmers.

Being in those bleachers, surrounded by others who understood and loved this sport as deeply as I did, was comforting. We were all part of a mystical aquatic clan that extended back for generations. Water, for many of us, is a passion. And I was immensely grateful that despite everything I'd done, despite all the poor choices I'd made, I was welcomed back into the aquatic fold with no questions asked.

As I sat there surveying the scene that day, the PA system suddenly burst into the R.E.M. song "Man on the Moon." And as soon as I heard that chorus, with the lyrics about believing, I burst into tears. I put my towel over my face and sobbed like a baby. The reality of what I'd done really hit me. I was at Senior Nationals. I was an elite-level swimmer again. Over the course of a single year I'd lowered my 200-meter backstroke time by an extraordinary eight seconds. By the end of the meet I would be down to 2:19.90.

I sat there, amazed at it all, and I remember asking myself how this all happened. *Was it luck, hard work, or something else? Why, out of all the struggling alcoholics in the world, had I been blessed with this do-over? Had my Higher Power been directing this energy toward me so I could reach my full potential, and if so, what was that potential? Was it about swimming fast and showing people what's possible, or was it something more?* I didn't have the answers, but I did know one thing: as I sat in those stands, I was enveloped with the purest gratitude I had ever experienced in my life. It opened up my eyes wide, my heart expanded to fill my chest, and every part of my body tingled, right down to my toes.

But there was still more work to do both in and out of the pool. First, if I wanted to qualify for the Olympic Trials, I would need to train harder and swim smarter to get my time down to 2:17.99. Second, if I wanted clarity as to my true purpose, I knew I needed to dig deeper into my soul and uproot those stubborn, limiting beliefs I had been holding on to for so long. *Uncover, discover, and discard,* the Program suggests. Of those two challenges, I wasn't sure which would be more difficult.

Eric and I got married in September of 1995, and we made sure the wedding was uniquely "us" and memorable for all who attended. The ceremony was at Glorietta Bay Park, next door to the Coronado Municipal Pool. About 300 people attended the event, dressed in their finest beach attire. Mom and Lloyd walked me down the aisle, and Kerri sang a version of "Edelweiss" with clever lyrics she had made up about the bride and groom. After the ceremony we staged a half-mile open-water swim at nearby Gator Beach. We distributed custom-made swim caps that read, "Eric and Karlyn's Wedding and Rough Water Swim," to the 150 or so swimmers who took part in the Speedo- and Paradowski's Swim & Sport–sponsored race. My friends Gerry Rodriguez and Randy Eickhoff duked it out for first place, and Gerry came out on top.

We went to Hawaii for our honeymoon and for the most part enjoyed ourselves. Bill Earley gifted us his time-share on Kauai for a week, and on Maui we stayed with our good friend and fellow Masters swimmer Jim Krueger. While most of the trip was idyllic, at some point I started picking little fights with Eric. As I was snorkeling one afternoon, enjoying the islands' beautiful tropical fish, it occurred to me that I was getting snippy because I was suddenly feeling a little trapped.

The older I get the more I realize that we are indeed products of our upbringing. Most of my exposure to marriage was what I'd witnessed growing up. My parents' relationship was nothing to aspire to. Just days into my own marriage, a small part of me was worried that, as was the case with my father's drinking, I was destined to repeat the same mistakes he'd made in his relationship with my mother. How, I wondered, was I supposed to prevent this?

CHAPTER 40

When You Swim, You Swim for Yourself

A FTER THE 1995 NATIONALS, I had roughly six months to shave two more seconds off my personal best in the 200-meter backstroke. In between my school and work schedules, I would need to find a way to get even faster. I wasn't alone. Fewer than thirty-five women would make the qualifying time standard for the Olympic Trials in Indianapolis next March, and any swimmer who had designs on being on that list had to go through the exact same qualification process. This is the behind-the-scenes aspect of the sport that resides far away from the gaze of television cameras. The sport doesn't come to a standstill when the Olympics end. Swimmers are fighting to squeeze just a little more speed out of themselves all the time, year in and year out.

I didn't harbor any illusions of actually making it to the Olympics. That would have required me to improve my 200 back time by a whopping ten seconds, not just two. But Eric and I were convinced that it was within my abilities to make it to the Trials. That in and of itself would be an amazing and satisfying accomplishment. Over the course of the next several months I continued to make improvements. But by year's end I was running out of time.

The University of Southern California (USC) announced it would be staging a "last-chance" meet at the McDonald's Olympic Swim Stadium in late February for anyone who hadn't yet reached an Olympic Trials qualifying standard. Palomar had a home meet scheduled for that morning, but since the USC meet didn't start until noon, Eric and I figured we'd have time to do both.

Last-chance meets are more like time trials than anything else. They're official meets, but there are only a handful of participants and even fewer spectators in attendance. The pressure is squarely on each swimmer to race as hard as he or she can to hit their time without the help of cheering crowds or competitors to race against. It's a far cry from the energy and hoopla surrounding a meet like the Janet Evans Invitational or the USA National Championships. In this case, nearly all of the competitors there that day were either collegians or were swimming for Coach Schubert's Trojan Swim Club.

As it turned out, I would be swimming the 200-meter backstroke all by myself. When it was my turn to race I hopped into the pool, grabbed the handgrips, looked over at the starter, and nodded once to let him know I was ready. He said, "Swimmer, take your mark." The horn sounded, and I took off. I knew exactly what my splits needed to be in order to go 2:17.99. Eric and I had worked them out over and over again on paper. I needed to be out in 33 seconds at the 50 and 1:08.50 at the 100. The plan was to even-split the race, or to "negative split," which meant I would swim the second half slightly faster than the first. To give myself a legitimate chance of making it, I needed to be around 1:43 when I hit the wall at the 150. At the USC pool, the digital scoreboard is located at the far end of the stadium in such a way that backstroke swimmers actually have an opportunity to see their splits if they wish. After I came up off the 150 wall, I glanced up at the clock and saw 1:44. I knew I could still make the standard, but I was going to have to dig deep and charge all the way home with whatever I had left.

I was all by myself. There was no one beside me to race. But this was exactly the epiphany I had had during my comeback—when you swim, you swim for yourself. Nothing else and no one else matters. It was just me and that clock. I knew the Trojan swimmers were waving towels and screaming for me, but I couldn't hear them. I threw my head back at the finish, drove my hand into the touchpad, and looked up. The scoreboard read 2:18.46. I'd missed the standard by less than half a second—roughly the time it takes to snap your fingers.

As I got out of the water, Eric threw his arms around me. All the other swimmers gathered around, clapping me on the back and telling me what a great job I'd done. The young collegians, in particular, couldn't stop saying what an inspiration I was. Coach Schubert came up to me and said, "If you've got any eligibility left, come talk to me. I'll take that kind of effort on my team any day."

I'd done everything I could do. I left the pool knowing I'd tried my absolute best. I didn't make the time standard, but it was okay. There would be other days. I wouldn't be swimming at the Olympic Trials, but there would be plenty of other racing ahead of me. The miracle was that I'd been at a last-chance qualifier meet in the first place. The real miracle, I kept reminding myself, was I was alive.

CHAPTER 41

A Perfect 54

As Eric and I rolled into 1996, I was no longer racing to be the fastest to go through all of AA's Twelve Steps. The Program's first three steps are about acknowledging that your life is unmanageable and that the path to recovery involves turning your life over to a higher power. It's on the Fourth Step that you start delving into self-analysis and are urged to look within to perform "a searching and fearless moral inventory." This step, compared to the first three, is a lot more demanding, as it requires critical self-reflection. No one likes to admit their failings, least of all people with addictive behavior. Alcoholics are adept at creating alternate universes for themselves, and they expect everyone else in the general vicinity to fall into orbit. But when you address that Fourth Step, you begin to realize how self-centered and hurtful that line of thinking can be.

My life was about keeping busy—particularly with school—staying active, and being healthy. It was about swimming and breaking records and staying sober. Sure, I could look back and acknowledge that I had drunk because I was unhappy, but the contemplation stopped there. I wasn't digging any deeper. I decided my Fourth Step could wait. Was it because I was still unprepared to deal with the pain, or was it because the old Karlyn, with her entitled view of herself, still believed that not all the Program's suggestions applied to her? In a lot of ways, I was still determined to do things my way, wisely or not.

Eric has always had a gift for coaching, especially when it comes to devising creative sets and workouts, and his intuition as a coach is second to none. He always knows what's going on in the pool. If an observer were to interrupt a workout at any given instant and ask Eric about Hillary's perceived effort over in lane 3, Eric would know—and his answer would be the same as Hillary's. If he believed his swimmer could increase his or her effort and go even faster, that swimmer would start to believe it too, and results would follow. Great coaches are like that.

Another of Eric's gifts is his flair for choreographing a ten-lane, 50-meter Masters workout for forty to sixty swimmers of all ages and abilities. When he coached at Coronado, Eric would have five or six different intervals going at the same time. He could roam the entire deck and know exactly how many swims were left in the set, each swimmer's pace, how much rest he or she was getting, and when the next send-off time would be. His attentiveness was remarkable. "Good job, Marcy," he'd say. "Okay, you're on number three now, right? You just went a 1:34. Now let's see if you can get the next one down to 1:32 or better." And then seconds later he would be doing the same thing for swimmers four lanes over. Eric was a maestro at making the entire pool flow.

But perhaps Eric's best attribute as a coach was his ability to recognize when someone was having one of those special days. He'd zero in on that swimmer and get them to do something they'd never thought possible. If Geary had a lifetime best of 1:23 in the 100-meter freestyle and was "on," Eric would say, "Geary, you're swimming great tonight! We're going to do a 100 free for time and I'll bet you can go a 1:18 or better." "There's no way," Geary would say. "That would be smashing my PR by five seconds, Coach." "Well, let's give it a try. I know you can do it."

And Eric would put a watch on Geary and, sure enough, Geary would pop off a 1:17 and he'd be over the moon about it for weeks.

Eric did that with me, time and again.

He'd look at me and say, "Spider, I think you can break two minutes in the 200 back at the next meet."

"No, I can't," I'd say.

"Yes, you can. Based on some of the things you're doing in practice, I'm convinced you can, and I'm going to write up some sets that will help you do it."

And lo and behold, the next meet would roll around and I'd swim exactly as he had predicted. Whenever I tried to give him some of the credit for what I'd done, he'd say, "It wasn't me who did it, Spider. It was you."

Eric made his swimmers feel good through their accomplishments. He believed in you before you believed in yourself. That's what the best coaches do, and that's one of the great gifts he gave me. As soon as I could see his belief in me reflected back, I became a convert. He gave me the confidence I needed to perform better than I ever imagined I could.

In June, I competed at the Janet Evans Invitational. I went toe-to-toe with some of the best backstroke swimmers in the world and qualified first for the finals against 150 other young women. It was a surreal experience parading across the deck and waving to all the cheering spectators who had no idea who I was or where I'd come from. As I was being introduced as the top seed, I fantasized about the announcer bellowing, ". . . and in lane 4, a recovering alcoholic from Coronado, California, who once registered an astonishing blood alcohol level of .52—Karlyn Pipes!" I'm sure seasoned Olympians Leah Loveless and Nicole Stevenson would have broken their goggle straps had they heard that one.

I didn't win that race, but I placed fourth and proved I belonged. Eric and I both proved we belonged. Mark Schubert, Frank Busch, and

Richard Quick, coaching fixtures on the U.S. Olympic team, all made
a point of remarking to Eric how well I was doing. Onlookers may not
have had a clue as to who we were going into that meet, but they sure
knew about us coming out.

The 1996 Olympic Games were held in Atlanta, Georgia, from July 19th
to August 4th. In the swimming competition the Americans, as usual,
took home the lion's share of the medals. Backstroke swimmers Beth
Botsford and Whitney Hedgepeth, two people I'd competed against
in the course of my do-over, earned gold and silver. And in August of
that same year, just a few short weeks after the Games were done, Eric
and I did it: at the USA National Championships in Fort Lauderdale
I placed tenth in the consolation final and swam 2:17.73 in the
200-meter backstroke, finally achieving the Olympic Trials qualifying
time standard. It was six months too late, but I had reached my goal. I
took great pride in knowing that at the end of the year my time ranked
me in the top fifty in the world. Not top fifty in U.S. Masters. Top fifty
in the *entire world*.

   One of the many things the Program has taught me is to keep looking forward. "We are going to know a new freedom and a new happiness.
We will not regret the past nor wish to shut the door on it," state the
Promises. From time to time I would reflect back and wonder what
would have happened had I started my recovery sooner by a year or two,
or even back when I turned twenty-five and broke that first Masters
world record. But no amount of conjecturing would make the least bit
of difference. The past was the past and there was nothing I could do
about it now but learn from my mistakes and keep moving forward.
Bringing that mindset to sobriety was not only cathartic, but wonder-
fully liberating.

The human toll exacted by excessive alcohol consumption in the United States is staggering. A study published by the United States Centers for Disease Control and Prevention found that some 88,000 lives are lost each year due to alcohol-related causes such as binge drinking, drunk-driving accidents, and diseases like cirrhosis.* That's a big body count. The study also attempts to put a dollar figure on alcohol abuse, calculating that in 2006 alone, the United States lost $223.5 billion in reduced worker productivity, health care costs, law enforcement, and motor vehicle accidents.

Alcohol abuse is one of those subjects we don't want to think about, yet we all know it exists. It's common to hear stories about people—maybe even our friends and acquaintances—blacking out at parties, getting arrested for DUIs, or crashing cars while drunk, but our minds try to separate those experiences from our own. We reassure ourselves that those things would never happen to us. Our relationship with alcohol is different. We control it. It doesn't control us. And, to a large degree, that's probably true. Not everyone who drinks too much is going to jump behind the wheel of a car and accidentally run someone over.

My father was a drunk for most of his life. As far as I know, he never got into a drunk-driving accident. He was never issued a DUI. He was never hauled into a court of law or thrown into a drunk tank. And, when he finally died at age seventy-one, his death certificate stated the cause of death as cancer, not alcoholism.

While the damage his drinking caused couldn't be measured in dollars and cents, as was the case with the CDC study, it could certainly be gauged by the emotional wreckage he left in his wake. His alcoholism destroyed his marriage. It scarred the lives of his children. To just what degree, I've often wondered, did it scar me? True, I had resurfaced from my own watery hole. Yet I still had an unexplained, hollow ache inside. I

---

* Marissa B. Esser, MPH, et al., "Prevalence of Alcohol Dependence Among US Adult Drinkers, 2009-2011." Prev Chronic Dis 2014; 11:14039. www.cdc.gov

was still searching for a way to get rid of that pain, and I wasn't sure yet if that was an attainable goal. Especially since I was having a difficult time putting my finger on why I hurt so much in the first place.

In 1997, Eric and I hatched a new plan. I would be aging up to the 35–39 age group in March, and we wanted to see if I could achieve Masters All-American status, or a number-one ranking, in every single event in every single distance in every single course during one calendar year. That totaled fifty-four different events—everything from the 50-yard breaststroke to the 100 short course meters freestyle to the 200 long course meters butterfly. Not only would the feat entail a lot of racing, it would entail a lot of *quality* racing. My performances would be going head-to-head with those of the best specialists in each event, including former National Team members and Olympians. Since logistically I would have the opportunity to swim many of the events only once, I had to swim fast all the time, and there would be no margin for error.

It was an audacious objective, particularly since I already had a lot on my plate that year between working and being a full-time student. We sketched out an itinerary on the calendar, circling all the biggest meets and trying to lay out a realistic plan of attack. Most meets have rules that restrict the number of events a swimmer can enter, so that was a consideration. Others offer only events of 100 yards or 100 meters or less, so that was another factor. And then there was the trick of getting enough rest between events to fully recover so I could perform at an optimal level at the next race. The biggest challenge of all, however, was keeping myself in tip-top fitness so that I could race any event on any given day. I would need to be able to swim a fast 1,500-meter freestyle and then immediately turn around and sprint a fast 50-meter breaststroke. I'd have to be ready to swim a hard 200-yard backstroke and follow it up with an equally hard 400-yard IM, 50-yard freestyle, or 100-yard fly.

Once we started this journey, striving to reach this goal, while exhilarating, was also exhausting. We modified my training so midweek practices took a backseat to weekend racing. The racing, in a sense, became my training. We were hitting USA Swimming age group meets, college meets, and Masters meets, big and small. The undertaking became a family affair. Mom, Lloyd, Eric, and I would sometimes go on the road together for meets and share a hotel room. I was so happy that the four of us shared something as healthy, challenging, and fun as our love of competitive swimming. It paved the way for countless adventures together. I cheered for Mom's and Lloyd's efforts and they cheered for mine. It got to the point where Eric and I were always bouncing from one swim meet to the next. Sometimes we'd go to a meet on Saturday, then jump in the car and drive a hundred miles so I could swim in another meet on Sunday.

And then tragedy struck. On May 10, 1997, during the Senior Olympics in Pasadena, Lloyd, who was only sixty-three, died of coronary heart disease. Less than two years earlier, he had been in the stands with Mom at that very same pool watching me compete at the National Championships, one of the high points of my do-over. Now, one day before Mother's Day, he was gone. Lloyd had shown me what real fatherly love felt like. Having him walk me down the aisle at my wedding was one of the most memorable moments of my life. I knew I would miss him very much.

Lloyd had been physically fit from training five times a week, giving him the appearance of someone decades younger. But what's on the surface can belie the truth underneath. Those close to him knew Lloyd suffered from gout and high cholesterol, and he wasn't always diligent about monitoring those conditions. And he never underwent a full medical stress test. Had he done so, his doctors may have been able to detect the partial blockages in his arteries.

During warm-up before the meet that day, Lloyd had mentioned to Mom that he couldn't catch his breath. That in itself was a bit unusual.

But swimmers are always out of breath. That goes with the territory for the level of physical exertion the sport requires. So he swam four of his events, and everything seemed to be fine. Then, as he was sitting in his lawn chair on the pool deck after finishing his fifth race of the day, the 200-yard backstroke, he suddenly toppled over. Bill Earley, who was trained for medical emergencies, was on Lloyd right away, administering CPR and rescue breathing. The lifeguards at the pool were on him too. But they were never able to revive him. Heartbreakingly, Mom witnessed the whole thing.

It was one thing to have lost my biological father. When he died, I was sad, but it was far from tragic for me. Losing Lloyd hurt on a much deeper level. With his death I lost the father figure in my life, and it saddens me that I never had an opportunity to thank him for all he had taught me. Mom was shattered. She felt guilty that she hadn't insisted on a stress test for him, particularly since she was in the medical profession.

We both agreed that Lloyd passing away at a swim meet may have been the best way for him to go, given how fond he was of the sport. He died wearing his swimsuit.

Losing Lloyd devastated me. I was grief-stricken at his funeral. Hundreds of people from the local swimming community showed up for the service. No one could believe Lloyd was gone.

For a while I considered shelving the 1997 racing plan. Swimming and meets and times and rankings can seem pointless when you've lost someone close to you. But after talking it over with Mom and Eric, I decided that Lloyd, who loved swimming as much as I did, would have wanted me to continue the quest. He was always one of my biggest fans. What better way to honor Lloyd's memory than to see if Eric and I could complete what we'd set out to do? So we rolled up our sleeves and went back to work.

It was a long, demanding process, but it was also great fun. Racing isn't just about climbing up on the blocks and waiting for the horn to sound. It's about good nutrition and hydration. It involves properly warming up beforehand and sufficiently warming down afterward. And the older you get, the longer both processes take. It's also exhausting—you're getting in and out of the water so often you feel you should be rewarded with fish, like a trained seal. I was racing so frequently that if Eric hadn't been there to keep track of what events were scheduled in what order, I would have climbed up onto the blocks without a clue as to what I was supposed to be swimming next.

Eric and I knew I was in the best shape of my life, and that December we set our sights on something else that had never been accomplished before in the Masters ranks. Call it a plan within a plan. We went to the Southern Pacific Masters Short Course Meters Regional Championships in Long Beach with the intention of trying to set ten world records in ten different events. Over the course of those three days at the Belmont Plaza facility, I had a little taste of what Michael Phelps must have been feeling in his lead-up to the 2008 Olympic Games in Beijing. He and his coach had made their intentions clear months in advance: Michael would attempt to break Mark Spitz's perfect record of seven gold medals in seven events. The audacity of setting such a goal, and then the mounting tension of winning one gold after another, some by the slimmest of margins, was must-see TV, and as Michael drew closer and closer to fulfilling his goal, competitive swimming had the country's attention in a way it rarely does. Eric and I didn't publicly proclaim what we were trying to do that weekend, but the margin of error for our unblemished record spree was slight. And by the time the meet finished on the night of Sunday, December 14th, we'd done it. Every time I dove from the blocks at that meet, I set a world record. The 50-, 100-, and 200-meter flys; the 50-, 100-, and 200-meter backstrokes; the 100-meter breaststroke; the 200- and 400-meter frees; and the 400-meter IM—all the strokes were represented.

When the final tabulations and rankings came through at the end of the year, I'd placed first in fifty-three out of fifty-four events. I had missed one: the 50-yard freestyle. Amy Pope, a swimmer from Kentucky, had just barely clocked a faster time than me. It was disappointing to have come so achingly close to reaching our goal, but Eric and I were confident we had accomplished something that would probably never be duplicated. And then a few weeks later we got the news that Amy's swim was unverified: it had occurred at an unsanctioned meet. So it was official—in 1997, we'd swum a perfect 54 for 54.

CHAPTER **42**

Is This Life Just a Test?

A FTER THE GREAT EXPERIENCE I'd had at Palomar, I was determined to try to compete again at a four-year college. My times were as fast as those of an elite high school swimmer, so it was just a matter of Eric and me finding the right fit. We were also both happy to relocate to wherever that might be.

The first coach I approached was Jim Montrella, head coach at Ohio State University. Our paths had first crossed when I was thirteen and Troy was trying to talk meet officials into letting me swim in the finals of a Senior Development Meet in Long Beach. Melissa Belote, the world-record holder in the backstroke at the time, had scratched, so there was an empty lane. Since I was the first alternate, Troy argued, it only stood to reason that I should be allowed to swim in Belote's place. The officials would have none of it. Jim came to our defense: "This little girl has waited around all afternoon and all evening for a chance to swim, and you're gonna tell her that she can't, even though there's an empty lane right there?" But the officials wouldn't bend. If there had been a spot in the consolation finals, they explained, I could swim. But I couldn't swim in the big finals. In any event, I never forgot how Jim Montrella had stepped up to the plate for me.

I called Jim and explained my unusual situation. I told him I was pretty sure I had some eligibility left, and that if he had an open spot on his team I'd love to swim with him in Ohio. The NCAA, I knew from my preliminary research, has a twenty-seven-year age limit for Division I athletes, but they'd made exceptions based on circumstances in the past. Given my alcoholism and subsequent recovery, I thought I had a pretty good case to make. Jim told me he'd check with his compliance department and get back to me. "I've got good news and bad news," he reported a few days later. "The good news is you do have some eligibility left. You're technically a fifth-year senior. The bad news is that Big Ten rules state that fifth-year seniors must have completed at least 80 percent of their credits to be eligible to compete, and you're nowhere near that."

So Ohio State was out. Eric and I explored a few more schools, including Arizona State University and Northern Arizona University. My times were fast enough to get a full scholarship at either one, but there were still some nagging questions about how much of my eligibility I'd used up while I was at Arkansas. In the meantime, I was contacted by Pat Skehan, the coach at California State University, Bakersfield, a Division II school. "We'd love for you to come for a visit and talk with us about possibly coming to CSUB," she wrote in her letter. Initially, I politely declined her offer. I was convinced I belonged at a Division I school.

But as the rules and regulations concerning my eligibility to compete at a DI school kept getting murkier and murkier, I decided to give Pat and her program a closer look. Bob Steele would be the men's coach at Bakersfield starting in the fall, and he was trying to keep the ball rolling from the incredible success of his predecessor, Ernie Maglischo. Maglischo's Roadrunners had won eight straight NCAA Division II titles in the late '80s and early '90s. The women's team had enjoyed some success over the years, but nothing close to the men's program. Eric and I drove up to do a meet at Clovis in the Central Valley, and on the way back we swung through Bakersfield. The first things we saw when we exited the freeway were an oil refinery and a barren desert. It was mid-June and it was hot—105° hot, to be specific—and unbearably dry. Eric and I raised our eyebrows skeptically at one another as we drove to the campus to check out the facilities.

While CSUB may have been small, with a student body of just 5,000 or so, it boasted an impressive eight-lane, all-deep 50-meter pool. Eric and I met with Coach Pat and athletic director Rudy Carvajal. They both confirmed that they could offer me a full ride, including a stipend for off-campus housing. "We'd really like you to join the team." We asked about Pat's coaching methods, and she was candid about her philosophy and what she expected of her swimmers. She valued high-caliber swimming and high academic performance. I liked her immediately.

On the drive back down to Coronado, Eric and I discussed the pros and cons. Bakersfield would offer me the opportunity to compete at a four-year college again. It was close enough to Coronado that if Mom suddenly needed anything, we could be there in a handful of hours. An added bonus was that we would also be only a few hours' drive away from Eric's mom in Alamo. Eric would give up his jobs back home, but with all my school expenses covered, financially it would not be a hardship. He was fine with the idea. Eric was like that—always so supportive. Bakersfield wasn't exactly the garden spot of California, but this wasn't a lifetime commitment either. For one school year, we finally decided, we could probably do anything. And that's how we approached it. It would be a nine-month adventure. Later, when I asked UC Berkeley's coach Teri McKeever about her impressions of the CSUB program and about Pat in particular, she said, "Her girls always look like they're having a good time." I found that insight to be not only telling, but reassuring. I signed the letter of intent and called Pat to let her know we'd see her in the fall.

Competing for CSUB and working toward getting my degree would be our next project. In the meantime, we could move Mom, who had been struggling in Solana Beach after Lloyd's passing, into our house while we were gone so she would be living near more people she knew. We'd move Lloyd's horticulture pieces down with her. After Bakersfield, the plan was that we'd return to Coronado and I'd finish up my studies at San Diego State University.

When it comes to competing at the DII level, an athlete has ten available semesters and a lifetime in which to use them. The moment you register for a full-time schedule (twelve units), that counts as a semester regardless of whether or not you ever set foot in a classroom. According to our calculations, between what I'd done at Arkansas and the various community colleges I'd attended, I had one available semester left. We took the news in stride and figured I would just redshirt in the fall. NCAA championships were in the spring, and I would make that my official semester.

But Pat had another idea. She suggested that if we could successfully petition the NCAA to grant me an additional semester, there would not need to be any redshirting. But, she explained, the plan would entail me making the argument that I was a one-time screwup who was now an exemplary student athlete. One of the patriarchs of CSUB, retired business professor Dr. Dick Graves, told me he'd help put my case together. We went back and retrieved my old transcripts from Arkansas, and I petitioned the university to strike my last semester. I then had to go back to some of my old bosses who'd fired me and ask them for what essentially were letters of *non*-recommendation. It was bizarre, to say the least. I approached Lindsey from Bula's; Chuck Chase, who was my boss when I was a state lifeguard; and Admiral George, who knew all about my trials and travails at NAB Coronado. I asked each one of them to pen negative letters as best they could. I needed evidence of what a mess I'd been during my alcohol-fueled days. Truth be told, I had been such a mess that it wasn't hard to prove. Thankfully, the strategy worked.

Eric and I found out that the NCAA was granting me a second semester. Now I had an entire school year to work with. It seemed like everything was working out according to plan.

And then, later that summer, my mother suffered a mild heart attack on the day of the annual Optimist Club of Coronado One-Mile Rough Water Swim. I was the overall winner that morning, and as I stood on the beach and watched my mother come in, everything seemed fine. She'd had a solid swim and posted a good result. As soon as we reunited, though, she started complaining about a bubble-like sensation in her chest. When it wouldn't go away, I drove her to the emergency room at Kaiser Zion Hospital, where they immediately whisked her away. The diagnosis was an arterial spasm. Even though my mother wasn't exhibiting signs of being in distress, the doctors wanted to keep her overnight for observation.

I remember lying in bed next to Eric's sleeping figure that night and being consumed with fear. I was terrified I was going to lose my mother next. The thought of losing her was incomprehensible, especially after just having lost Lloyd. After all these years, we finally had a solid relationship, and it was something we both treasured. Was I being tested? Thankfully, the thought of using alcohol to douse the uncertainty I was feeling never once crossed my mind. But for the first time in half a lifetime I was being forced to experience a broad range of emotions head on, without an anesthetic, and it wasn't easy. Fortunately my mother's episode turned out to be nothing more than a scare. Eric and I could move up to Bakersfield as we'd planned.

A few years later, the local Masters community in San Diego suffered another blow when Bill Earley, who'd attempted to resuscitate Lloyd on the pool deck in Pasadena, died during the Coronado Annual July 4th

Rough Water Swim. Eric, as fate would have it, was the race director that day. Bill, a lifelong swimmer, had been a star at Yale back in the 1950s, and his love of the water had continued during his many years as a UDT (Underwater Demolition Team)-SEAL and as an MWR lifeguard. He was quirky and opinionated, and Eric, who had gotten to know him well both in and out of the water, adored him. Bill was like a second father to Eric. His passing rocked Eric almost as much as Lloyd's had rocked me.

CHAPTER 43

The Exclamation Point on My College Career

W HEN WE ARRIVED IN BAKERSFIELD, life got a lot less complicated because I could focus entirely on swimming and school. Up until that point I had been working full time, going to school full time, and swimming "full time." Looking back, I'm not sure how I managed to get it all done. I was able to do it thanks in large part to the love and support I received from Eric. He handled many of life's details, so it was easier for me to show up and perform, whether in the pool or in the classroom.

After the move, Eric was open to whatever work he could find. Pat gave him a tip on a job at the Adaptive Aquatics Center, a warm-water therapy and rehabilitation pool. It was a good fit. Eric became program manager and a certified pool operator. Throughout the years, Eric was always bolstering his credentials. He was a certified masseur, an American Swimming Coaches Association Level 4 coach, and now a certified pool operator. Eventually he would also go on to earn his ACE (American Council on Exercise) Personal Trainer Certification. Eric is a sponge when it comes to knowledge, and he has a knack for being able to translate everything he learns into practical applications.

As my new coach, Pat Skehan became another in a long line of influential souls who appeared in my life during my recovery. Pat wasn't much for chitchat. She wasn't the touchy-feely type either. But she absolutely loved her "girls," and they loved her back. Pat had been swimming all her life and came from a long line of swimmers. Her father used to organize a swim camp in the Catskill Mountains in upstate New York. From 1980 to 1989 she was the head coach of women's swimming at the University of Rochester, and then moved to Cal State Bakersfield in 1990 to lead their women's team. She was at CSUB for twenty-two seasons, and during her tenure with the Roadrunners she led the program from inception and successfully elevated it to one of the nation's top Division II programs. You will never hear Pat talk about her litany of accomplishments—she is one of the most self-deprecating coaches I have ever met.

Pat sat me down at the very beginning and we discussed the type of training I'd been doing. "We do a lot of training based on science," she said. "We do a timed thirty-minute swim at the beginning of the year to establish your pace, which will then serve as a benchmark for your intervals for the season. We're going to be training different energy systems. Too many swimmers, we've seen, focus on only one type of training. Here at CSUB there is no gray area. We hope to balance your effort levels between Endurance 1, Endurance 2, Endurance 3, Anaerobic 1 and 2, and so forth." Eric was an instant fan of the plan.

Before moving to Bakersfield, I was averaging 25,000–30,000 meters a week, plus weights and an occasional run. While I would be doing roughly the same amount with Pat and her program, she would be placing a greater emphasis on quality over quantity and a great deal of race pace training. From the get-go I appreciated Pat's workouts because there was no ambiguity. We had our laminated pace charts right there on the pool deck, so when a set was called out we knew exactly how much effort was expected and what times we were targeting. No surprises. No mind-numbing mega-hard sets designed to demoralize you or tack on extra miles. Pat created a training program for us with specific and measurable goals in mind, and it seemed everyone flourished in this positive environment.

Outside the pool, I was a little concerned with how I'd fit in with the young women on the Roadrunners' team. I didn't want them to think of me as some old lady who'd be monitoring and judging what they did in and out of the pool. As it turned out, I had nothing to worry about. Carrie Smith, who picked me up from the airport the day I arrived, was the first to welcome me, and our instant friendship set the tone for my relationship with all the others.

Memories of my time in Arkansas came flooding back to me as I went to a few parties with my new teammates and watched them party to excess. It didn't make me want to drink, but it did set off a few alarm bells in my head. I secretly worried that one or more of them might be opening up a trapdoor like the one I fell through. Later, after I got to know some of them better, I confided in them about my history, but I refrained from trying to lecture them or curtail their "fun."

Bakersfield turned out to be the ideal situation for Eric and me. The city was laid back and unpretentious, and I enjoyed getting around on my beach cruiser bicycle. One of Pat's greatest skills was cultivating the local California talent that came to her. By the time these women were seniors, Pat had them swimming much faster than they had as freshmen. We had a great group of seniors, including Carrie Smith, Cory Snow, Amy Hurst, Rebekah Solomon, Annika France, Kate Slabodnik, Corene Vieira, and Charli Shearard, a transfer from South Dakota who showed up one day out of the blue and walked onto the team. Eric was encouraged to swim with us in the mornings, and Pat often assigned him to train distance with Skye Flocco, the only freshman on the team.

It was truly magical to watch this pool full of swimming talent begin to put together some amazing performances both in practice and in our dual meets against the likes of UC Davis and UC Santa Cruz. The school newspaper caught on to the fact the new kid on the block was actually in her mid-thirties and began to refer to me as the team's "secret weapon." Local news stations also caught wind, and eventually each of the three networks did a feature on me. It was fun to be something of a local celebrity.

In December we traveled to Long Beach to compete in the Speedo Meet of Champions, a huge event that attracts many of the best college teams. I placed second in an exciting 200-yard freestyle race against Limin Liu, a Chinese Olympic silver medalist who was swimming for the University of Nevada, Reno. During that race, Bob, our men's coach, happened to be standing on deck next to Sam Freas, who had left Arkansas some years back and was now coaching at the University of Hawaii. "You know, Bob," Sam said as they watched my performance, "I used to coach her." When Bob reported this exchange to me later, I just about fell into the pool laughing. All these years later, Coach Freas, who could never manage to say a word to me during all of my early morning practices with his men's team, was suddenly trying to take some of the credit for my success.

The first thing I realized as I walked out onto the pool deck at the C.T. Branin Natatorium in Canton, Ohio, in March 1998 for the NCAA Division II championships was that the banner at the far end of the pool read "NCAA." It didn't say "NCAA Division II." It simply said "NCAA." The whole stigma attached to DII and DIII teams became completely irrelevant. I was at our college national championships, and the swimmers in attendance were the very best of this division. While it may not have been the stage I'd envisioned when I first decided to resume my collegiate swimming career, it was pretty darn close.

From the very first morning session, my teammates and I were on fire. We were placing swimmers in the finals and consolation finals in nearly every event, which is exactly what we needed to do to accumulate enough points to finish high in the standings. Our goal was to finish in the top three, which would be the best women's swim team results in Roadrunner history.

Mom flew in for the event, and having her at the meet meant a great deal to me. Eric had been given the role of team masseur, so he had a front row seat right on the pool deck. In my first event, the 200-yard IM, I placed second behind Clarion's Christina Tillotson. I was disappointed because I knew I had mentally given up on the breaststroke leg and had literally watched Tillotson swim away with the title. Later, when I found myself alone in the locker room, I moved in front of the mirror and gave myself a heart-to-heart talk. I stared at my reflection and asked myself why I'd fought so hard to compete again in college if I wasn't prepared to give it my very best, my absolute all. The reinforcement worked. I quickly bounced back to win the 100 backstroke, which made me, at age thirty-six, the oldest swimmer in history to capture an NCAA title. Charli won the 100 fly and placed second in the 100 free. Everyone was swimming phenomenally. But the team competition remained nail-bitingly close between Drury University, the defending champion from Missouri; the favorite coming in, Truman State, also from Missouri; Metro State, from Minnesota; and us, the ladies from California!

My next individual event was the 400-yard IM, and we needed points to pull ourselves out of fourth place. I would be going head-to-head against Tillotson again. It seemed that no matter what transpired over the course of my swimming life, I was destined to be challenged by that daunting 400 IM. Once the gun went off, I raced ahead on the fly and on the backstroke. This time, instead of tightening up and losing ground in the breaststroke leg, I stretched out my lead and never looked back. I blazed through the freestyle with a 58 split and hit the wall a full two body lengths ahead of Tillotson. I not only won the race going away, but I did it with an impressive time of 4:24, a full eight seconds faster than the 4:32 I'd swum as Troy's fifteen-year-old prodigy at the Junior Nationals in Dallas.

My last individual event of the meet, two days later, was the 200-yard backstroke. All weekend long I'd been staring at the pool records, which were prominently posted on the wall of the natatorium. Linda Jezek, the 1976 Olympian who had broken the world record in the 200-meter backstroke, held the pool record with a 1977 time of 2:00.52. Since my best time was 1:59, I kept telling myself I could get it. This was the swimmer I had idolized as a kid, and I thought how cool it would be to leave my mark on the wall just like her. In the prelims I swam a 2:01.77 and it felt easy, relaxed. In the finals, I swam a great race and won my third individual event of the meet, scoring even more points for the team. The win was bittersweet, however, as my time, a 2:00.54, missed Jezek's pool record by a mere two-hundredths of a second. But I did swim faster than the Division II record in that event, making me the oldest athlete to ever set an NCAA record.

The last event of any team competition is usually the 400-free relay. There are more points at stake with relays, and the excitement from the long meet reaches a crescendo as the top four sprint freestylers from each school line up behind the blocks for the grand finale. We were seeded third, but Charli, Corey, Amy, and I knew we could swim faster. At this point we were out of the running for the team competition, but a good final showing would get us close. With the roof of the small natatorium about to topple off from all the boisterous cheering and whistling, our foursome powered through the final, winning by a very small margin. Later, as we marched up to accept our trophy, the loudspeaker was playing the Beach Boys' "California Girls." We unzipped our sweat tops to reveal t-shirts that read "Victory." That relay triumph propelled the Roadrunners into second place overall in the team standings, just behind Drury. When we arrived back in Bakersfield the next day, there were hundreds of fans there to greet us, and our accomplishments were detailed in full in the local news.

While my individual titles were certainly rewarding, helping bring Pat and the team success put the exclamation point on my collegiate experience. Everyone on the team had a role in securing that second-place trophy, and that type of positive, team-oriented environment is exactly what attracted me back to college swimming in the first place.

Competing at Cal State Bakersfield was an unforgettable experience for me. Sometimes I look back and wonder how I ever could have been so fortunate as to land in that situation. To this day, I'm still connected to many of my Bakersfield teammates, and it's been a real treat watching them mature into accomplished young women. None of this would have happened, of course, without Pat. She laid the groundwork that made the magic possible.

CHAPTER 44

Taking the Right Kinds
of Risks

E RIC AND I WERE ENJOYING OUR TIME in Bakersfield so much that we decided to extend our stay. Judith Pratt, my academic advisor, also made the argument that I'd probably be better off remaining at CSUB than transferring to SDSU. If I transferred to San Diego, going from the quarter system to the semester system would cost me some units. Plus, Judith explained, because of the size of CSUB's student body, I'd have a much easier time getting into the classes I needed for my major, which was communications and public relations. Eric was happy with his job at the Adaptive Aquatic Center, which included meeting with physicians in the community to discuss the merits of warm-water therapy. He wasn't coaching, which he missed doing, but at least he was still around aquatics. Judith was right: it was a sound decision to stay.

We analyzed my transcripts and I realized that if I could do summer school and up my class load, I'd be able to graduate in June of 1999. We told Mom about our plan, and I said that if she had any reservations, we would come back to Coronado. She insisted she was getting better little by little.

"Of course it's lonely without Lloyd, but you and Eric need to do what you need to do," she said.

"I miss him too, Mom," I said. "I didn't have a chance to say goodbye to him."

"None of us did," she said.

I took a part-time job with the Joshua Tree—Girl Scout Council helping to run their sports programs. Pat had connected me with Dianne Campbell, an energetic and enthusiastic manager of the program department. I enjoyed the work, mostly because I loved helping to empower young girls. All summer long—and it was a hot, hot summer—I juggled my classes with my job and my swimming.

Pat organized a twenty-four-hour relay to raise money for the team. The idea was that each swimmer would swim as hard and as far as she could over the course of an hour and then hand off to the next swimmer. A group of volunteers was assigned the task of sitting on the pool deck and counting each lap. I drew the 1:00 a.m. slot. When you're in the pool all by yourself late at night like that, your mind and body gradually sink into something of a trance. You lose track of the number of lengths you've swum and eventually even the direction you're traveling across the pool. Senses of time and space blur. While I was fatigued and in a state of sensory deprivation crossing back and forth across the darkened pool, I suddenly heard a voice.

Karlyn!

It was Lloyd's voice.

L-Lloyd? Is that you? I said, startled, but fighting not to miss a beat in my stroke turnover. *I've missed you so much.*

I've missed you and your mom too, Karlyn, he said. I miss you both a lot. I just wanted to tell you how proud I am of you. You're doing so amazingly. You're going back to school and you're swimming so well and you're taking care of your mom.

I'm trying, I said, the lenses of my goggles starting to fog from the dampness in my eyes.

The pain and discomfort I was feeling immediately disappeared. Having Lloyd in the water with me was giving me an incredible second wind. I started to swim even faster as he illuminated the darkness around me.

H-how's heaven? I said.

Oh, it's great up here, he said. *I'm gardening all the time.*

Do you get to swim too?

Oh yeah. I get to swim all the time.

And the pools—are they beautiful? I asked.

They're really, really beautiful. You won't believe it when you see them, Karlyn. And they keep the water nice and warm, just the way you like it.

I had no idea parental love could be so everlasting—that it could out-last even mortality. As I continued to swim and listen to Lloyd rattle on about how wonderful everything was in the afterlife, I thought back to how cute he was whenever he raced the 200-yard backstroke, the last event he swam here on Earth. Lloyd never counted his laps and, as he got older, he'd often get confused as to how many he'd done. One day my mom and I decided we'd start counting for him. We stood at the end of the pool and held up a lap counter with big black numbers for him to see. I couldn't help but smile at the memory. And now here he was, the spirit of my adopted father, helping me get through my challenging relay leg just as we used to help him.

Dianne, my think-outside-the-box supervisor at Girl Scouts, decided we needed to offer fresh and innovative programs to our membership. She had heard of a new event called Sports and Slumber and thought CSUB would be a perfect place to host one. Even though I had no experience in event planning, she had faith in my ability to organize and deliver it. The idea was to place girls in close contact with female student athletes at a sports-oriented sleepover. We wanted to teach the girls about healthy, active lifestyles and to inspire them to pursue their own dreams of com-peting at the high school or collegiate level. The event was a huge success.

Being around all those energetic, bright-eyed Girl Scouts was stirring up feelings buried deep inside me. Maybe it was time to think about starting a family of my own.

That summer of 1998, Senior Nationals were scheduled to be held in nearby Clovis. For the past three years I had been reaching the qualification time standards with ease. In addition to training with Pat and the CSUB team, I also started practicing with the Golden Empire Swim Team. It was kind of comical—as I kept getting older, my lane mates kept getting younger. I loved swimming with the kids, and I found their youthfulness infectious. The head coach, Sage Hopkins, was trying to qualify a women's 400- and 800-meter relay team, and I offered to help. My teammates Jenny, Courtney, and Emily were barely teenagers, but we hit the standard on our first try. The girls and their parents were understandably excited about having the opportunity to go to Nationals and thanked me profusely. I told them I didn't have much to do with it. It was the girls' hard work in the pool that had gotten them there.

Throughout my lost years, I had had a risky lifestyle that affected everything: my safety, my health, and my emotional well-being. It was a dangerous way to live, and to this day I am incredibly grateful that my destructive behavior did not get me incarcerated, institutionalized, or killed.

I was still taking risks, but now they were the right kinds of risks. Eric and I giving up our jobs and moving to Bakersfield? That was a big risk. My going back to school to swim as a college athlete in my mid-thirties? That was another risk. A healthy risk. A risk with the goal of improving my life. Taking those kinds of risks is good for the spirit and the soul. By changing nothing, to paraphrase the saying, nothing changes. And while staying the same may have seemed like a good option when I was in the grip of my disease, it was no longer an option in my recovery.

I worked hard in school and made the dean's list every quarter. In June of 1999—a full nineteen years after I'd first started my college education—I graduated with honors, *cum laude*. During the entire commencement speech, all I could think was, *Better late than never.* I was finally finishing what I had started all those years ago, and I felt extremely pleased with myself. For so long, my life had been about inaction, but now it was all action. In the pool, Eric and I were continually setting goals that were increasingly more challenging. Even well into my mid-thirties, my times were getting faster, which at the time was unheard of in swimming. As the guest speaker at the graduation ceremony spoke at length about life's infinite possibilities, about dreaming big and never settling for anything less than greatness, I reflected on how far I'd come since the day I finally acknowledged my alcoholism to my mother. It's odd to think that those six little words— "Mom, I think I'm an alcoholic"—had the power to change my life forever, and in so many positive ways.

Just before Eric and I were about to make the move back to Coronado, we got word from Joe Kernan, our landlord, that he and his family were moving back to the island. They needed their house back. Mom scrambled to find us a new place to live. She managed to lease a 1,000-square-foot, two-bedroom, one-bath house a couple of blocks from the beach, and that's where the three of us lived for the next year. It was a tight squeeze, but we discovered that we got along very well together. Mom adored Eric. She enjoyed cooking and he enjoyed eating, so that, coupled with his skills on the pool deck and his easygoing nature, made him a perfect son-in-law for her.

That summer Eric took over the head coaching position at CNSA. Again, it's funny how life works sometimes. I was now married to a successor to Troy, one of my greatest influences. All roads for me, it seemed, led back to Coronado Navy. Eric loved his job, and the kids all adored him.

After graduating from CSUB, I thought it would be fun to take a light job for the summer. Ironically, I ended up waiting tables at the Bay Beach Cafe, the same restaurant I used to launch my drunken open-water swims in the San Diego Bay from. Steve Lindsey had since sold his share of the business to his partner, Ray Carpenter, so he was not on the scene anymore. Our paths had crossed over the years, however, and I knew he was happy I had gotten my act together. He had seen many of his friends and former employees die from alcoholism or drug abuse, and he was relieved I would not be one of them. People forget that addiction is often deadly. I try to remind myself of that fact every single day.

In the fall, I started a job as a program specialist with the Girl Scouts San Diego–Imperial Council. There were about seventy staff at the offices on Upas Street, mostly women. My role was to develop interesting, innovative programs for our membership, at the time 30,000 strong. After my stint at the Joshua Tree Council in Bakersfield, I now had plenty of experience. With the support of the CEO, Jo Dee Jacob; my manager, Nancy Palmer; and my assistant, Eliina Lizarraga, over the next four years we created very successful events, many of which focused on the sport of triathlon. We offered a series of triathlon seminars and had a three-day triathlon camp in the Cuyamaca Mountains, culminating in the fall with the first-ever Girl Scout Try-Athlon. Over 250 girls and leaders participated. We also offered surfing, rock climbing, tennis, golf, basketball, fencing, and the ever-popular Sports and Slumber, which attracted over 500 participants the first year. I was affectionately known by our membership as the Sports Lady, and I loved my job. It was rewarding and inspiring to watch girls and leaders became empowered and emboldened to step outside of their comfort zones.

At home Mom and Eric and I got along so well that we pooled our resources and purchased a house together in Point Loma. In that small-world way, our real estate agent was my former CNSA teammate Neil

Purdy. Eric was always great managing our money, and even when we were in Bakersfield and I wasn't working, we were debt free. Buying a house with Mom was a good investment for everyone concerned, and we all looked forward to this next stage of our lives. Since we hoped to start a family soon, we bought in a family-friendly neighborhood with a great elementary school right across the street. It was a perfect home, with a room for a baby and a separate living area for Mom. Since she was retiring soon, the plan was for her to become our live-in babysitter while Eric and I continued to work. Like so much of my life in sobriety, everything was falling neatly into place, and I looked forward to what the future would bring.

CHAPTER 45

The Do-Over Took On
a Life of Its Own

I 'VE OFTEN WONDERED WHERE THE DRIVE comes from—the drive to be the best. True, I've never liked losing, and I have an innate competitive drive. But every time I stepped up onto the blocks to race, it wasn't about losing to another swimmer; I didn't want to lose to myself. Sobriety cleanses away a lot of things, but it doesn't necessarily wash away self-doubt or instantly boost your self-esteem. Over time and with each race, I was finding the courage to face down my own fears, my own demons. I was proving to myself that I was valuable after all.

In a sense, my strength was coming from a place of weakness. It wasn't confidence that drove me; it was lack of it. Every time I signed up for a meet, I wanted to prove to myself that I possessed follow-through. That I could succeed. That I wasn't a quitter.

One of the Program's most well-known mantras is about living life one day at a time. Focusing on the little tasks, it is suggested, helps make the greater journey seem less daunting. I was swimming life one length at a time, gradually gaining strength and momentum through my successes and failures. Back in 1996 at the age of thirty-four, I swam the 1,500-meter (almost a mile) freestyle in 17:48.44. Karen Burton recorded the fastest time in the world that year in my age group with a 17:38.70, and Lisa Hazen had the third-fastest time with a 17:48.60. None of us was born seventeen-minute milers. It took years of patience, perseverance, and stamina to produce those swims. When I first attempted to swim a mile in front of Mr. Cully all those years ago, it probably took me close to forty-five minutes to complete it. I was overwhelmed by the magnitude of what I was attempting to do. My young mind couldn't grasp the distance I was trying to cover. But I succeeded in reaching that goal, just as I later succeeded in swimming across Lake Sequoia, by breaking the challenge down into small, manageable steps. What I learned in sobriety is that all of life's biggest challenges need to be approached in the same way: one small step at a time.

Every race, every win, every record; all these little tests were happening over and over and over again. They challenged me. Externally, people would look at what I was accomplishing and say, "Wow, that Karlyn, she's really, really driven. She's so incredibly intense." What few realized, though, was that what was really driving me was the internal battles I was waging against myself.

At some point, the do-over took on a life of its own. Success begets more success, and there was an insatiability associated with the quest I was on. Once I raised the bar to a certain level, it didn't seem to be enough. I wanted to raise it higher. Take the 100-meter long course butterfly. In August of 1993 as a thirty-one-year-old, I swam a 1:12.70, and I was excited to have placed eighth in the 30–34 age group. A year later, I made a huge drop, and my 1:06.62 moved me up to first in the country and second in the world. A year after that, as a thirty-three-year-old, I swam 1:05.23, which led to a number-one ranking in the world and a new world record. I improved upon that mark still further a year later. You get a little greedy with it. *If I can do a 1:06, why can't I do a 1:05? If I can do a 1:05, why can't I do a 1:04?* At the end of the day, you want to see just how far you can take it. I think that's probably the case with most great athletes.

The motivation comes from never being satisfied, from searching for that one perfect performance, which of course ultimately doesn't exist.

The record-breaking I was doing, while certainly an accomplishment, was really just the by-product of a lot of hard work, dedication, and narrow-minded focus. I enjoyed the training. I liked being a workhorse. I didn't mind working hard and feeling the discomfort that accompanies that. I also loved the competition, because that's where I got to see the results of my hard work. And I certainly loved to race. I took great pleasure in pushing myself to see exactly what I was made of, and, when I did, I could see I was made of some pretty tough stuff.

All throughout this time period, Eric and I were a team. I was the one who was front and center, but he was the one behind the scenes who made it all possible. Eric was very comfortable with this division of labor. In fact, he preferred to be away from the limelight. But I sometimes wondered whether my strong personality was harmful to the health of our relationship. Addiction is the most selfish of pursuits, and I wasn't deluding myself that just because I was sober, I'd somehow gotten control over my selfish side.

Like an addict in denial, at that time I couldn't see that my record-breaking feats were just as self-centered as my eating and drinking binges from my lost years. I'd merely substituted one addiction for another. But society tends to reward and embrace some forms of compulsive behavior while castigating others. My swimming accomplishments were providing me with validation I felt I needed, and the feeling was intoxicating. Winning gold medals and setting world records made me feel higher than any alcoholic beverage ever did. Swimming was a healthier addiction to be sure, but it was an addiction nonetheless. And it was all driven, in my eyes, by a sense of inadequacy, a sense that I needed to prove myself.

CHAPTER 46

Baby or Bust

E RIC AND I STARTED TRYING to get pregnant in January 2000. I was thirty-six going on thirty-seven. So much had gone exactly the way I planned during the do-over: I'd gotten sober, met my husband, earned my college degree, and became a record-setting Masters swimmer recognized all over the world. Now it was time to settle down and start a family, which we were both very excited about. I continued to train hard and race hard, including competing at the President's Day Classic, where I swam nineteen events over the three-day weekend, earning the high-point award against athletes less than half my age. A few weeks after that meet, just before my birthday in March, I found out I was pregnant. Eric and I were elated.

The joy was short lived. At about seven weeks, I miscarried. It was devastating. One day you're excited about this new life, and the next you're deflated like a balloon that has lost its air. The only consolation was that it had happened early in the pregnancy. In hopes of preventing another miscarriage, I gathered as much information as I could about what might have gone wrong. I was surprised to learn how often women miscarry. I knew many female athletes stopped having regular menstrual cycles because of their intensive training. I was lean from all my training, but I had very regular cycles, and that indicated that I was ovulating. Dr. Ron Reinch, my physician at Kaiser, ordered some tests, including a hysterosalpingogram to gauge the health of my uterus and Fallopian tubes. The results didn't raise any red flags that precluded me from carrying a baby to term. Dr. Reinch did recommend that Eric and I pursue fertility treatment since, factoring in a miscarriage I'd had in my twenties, I'd technically miscarried twice in succession.

I was put on Clomid, a drug to stimulate my ovaries. To be on the safe side, I decided to reduce my swimming, increase my sleep, and tweak my nutrition. That spring I went to the 2000 Short Course National Championships in Indianapolis, Indiana, and, despite all the setbacks and the emotional turmoil I was in, I won all my events and set a national record in the 100-yard IM. It was difficult for Eric and me to plan or to schedule meets very far down the road, but I was fine with that. The expectation and hope was that I'd get pregnant soon and, once that happened, competition would end for the duration of the pregnancy. I would still practice, but I wouldn't be swimming nearly as hard or as long.

I got pregnant again, but a few weeks later I had another miscarriage. I was in shock. Again? With the advice of Dr. Reinch, we took a more aggressive route and added injectable hormones and inseminations into the equation. I became a regular at Kaiser Hospital Fertility Clinic in Loma Portal. The protocol called for me to self-inject for a period of time during a cycle, with the dosage being dependent upon the results of blood tests and ultrasounds. Fortunately, my schedule with the Girl Scouts afforded me the time I needed to shuttle from the hospital to the doctor's office. Everything in our home life became painstakingly exact. Our sex life became reduced to charts and lab readings. The insemination procedure itself was painful enough, but the toll the entire process was taking on our relationship was just as agonizing.

But Eric and I were up for the challenge. We had started this journey together, and we were going to see it through to the end. It was baby or bust. The first time we used injectable hormones, I got pregnant. We were relieved. I backed down my swimming and became less active overall. But at seven weeks, I miscarried yet again. After three consecutive losses, I was feeling distraught, depressed, and utterly defeated.

For the first time in my life, my body wasn't cooperating. It wasn't responding the way I wanted it to respond. If I wanted to break 4:30 in the 400-yard IM, I knew the type of training I needed to do to get there. Eric would write me up workouts that would act as guidelines, and I could push myself harder and harder until my fitness level peaked and I achieved my goal. But this was different. The women in my family had never had any problems with fertility that I knew of, so I never once imagined that I would. Like many women, I had spent the majority of my reproductive years avoiding pregnancy with the help of birth control. I never thought it was a matter of *if* I wanted to get pregnant. I had mistakenly thought it was simply a matter of *when*.

I decided I had to buck up and be strong. Not just for Eric, but for myself. That's the world I was brought up in. I needed to be tough, to shut down my emotional side in order to persevere, in order to survive. Inside, though, I was crumbling. Eric tried to reassure me that we didn't need to experience parenthood to lead fulfilling lives. But nothing he could say or do was going to stop me from plowing ahead. I kept thinking that there was something I could be doing better. If I could just find the secret ingredient that was missing, then maybe I could have a baby. *I can solve this thing,* I told myself.

I got pregnant again. A month and a half later, Eric threw a surprise party for my fortieth birthday at my Uncle Bill and Auntie Gracie's house in Mission Beach. Here I thought we were going to a simple St. Patrick's Day celebration, and instead I walked into a house overflowing with friends and family. I was seven weeks into my pregnancy. This, I knew from recent experience, was the scary time. Sure enough, in the middle of this huge party—a party I knew Eric had planned in part to help me get over the physical and emotional turmoil I'd been through—I could feel myself starting to miscarry again. I sat in the bathroom, alone and shell-shocked. It was cruel, what was happening. I didn't know how to break the news to Eric. I could hear all the revelry on the other side of the door, and all I wanted to do was turn out the lights and hide in there for the rest of my life.

With each previous miscarriage, I had told myself, *Okay, I'm tough. I can handle this. I can keep on going.* But the fourth one broke me. I lost hope. I couldn't for the life of me figure out a way to *make* it happen. I felt so utterly powerless. Naturally, given the insecurities I'd battled my entire life, I started to view what was happening as a personal failure. My mom had five kids. Kirsten had five kids. Was it really too much for me to ask to have just one?

Later, after we got home and Eric and I were trying to come to terms with the latest blow, I finally said, "I want to try again."

"Karlyn . . . " he said.

"I want to keep trying, Eric," I said. "I'm not giving up on this."

"Let's just let it go."

"I can't. We haven't exhausted all of our resources yet."

"We don't need to do this, Spider," Eric said. "I didn't marry a baby. I married *you*, and you're the only thing that matters to me."

But I insisted. I refused to quit. It was the same blind stubbornness I'd exhibited when I swam across Lake Sequoia as a child.

"I'm sorry, Eric," I said quietly, "but I've gotta run this thing through its entire course."

For the next six months we went through the heartache again and again. By this time, we were both on autopilot, just trying to survive the ordeal. Upon reflection, I have wondered if one of the reasons I continued to fight so hard was a fear of what failure might mean to our marriage. Finally, just before our final round of insemination, Eric said, "Let's stop, Spider. Let's just stop." We'd gone through the process so many times we had lost count. He was over it. He was tired of the hurt, and tired of seeing me get hurt. Sex had become passionless and mechanical. In order to cope, I had to treat what we were going through like training for that damn 400 IM. There had to be something *I* was overlooking, and it was just a matter of time before *I* found it. And I *would* find it. When it came to my swimming, I always found it.

But with this, I never could. Everywhere I looked there were mothers with babies. What did those women know that I didn't? Was there some secret no one was sharing with me? It didn't help that we lived across the street from the school. Sometimes I'd stare out the window and see all the kids playing during recess. They'd be laughing and chasing each other across the blacktop. It finally became too painful to watch, and I simply closed the curtains.

Ultimately, when I began to examine my deepest, darkest fears, the thought occurred to me that God didn't trust me to raise a child. That was difficult to swallow—that my Higher Power didn't think I had it in me to be a good mother. That line of thinking, of course, fed directly into my insecurities and sense of unworthiness.

At some point, Kaiser informed us that they'd done everything they could for us. There was never a clear explanation as to why I couldn't carry a pregnancy to term. I fell into the category of "unexplained." As I finally closed the door on ever having a child of my own, I tried to figure out what it all meant. Throughout my do-over, I had learned that every challenge, big or small, should bring insight. During my sobriety, God had been extremely generous to me. He'd given me back my health, my body, my intellect, and my talent. From 1993 to 2002, I had achieved nearly everything I had worked for. Now, for the first time in my sober life, I had failed.

As it was with my entry into sobriety, the pool was my escape. Whenever I wasn't pregnant, and especially after a miscarriage, I'd lose myself in the numbness of training. Our dream of having a family had disintegrated before our eyes. Instead of going to a therapist or grief counselor, I went to the pool and dumped all my frustration, sorrow, and anger there. In the water I knew I had a say in the final result.

CHAPTER 47

Why Do We Act the Way We Do?

E RIC HAS ALWAYS BEEN AN OPTIMIST, with his glass half full. Even when he was dealt the blow of his father leaving when he was thirteen, he soldiered on. That's just his nature. When it came to our infertility issues, he reassured me that our inability to become pregnant was not my fault and that we could live just fine without children. "You're all the family I need," he would say. While most people would treasure a love like that, I found it suffocating at times. I just couldn't comprehend it. I grew up in a contentious household where my parents always fought. Peaceful, noncombative relationships made me uneasy; I didn't understand them. When you don't understand something that is clear to someone else, you can get frustrated and even angry. I did this with Eric, turning the brunt of my frustration and discontent on him. Maybe I wanted him to be a little disappointed in me to validate some of the ugliness I was feeling inside.

Looking back, Eric should have stood up to me more, but I was a formidable opponent. A lot of times—most of the time, if I am truthful—it was Karlyn's way or the highway. Much of that, I realized, was tied to my addictive personality. When I wanted something, I'd go to any length to get it. But Eric could seem almost indifferent to things. He just wanted to please me. "I just want to love you, Spider," he'd tell me. "I want to love you completely and wholly. Let yourself go and accept that." But I couldn't. Even though we were husband and wife and we'd gone through the highest of highs and the lowest of lows together, I couldn't let him in. And I couldn't for the life of me understand what was causing this resistance. It was becoming more and more apparent to me that I had issues with intimacy, as many alcoholics and children of alcoholics do. But was it something else as well?

The alcoholic's personality is complicated. If an alcoholic's addiction is the most selfish of pursuits, an alcoholic's sobriety may be a close second. When you were drinking, your focus was self-centered. In sobriety your focus is self-care. The transition can be a difficult one. But you learn that you have to take care of yourself before you can take care of anyone else. Twelve-step programs encourage you to establish boundaries, and when your well-being is threatened, to learn to detach. With love, of course, but still to detach.

After our miscarriages, Eric and I kept busy with new projects. Our relationship had changed, but from the outside you would never have known. When Eric started running marathons and spending a lot of time training with his mentor, Hal Goforth, I was more than happy to let him go off and do his own thing. Ever since we first met, he had been supportive of my hopes and dreams. He was my biggest fan, bar none. But when it came to a role reversal, sadly, I was hardly ever there for him.

I rarely went to any of Eric's races. He ran a 2:56 in the Boston Marathon and had spent months in preparation, but it was too much of a hassle for me to come and watch. I always had some kind of reason, some other commitment I'd made. He also enjoyed playing guitar, but I shut him down on that front by letting him know I didn't care for his singing voice. At one point he wanted to learn German because many Germans come to Kona, where we later lived, for the Ironman triathlon, and he thought it would be fun to speak to them in their own language. But I wasn't supportive of that goal either.

This pattern of behavior was nothing new. A few months into our relationship, Eric had announced he wanted to put his name in the lottery for a slot to compete in the Hawaii Ironman. If anyone understood sports-related goals and commitment, it should have been me. I put in hours upon hours of intense training for my swimming week in and week out, but that, I knew, paled in comparison to what it took to prepare for a competition made up of a 2.4-mile swim, a 112-mile bike ride, and a 26.2-mile run. When he described how much training the race would entail, my initial reaction was, "Well, I think you might need to find yourself another girlfriend." I didn't even try to beat around the bush about it. I wasn't joking. I wanted that attention. I wanted that time. Essentially I was warning him not to do anything that would take his attention from *me* and the pursuit of *my* dreams.

Why do we act the way we do? How can we be so hurtful to the ones we love? Was my inability to support Eric the way he supported me a conscious decision? We all have wants and needs. What happened in my life that allowed me to even consider that my aspirations were more important than his? Yes, I had had an absentee father, but so had Eric. And yet he had somehow found it in his heart to become a caring, selfless, compassionate individual, while my personal evolution had led to something quite different. Was Bill W., the AA founder, the same way? Is that why he emphasized within the Program and the Twelve Steps the need for a "fearless moral inventory" of our wrongs and shortcomings? Because he knew firsthand that while sobriety may help someone gain control over their drinking, it doesn't completely resolve their addictive behavior?

Eric knew I wasn't supporting his dreams. It was blatant. But instead of griping about it, he just went about fulfilling them on his own. That is what a healthy non-addict does: they live life on life's terms and take ownership of their own happiness. And not only did Eric fulfill his dreams; he fulfilled them spectacularly. His resilience and tenacity were remarkable. But I was a no-show for him in so many ways. I had so much work still to do.

CHAPTER **48**

You Never Have to Go Solo in Swimming or Sobriety

T HE PROGRAM'S FELLOWSHIP, I discovered, operates in much the same way as lane-mate dynamics work in the pool. You support each other through thick and thin, and in the end everyone is better for the experience. While getting sober or reaching an aquatic goal are certainly individual pursuits, the truth is that in swimming or sobriety you never have to go it alone.

In a Twelve-Step meeting, the group offers support and encouragement; they want the best for you. It's like that in the pool with your lane mates. They're the people who inhabit your little universe each and every practice. Some days there might be only two of you; others days as many as seven or eight. There's a unique, subtle rhythm to swim workouts. Everything runs according to the clock. In the old days, we used a round pace clock to keep track of our progress. Troy would describe a set, such as 10 x 100s on the 1:30, and he'd instruct us to leave "on the top," which meant starting when the sweeping red secondhand reached the 60 on the clock. Or he told us to leave "on the bottom," which meant when the secondhand was at the 30. Swimmers are sent off in waves, every five or ten seconds. The fastest swimmer takes the lead, the second fastest swimmer goes second, the third fastest third, and so on. We circle-swim in a line, which means that, much like vehicular traffic on a road, we continually swim on the right-hand side of the lane.

There's generally not a lot of discussion when it comes to who will be swimming where in the order. The hierarchy is established from recent experience and according to the requirements of the particular set. At the Center, if one of my lane mates was feeling ambitious, he or she might ask to lead. If someone else felt tired or achy, they might elect to move down the line.

In many ways, your lane mates are as important as your coach. You rely on them to show up at a 5:00 a.m. workout no matter the day, and they rely on you to do the same. Over the course of my career, I've had lane mates who were national champions, world-record holders, and Olympic gold medalists. I've swum with Masters swimmers twice my age and age-groupers one-quarter my age. They hold you accountable, they challenge you to swim your best, and they're there to pick you up if you're having an off day. Looking over the course of my career, I can honestly say that each and every one of those individuals became a part of me during the journey. Their friendship, encouragement, strength, humor, competitive drive, empathy, and playfulness helped make me the swimmer I am today.

That said, competitive swimming is still a cut-and-dried sport. You wake up in the early morning darkness and you either go to practice or you don't. You finish a hard training set, sign up for a meet, win a race or achieve a certain time or you don't. There are outside influences helping you along, but in the end, it is up to *you*.

Looking back, I am amazed at what Eric and I accomplished. So many of my performances seem preposterous to me now. I wanted to set a world record in every stroke during the course of my career, and I managed to do that. When I was thirty-five, my 200-meter backstroke was the second fastest in the country for any Masters swimmer, any age, male or female. The only swimmer who recorded a faster time than me that year was Joe Tristan, a twenty-one-year-old from Michigan.

We were on a rampage, Eric and I. I was blessed to have a lot of sponsors during this time. Companies like Zoot, EQ Swimwear, Zura, FINIS, Speedo, View, XTERRA Wetsuits, Mizuno, Accelerade, and PureFit provided plenty of awesome product, and I was appreciative of their support. I was now considered a professional athlete since I occasionally won prize money at events like the Kerr-McGee Elite Meet (now the Chesapeake Elite Pro-Am) or the Speedo Grand Challenge. We received no financial assistance, though, and paid our own competition and travel expenses. And we traveled a lot. We were crisscrossing the world, going to countless meets in order to achieve our goals.

I had reduced my approach to life to three rules. Rule 1: Don't drink. Rule 2: Swim. Rule 3: Break records. On the surface, I was skimming right along like one of those water skeeter bugs that dance on the surface of ponds and swimming holes. I was a poster child for Masters swimming. I was healthy, fit, youthful, and outrageously fast. I was appearing in magazine and newspaper articles, endorsing products, and jet-setting around the world. But, just as a poster is two-dimensional, underneath my facade there wasn't a lot of growth going on. If I had taken the time to stop and look inward, I would have realized that emotionally and spiritually I was stuck in an eddy, swirling around and around and making no forward progress.

Donna, my sponsor, had passed away, and I never sought to replace her. Maybe I didn't want to disrupt my wonderful carpet ride. A new sponsor would have seen what was going on and called me on it. She might have said, "Do you know, Karlyn, I'd recommend that you back off from swimming for a while," or "Karlyn, maybe you should consider which is more important—your swimming or your recovery?" *Recommend . . . Consider . . .* That's one of the many great things about the Program: everything is merely a suggestion. Sobriety works only if we choose it for ourselves. It's an inside job.

I was still showing up at meetings here and there, so I still had my foot in the door, but I wasn't really working the Program. I was still doing it my way. I was picking and choosing which elements I wanted to absorb. It was "AA á-la-carte."

CHAPTER 49

The Big Island Exudes
a Spiritual Energy

E VER SINCE I FIRST SET FOOT in Hawaii, the islands have always been a special place for me. For years, Eric and I would go on an annual vacation to Maui with Eric's mother, Janet. One year we happened to have a five-hour layover in Kona. The Big Island left such an impression on us that it replaced Maui as our go-to getaway spot. I've swum in countless bodies of water around the world, but there's something different about Kona. It isn't just the crystal clear water teeming with tropical fish, turtles, dolphins, and manta rays. For me there is something magical and restorative there as well.

In the spring of 2003, Mom and Eric and I started thinking seriously about making a permanent move to Hawaii. The decision was partially motivated by a need to heal from the trauma of the miscarriages. Our good friend Heather Catchpole was renting what had been intended as the baby's room in the Point Loma house, but it was becoming increasingly painful to walk past it every day. A move to one of the Hawaiian Islands would be about new beginnings. Unlike my "geographical" moves of the past, this one was done with healing in mind. But first we needed to make sure that such a thing was manageable. It's one thing to vacation on a tropical island, we'd been warned. It's another to live there.

Each of the islands, we discovered during our research, had its pluses and minuses. My cousin Dain, the surfing pastor, lived on Kauai, so that definitely was a plus. Kauai is also very green and picturesque, but at that time there were no public pools or Masters program there, and, surprisingly, the open-water swimming scene was limited. Oahu was too busy for our liking, and Maui seemed too trendy, homogenized, and expensive, especially if we wanted a house with a view. The island of Hawaii itself, though, seemed to have it all. For starters, there's the vastness. It's called the Big Island for a reason—its expanse is enormous. There are lush valleys, dense rainforests, and majestic peaks like the 13,796-foot Mauna Kea. The island also boasts a wonderful diversity of people and cultures. Even the weather is diverse, offering eleven of the world's thirteen climates. More importantly, though, the Big Island exudes a spiritual energy that is both unique and inspiring.

The plan was for Mom to retire from her job at Quest Diagnostics, for Eric to resign from his coaching positions, and for me to parlay my current job with the San Diego–Imperial Girl Scouts into a position working with the Girl Scouts Council of Hawaii. We would rent out the Point Loma house until we were sure that Hawaii was where we wanted to be. In Kona, Eric would work at a private gym and start offering elite-level personal training with an emphasis on preparing clients for running, swimming, or triathlon events. Eric and I flew to the Big Island in August and found a house to buy pretty quickly. I moved in January 2004, immediately starting my new management position with the Girl Scouts. Eric and Mom went to work packing up the Point Loma house, shipping the car, and arranging for a container to get our things moved, and arrived two months later.

This new chapter in our lives was intimidating because we didn't know how we would adapt to such a drastic change. How long would it take Eric to build a client base? Would we get bored or contract island fever?

And what about the ocean? If one of the main reasons we were moving was to have access to that luxurious water, how could we be sure it would always be as warm and welcoming as we envisioned?

My first day in Kona, I went down to the Kailua Pier. I was apprehensive as I stood on the sand. I took a deep breath and slowly waded into the water. Few things have ever felt as good as that very first swim as a Hawaii resident. I exhaled deeply, and was overcome with a profound feeling of peace. The tension and stress of the miscarriages, which I had been carrying around for the last few years, slowly began to trickle out. I could finally release some of the anguish I had been holding on to for so long. So much pain, so much time and energy spent covering up the hurt. As I took a few strokes in the refreshing, healing water, I wondered what it would feel like to let it *all* go.

CHAPTER 50

In the Water, You Are Ageless

A s anyone who has ever visited Hawaii knows, "aloha spirit" refers to a peaceful, compassionate, and spiritual state of mind often evident on the islands. What I first experienced when we moved to Kona, however, was anything but.

On the swimming front, I was training with one of the local age group teams and a fast group of Masters. The coach, an All-American swimmer and water polo player back in the early 1970s, had a state-wide reputation as an excellent motivator and leader. He was an accomplished Masters swimmer, having recently set four FINA world records. He also had a territorial streak.

While his age group team was the biggest program on our side of the island, he wasn't the only game in town. The Kona Dolphin Swim Club, coached by Harry Canales and Kathy Clarke, not only shared some of the spotlight with this team, but actually shared the same pool and pool time. Each team would divvy up lanes for practice, four lanes each. My new coach made it clear that he didn't care for Harry, so there was an undeniable tension permeating the pool deck. Throughout my swimming career I'd seen my fair share of "poolatics," as I've dubbed pool politics, but this felt as if I was walking straight into the Hatfields and McCoys. Since I was new to the island, I adopted my coach's attitude, unfairly judging Harry before I'd had an opportunity to get to know him.

Previously when I swam with an age group team, the coach would often encourage me to give the kids technique tips here and there. I was considered an extra set of eyes and ears in the pool, and since I was in the trenches with the kids, they listened to me. I was considered an asset to the coach and an integral part of the team. With this coach I offered only a few small suggestions, such as reminding the kids to streamline off the wall or to keep their heads still on backstroke. Apparently, however, my contributions were not welcome. One day I showed up on deck and the coach said, "This isn't working out."

"What do you mean?" I asked, confused.

"I don't want you swimming with us anymore," he said. I still had no idea what he was talking about, and he must have sensed that from the look on my face because he repeated, "You're not welcome to swim with my teams."

"Teams, *plural*?" I said.

"Yes."

"Let me get this straight. You're kicking me off both your age group team and your Masters?"

He then proceeded to unload a stash of resentments he'd been harboring toward me since I first joined the team. I was devastated. Lacking children of my own, I had found that swimming with the kids helped assuage that pain. Now that would no longer be available to me.

So here I was, a few months into the move, and I was without a team to train with. Not quite the aloha spirit I'd been hoping for. I eventually managed to talk my way back onto the Masters team, but the coach had little or nothing to say to me. I'd diligently show up for practice, and he would call the workout with barely a glance in my direction.

Once I started my job with the Girl Scouts Council of Hawaii, I discovered I was the office. I was put in charge of monitoring the entire island, with a membership of about 500. My first goal was to get a handle on whether the girls and leaders were happy. During my time with councils in Bakersfield and San Diego, I'd become program driven. I believed that the best way to serve our membership was to create innovative programs and events designed to motivate and inspire both the girls and the leaders. I set up meetings—we had about twenty-five troops in all—and was encouraged to hear that the leaders also wanted improved programming to keep the girls engaged and involved. They seemed excited to have an enthusiastic person like me on board.

One of the first things I came up with was a take on the "101 Things to Do on the Big Island" list for tourists. I would collaborate with local businesses and create a list of "101 Things for Girl Scouts to Do on Hawaii," including the opportunity to earn badges in surfing, outrigger paddling, swimming, jewelry making, and even car care. The possibilities were endless. When I pitched the concept to the CEO, who worked out of the central office on Oahu, I was told to hold off.

"It's not your job to administer programs," the CEO explained.

I also had taken a Red Cross instructor course to become certified to teach CPR and first aid. Girl Scouts requires its leaders to have training in these skills, but no classes had been offered on the Big Island for some time. I was now qualified to do something about the situation, so I eagerly pitched that idea as well.

"I'd like to get my troop leaders the training they need," I told the CEO. "Can I get the green light to get started on that?"

"We have trainers, Karlyn," she said. "When our schedule permits, we will send someone over from Oahu and offer a class."

"But I can do it," I said. "You don't need to spend resources on that. I'm now a certified instructor."

"Well, that's not your job either."

I was beginning to wonder exactly what my job *was* supposed to be. If it wasn't programming and it wasn't training, where did that leave me? Selling eighty-five-cent badges? I'd arrived with so much exuberance, but I was quickly becoming disheartened and disappointed. I truly believed in the Girl Scout movement and for the previous six years had enjoyed very positive experiences with the organization. But I came to the conclusion that in a situation like this I wasn't going to be able to make the least bit of difference.

The poolatics and the politics—this was happening within the first couple of months in Hawaii. The vibe I was getting was, "Aloha. Welcome to Hawaii! Are you sure you want to stay?" Everything was caving in on itself. Ironically, the Big Island centers around Kilauea Volcano, which has been in continuous eruption since 1983 and is symbolic of constant growth. The volcano is a life-giving force, and the land mass, both literally and figuratively, is expanding on a minute-by-minute basis. But what I was experiencing in this most dynamic of settings was individuals who either wouldn't or couldn't grow along with the world around them.

That summer I was asked to be a guest speaker at the American Swim Coaches Association's Annual World Clinic in Fort Lauderdale, Florida. As I joined the crowd milling about in the conference hall, I saw Coach Harry across the way. I had been toying with the idea of asking him if I could swim with his team, but I knew it would be a delicate matter. I made an appointment to meet with him. As soon as we got together, I made amends.

"I want to apologize," I told him as I explained the situation. "I didn't know you at all, and I never took the opportunity to even try to get to know you. I formed an opinion based on what someone else said to me, and I'm sorry for that."

And Harry, being who he is, said, "No worries, Karlyn."

I took a hard swallow. "Do you think I could have an opportunity to swim with your kids, Coach Harry?"

"Of course," he said.

"Are you sure?"

"Karlyn, you are such a positive role model. I'd love to have you swim with us."

"If I ever say or do anything that oversteps my boundaries, please tell me right away," I said.

"Please swim with us," he said. "The kids will love it, and so will I."

So in 2005 I joined Coach Harry and the Kona Dolphin Swim Club, and I've been a proud member of the team ever since. Joining the Dolphins was just what I needed. There is so much aloha spirit that the team feels like a family, or *ohana*, in every sense of the word. Since Eric and I were not able to have a family of our own, the kids on the team became my kids. I became a part of their lives, and they became an important part of mine. I've had the privilege to proudly watch them grow up and become successful student-athletes and hard-working, goal-oriented individuals. In turn, I hope that my passion for swimming rubbed off on them and has shown them, by example, that swimming is a lifetime sport. No matter what the circumstances of your life, the water accepts you as you are. In the water, you are ageless.

I had long toyed with the idea of one day forming a business offering private swimming instruction, swim technique clinics, and multi-day training camps. In early 2005 Eric and I decided to give it a try. The genesis for the idea was simple: we wanted to teach people how to swim faster with less effort using easy-to-understand drills and techniques. Learning to swim with more efficiency isn't rocket science, but given some of the suggestions online, you might think so. The Internet also offers a huge amount of conflicting information, so our main goal was to simplify and demystify the sport so that swimmers and triathletes could feel successful right away. We see swimming basically as paddling, akin to what you'd do on an outrigger canoe, kayak, stand-up paddleboard, or surfboard. Move forward with the least amount of effort, keep the vessel stable, try not to lose your balance, and don't tip over! In swimming it's okay to rock gently, but rolling from side to side wastes energy and time and can create a huge amount of drag when your feet split apart to keep you from capsizing.

We called our method Faster Freestyle, and while it might have seemed revolutionary and new compared to what other coaches were teaching at the time, the stroke was actually quite old fashioned, just with a few modern twists. In fact, if you look back at the history of the sport, it is very similar to what swimming legends like Duke Kahanamoku, Johnny Weissmuller, and Esther Williams used to win Olympic gold back in the earlier part of the century: shoulder-width hand entry, early catch and pull, and loose, relaxed, "anything goes" recovery. The only real difference between then and now is that now we swim with a neutral head position instead of looking forward, and we suggest a glide at the top of the stroke to rest, extend the reach, and help set up the next pull. This is often referred to as "catch-up" swimming, and it looks as if the swimmer is loping through the water, but it is a very fast and efficient way to swim. The clients we had worked with previously loved the simplicity of the technique as well as our easy-to-understand and easy-to-apply teaching methods. And they found themselves rewarded with immediate improvements.

We already had a foothold in the market. Whenever I was in a pool, no matter what part of the world I was in, swimmers would approach me and ask how they could go faster. In particular, triathletes who had no competitive swimming background were always asking me for tips on how to better tackle the swim portion of their races. Since Eric and I were now in Kona, home to the Ironman World Championships, the most famous annual triathlon in the world, it seemed like a serendipitous location to establish our business, which we named Aquatic Edge.

My old friends the Hubbards still lived on Oahu, though Dick had retired from the navy. I knew Dick would be a wealth of knowledge on how to set up a business and would also have some ideas about inspirational speaking, another career I wanted to pursue. Eric and I decided I would swim in a meet called the Keo Nakama Invitational in Waipahu, and while there we would meet up with Dick in nearby Mililani. While I love competing in Masters meets, this invitational would give me a chance to race against the fastest kids from all over the islands. My former CNSA teammate Katherine Nichols, now a writer for the *Honolulu Star-Bulletin,* caught wind of my endeavors and wrote a story entitled "Swimming against the tides: A record-setting 44-year-old swimmer gives and gains inspiration at youth competitions."* It ran on the front page.

I swam well, and afterward we drove up to see Dick. As always, it was great seeing him and Dougie, and he was able to give me valuable advice on how to successfully transition from my position with the Girl Scouts to a career as a successful swimming technique guru and inspirational speaker.

When we returned to Kona, Eric and I went on a hike and planned our future, just as we had done in Southern California. We talked about setting up Faster Freestyle and Multi-Stroke clinics across the country, maybe even worldwide, and of bringing clients to Kona. We also visualized creating open-water swim camps on the Big Island so that we could share our slice of paradise with guests from around the world. Eric and I hoped not only to be able to share our passion for swimming and instruction, but also, with any luck, to position Aquatic Edge to allow us to touch many lives and make a positive contribution to the sport.

In keeping with our goal, I signed an endorsement with James Murdock, the owner of Endless Pools. The next thing we knew, Eric and I had a state-of-the-art "swimming machine" in our yard and we were off and running. The Endless Pool would allow us to innovate, fully embracing modern technology to provide science-based feedback to our clients. In the Endless Pool, mirrors on the bottom allow you to see yourself in

---

* Vol. 11, Issue 181. Friday, June 30, 2006. archives.starbulletin.com/2006/06/30/news/ story04.html

real time while you swim into resistance that keeps you in place. We would also offer video recording with analysis to help speed up the process. We found that the more our clients saw themselves swim, the more able they were to make change and see improvements.

Initially I had my reservations about the efficacy of a "swimming machine." But my first dip into our new pool proved to be a life-changing experience for me. It was fun and dynamic, not at all like the static experience of running on a treadmill. More importantly, swimming in the Endless Pool allowed me to experiment with my technique. When I made an adjustment to my stroke that made me faster, I surged forward. Conversely, if I did something that slowed me down, I was pushed back. The current renders it obvious which techniques are faster or slower, easier or harder, so learning and teaching are based on data and direct, immediate feedback, not personal opinion. Over the last ten years, so much of what I have learned about faster swimming has come from trial and error in the Endless Pool. Not only has it been a revolutionary training tool for me, but it has also been invaluable for my clients who travel to Kona to work with me privately so that they can enjoy the benefits of a Faster Freestyle.

CHAPTER 51

Just Keep Swimming, Just Keep Swimming

W HEN IT COMES TO MY swimming career, I've always been able to celebrate my accomplishments. For many athletes nothing is ever good enough, and they're cursed with an inability to pat themselves on the back. More important than a capacity to accept your triumphs, though, is the ability to leave disappointments behind in the pool. I don't carry those with me. I don't dwell on them. I don't beat myself up over them. My attitude has always been about putting forth my best effort, whether in practice or in a race. *Let me see if I can do this . . .* And if it doesn't work out the way I hoped, I take comfort in the fact that I tried.

That said, I wasn't disappointed very often. One of the few times I've been beaten in my Masters career was in the 200-yard butterfly. I had been on a tear, breaking records left and right, when I showed up to race at the U.S. Masters Nationals in Santa Clara, California. Tracie Moll, who had qualified for the Olympic Trials in the 50- and 100-meter free-styles and was the world-record holder for the 35–39 age group in the 100-meter fly, was known for being a sprinter. But she'd signed up for the 200 fly and was seeded right next to me. I didn't think Tracie was much of a threat until I reached the last wall and saw I hadn't shaken her. She was still right there beside me and didn't seem to be dying in the least. I, on the other hand, felt as though I had the proverbial piano on my back. Tracie beat me to the wall—and in one of my best events, no less. Not surprisingly, she was elated. I was stunned.

Tracie and I had been selected as two of the Top 10 Masters Swimmers of the Year, so losing to her was certainly nothing to be ashamed of. Whatever her mental strength was that day, it was stronger than mine. I congratulated her after our race, and we've been friendly rivals ever since. I didn't dwell on the loss. It was on to the next race, which I see as an important attitude for athletes to cultivate. Steve Scott, one of the greatest track milers in U.S. history, would give himself exactly twenty-four hours to put a poor race behind him. He allowed himself to be as frustrated, disappointed, and angry as he wanted to be for one day, but as soon as that twenty-four-hour window passed, he forced himself to close the door and move on.

At AA meetings that I've attended over the years, I've noticed that many recovering alcoholics seem incapable of leaving their failings or shortcomings behind. They become so intimate with the ugliness and the pain that it is hard for them to imagine life without it. It becomes part of their persona. It's safe, because it is familiar. For me, I found the safe and familiar in the pool. It washed away the guilt and shame I still harbored about my past. It melted away the hurt and anger I felt about the miscarriages. It numbed the ache when I spent any time at all contemplating my internal emptiness. It seemed like the perfect pain reliever.

I was still going to meetings, but mostly for maintenance. Truth be told, sometimes I felt like an imposter. Here I was with a good amount of time in sobriety, and yet I had not even come close to finishing the Twelve Steps. I had stalled on that darn Fourth Step of taking a moral inventory. When I contemplated it a little bit further, I came to realize that I was really stuck on the Third Step, which recommends trusting God with my recovery and admitting my powerlessness to overcome my addiction on my own. I knew I was being stubborn, but I thought I had things pretty much under control all by myself.

As for the personal inventory of my character defects to be addressed in the Fourth Step, well, I wanted the past to stay right where it was—in the past. I didn't want to take out a microscope and examine my dark side, the one riddled with failures, faults, flaws, and fears. Never mind that every person I had talked to in the Program told me how cathartic and life-changing the personal inventory experience had been for them. I resisted. I was convinced I was fine the way I was.

With swimming, I'd found a new drug. It made me feel good. It made me feel high. But as healthy as it may have been and as innocently as I may have approached my do-over, the truth was I'd simply established a new addiction. Don't get me wrong—it was a much more positive addiction than drinking or bulimia, but it was an addiction nonetheless. My higher power became swimming and everything that went along with it. I was hooked on the training. I was fixated on the racing. I was addicted to the winning, and I was becoming obsessed with the records.

The mind has an amazing ability to pick and choose what it pays attention to. I was leading a dynamic life, being showered with attention and acclaim, and for the longest time I was able to convince myself that everything was 100 percent great. The reality was that there was something else I should have been doing. There was work to be done, and I was avoiding it. In retrospect, I should have been going to more meetings and fewer meets.

For so many years, it was easy to tell myself that it wasn't the right time to address the Third and Fourth Steps, along with whatever else I was running away from. In all honesty, I had simply stopped when I got to the hardest step, the one that required introspection and change. All over again, I had become my father. I again became precisely what I'd been fighting so hard to avoid—a quitter.

There were things I could have done differently to make my approach to these steps easier or different. But one of the many wonderful things about the Program is the dictum to *seek progress, not perfection*. There is no perfect path to recovery; it's a winding road with many directions to choose from. I don't regret having lived my do-over the way I did. Up to this point I hadn't been ready to deal with the true reasons behind my addictive tendencies. But Hawaii, I hoped, was going to change that. Perhaps in the healing waters off Kona I would find the strength and courage I needed to finally dig into that "fearless moral inventory" I'd been avoiding for so long.

"Just keep swimming, just keep swimming" is a key line from the now-classic movie *Finding Nemo*. As the character Dory navigates the dark and scary parts of her oceanic journey, she sings these words over and over again to shore up her confidence. That's what I was doing too. Since moving to Hawaii, I had redoubled my efforts in the pool with that same "just keep swimming" attitude. As a forty-two-year-old, I notched up national number-one rankings in thirty-eight different events. That year I was again named one of the top Masters swimmers in the world—a feat I would duplicate in 2007, 2008, 2009, and 2012. I owe a lot of this success to Coach Harry and the Kona Dolphins. Swimming with them, I had some super-fast teenagers to train with on a regular basis. Nick Garrett and Jade Morton were both Hawaii State Champions, and J.P. Friend and Shasta Montgomery were up and coming. We pushed each other to be our very best, and the results followed.

There was a problem, though. I was getting greedy. In 2007, I aged up to the 45–49 age group, and I set my sights on breaking every short course yards national record in that group in a period of twelve months. All four strokes in every distance. And I did it. I also set a total of thirty-one FINA world records that year, sometimes swimming as fast or faster than the times I had posted ten years earlier. But I knew a slowdown was inevitable, and then what? Breaking records was my go-to method for covering up my insecurities. What if that ride was coming to an end? I was beginning to measure my self-worth, I realized with a sinking feeling, by my performance.

On September 28, 2007, I was inducted into the International Masters Swimming Hall of Fame (IMSHOF). The ceremony, part of the annual United States Aquatic Sports Convention, took place in Anaheim, California. Mom, Eric, and a whole posse of swimmers from San Diego attended. The criteria to be considered a candidate are a minimum of sixteen years of active participation in the sport and competition in four age groups. Emphasis is placed on international and regional performances, dominance in the sport, and a genuine contribution to the sport in general.

Other inductees in my class included Woody Bowerstock, Suzanne Heim-Bowen, Sandy Galletly, and the legendary Ron Johnson. I was thrilled to be in the same class as Ron because, whether he was aware of it or not, he had played a huge role in my success as both a swimmer and a technique coach. Some seven years previously, back in 2000, Ron had written an article entitled "The New Australian Crawl: Easy Speed!" for *Swimming World* magazine in which he analyzed the freestyle strokes of superstars Ian Thorpe, Grant Hackett, and Kieren Perkins and compared them to the strokes of the top American swimmers. After reading the publication, I made a big decision. At the age of thirty-eight, at the peak of my swimming career, I decided to change my stroke. And it worked—my times got faster. To this day, I'm a proponent of Johnson's theory that strongly discourages "fish-like" swimming, with rolling from side to side and pushing at the back of the stroke. Sadly, Johnson passed away in 2009, but his insights and expertise on swimming technique live on through me and many others.

To be recognized by the Masters swimming community and the Hall of Fame selection committee was a huge honor. In hindsight, I wish I'd thought to invite John and Patti Waterman, Pat Skehan (my Bakersfield coach), Jon Larson (my Coronado coach), John Baker, and a few others, because they'd all played such instrumental roles in my achievement. But I had no idea of the significance of the occasion until the ceremony began.

Mark Gill, a friend and a swimmer with Swim Kentucky Masters, was MC of the event. As I listened to his remarks, I was fascinated by how the Hall includes talented Masters athletes from around the world and from all aquatic sports, including diving, water polo, and synchronized swimming. In my acceptance speech, I shared how I had become smitten with Masters swimming at the tender age of eleven. I described how watching my mom compete at an early meet way back in 1973 and seeing her win a big shiny medal piqued my interest. "Who knew," I said, "that it was possible to earn gold medals even as an adult?" I made a point of thanking Mom for sharing her lifelong passion for swimming with me, and I of course thanked Eric for being an amazing partner, friend, and coach. I also expressed gratitude to U.S. Masters Swimming for providing an environment where people of all ages and abilities can train and compete, allowing adults to feel like kids all over again.

When fellow IMSHOF member Tod Spieker placed the mantle around my neck and we posed for pictures, I couldn't help but reflect on how far I'd come since I stood on the pool deck at the George Worthington Baths after my stint in rehab and, after a lot of deliberation, found the wherewithal to coax myself back into the water. I wondered what the audience would think if they knew the real story behind my do-over.

I also wondered what it would feel like if one day my accomplishments might earn me a place in the International Swimming Hall of Fame (ISHOF) alongside my coach Mike Troy and the other swimming legends I revered so much. Troy was inducted in 1971, largely in recognition of the multiple world records he broke over the course of his career, in addition to his two Olympic gold medals. An induction into the ISHOF would be the best "Attagirl!" ever!

CHAPTER **52**

The Day That Everything Changed

D URING MY RECOVERY, SWIMMING had become my salvation. It had given me back my mental and physical strength. It had supplied me with an identity, garnered me attention and acceptance, and was now the lynchpin of my livelihood. I was writing a monthly column for *Swimming World* magazine that featured, in large part, my love affair with the sport. I was refining my Faster Freestyle instruction skills and becoming a better teacher. Swimming had also helped me mend my relationship with my mother. Eric had come into my life because of swimming. Swimming had helped me turn my life completely around in so many ways. But why, I began to wonder, did I still have that gnawing emptiness inside?

Even after all we'd been through together—the triumphs we'd had in the pool and the heartache we'd endured in our personal life—there was still some part of myself I wouldn't let Eric get close to. It frustrated me, this inability to let him in, to really connect with him on a deeply intimate level, and I could not understand what my resistance stemmed from. Here I had this wonderful, trustworthy man in my life who simply wanted to shower me with love. Why wouldn't I let him? Most women dream of that type of love and devotion. I chalked up my apprehension to the hurt I'd felt as a young girl. Maybe the genesis of my struggles with intimacy came when I realized that in order to survive in the Pipes household I needed to turn myself into a hardened tomboy.

For the next few years, Eric and I were frequently flying to the mainland to do swim meets and clinics—yet our lives were slowly drifting apart. It's difficult to pinpoint exactly when it started. The distance got to the point where he was coaching me only once a week. The rest of the time I was either swimming with Coach Harry or training on my own. That in and of itself was a change from what we were accustomed to. Eric had always been there on the deck, pushing and cajoling and working to get the best out of me in practice. But our schedules didn't allow for that anymore. Whenever Eric and I did have one-on-one time, most of our talk revolved around the business, specifically scheduling and our upcoming travel plans.

In December 2008 when I told Eric I'd found a therapist, he was all for it. In his mind, he thought everything between us was perfectly fine. In reality, the biggest reason I started seeing Lee Ann was to explore my frustration over our marriage. I wanted a more intimate, fulfilling relationship with my husband. I told Lee Ann that my conversations with Eric weren't in the deep end of the pool; they seemed permanently stuck in the shallow end.

"I need someone more spiritual and deep in my life, Lee Ann," I said.

"It sounds as if you're making Eric your scapegoat, Karlyn," she said. "Do you think that's fair?"

"I don't know," I said. "All I know is I'm not as happy as I should be."

"How long have you and your husband been together?"

"We've been married for thirteen years," I said.

"That's a good chunk of time. Why do you think this is all coming up now?"

"I have no idea. Maybe because I've been getting the sense that this island speaks the truth."

"So are you implying that what you and Eric have is not true?"

"I'm the one who's the fraud, Lee Ann. At least that's what I feel like a lot of the time. How can there be truth in our relationship if there isn't truth in me?"

The more I looked inward, the less I liked what I saw, and this internal focus started bringing up old feelings about my self-doubts, my low self-esteem, and my insecure childhood. Going to therapy is a lot like addressing the Program's Fourth Step. It's uncomfortable, it's challenging, and it can be painful beyond belief. No one enjoys admitting his or her character defects. Alcoholics in particular are masters at holding on to resentments and notorious for pointing the finger at everyone but themselves for their problems. But I wanted answers, and I was committed to gaining more insight into why my life felt so unfulfilling at times.

As my frustrations continued to mount, I started snapping more at Eric, the very person who least deserved that. I felt he wasn't really listening to me. If I had to repeat myself, I'd get nasty and angry. Here I'd embarked on this insightful journey and he wasn't a part of it. Did I want him to be a part of it, or was I closing him off? For so much of our relationship, I wanted to have things my way. Some things weren't even negotiable. But now, suddenly, my needs were not being met—not in my mind anyway. And I started blaming Eric for that. It's ironic, when I look back on it, because Eric had always been so supportive of me, especially when I was absorbed in the whole Karlyn-conquering-the-world swimming project. But for some reason I couldn't help myself. Instead of calmly trying to have a conversation, I would immediately go on the offensive.

"I don't get it. Why are you so angry with me?" an exasperated Eric said one day. "I'm just trying to love you. It seems like you're taking whatever you're going through out on me." He was right, of course, but I didn't want to acknowledge it. Lee Ann was right too: Eric had unwittingly and unjustifiably become the focal point of my discontent.

Eric, meanwhile, was on his own quest. He had fully embraced Ironman triathlons, which only made sense when we were living a stone's throw away from the sport's symbolic home. He would disappear for hours at a time on long runs or rides with other triathletes. Maybe that was his way of coping with my mood swings. I'd always thought San Diego was the place to be for people who enjoy fit, active lifestyles, but Kona takes it to a whole new level. The sense of athletic community here is strong, with a large percentage of the population dedicated to healthy living. Maybe it's the weather, with an average temperature of 85 degrees making year-round activities not only possible but pleasant. Maybe it's the isolation. After all, the Big Island sits roughly 2,400 miles from the nearest continent. I think the water inspires many of us. And while I loved swimming in the deep blue water off Kona, the thoughts I took into the ocean with me were becoming more turbulent by the day. Change was on the horizon, and I wasn't sure I was ready for what lay ahead.

While Eric was more than willing to do Aquatic Edge clinics with me, it wasn't his dream. It was my passion, and looking back I think he went along just to keep peace in our relationship. He wanted to focus on more hands-on personal training, especially coaching triathletes. His idea of a perfect Sunday, for example, would be to take one of his clients for a 100-mile bike ride and follow that up with a swim training session in the ocean. Because the clinic side of Aquatic Edge had grown so successful, though, he wasn't able to do much of that. He barely had enough time for his own training, let alone someone else's.

In February of 2009 Eric and I were scheduled to fly to Dunkirk, France, for the French Short Course National Championships and then a European clinic tour. I had been to the UK and France on a very successful business trip two years before. Because of a loophole in the FINA Masters rulebook, in 2007 I was able to compete for Athletic Club Boulogne-Billancourt (ACBB), a French multi-sport team located in Paris. We even set a relay world record. I enjoyed the camaraderie and team spirit of ACBB (now Boulogne Billancourt Natation) so much that I represented them at FINA Masters world championships on two separate occasions. Regretfully, I don't get to see these teammates very often, but when I do, we pick up right where we left off.

As for our business, it was booming. We were offering over fifty Faster Freestyle multi-stroke or open-water clinics a year with bookings all over the world. On deck, we made a great team, and Eric was a patient, skillful teacher. Even though we were having personal problems, it didn't show in our work.

We enjoyed sharing our swimming technique with swimmers and triathletes of all ages and abilities, and we took pride in the influence we were having. As a nice reward, we were receiving emails from clients reporting they had slashed seconds off their personal bests in the pool or minutes off their triathlon swim times. Parents of age-groupers also reached out to tell us that their children had improved greatly or had developed a renewed interest in the sport. We heard from athletes with swimming-related injuries who were now pain free thanks to our instruction. All the positive feedback made us feel that what we were doing was making a real difference in people's lives.

Now it was time to hit the road, but I wasn't looking forward to the trip. There were so many things I was trying to work out, and I needed space and time to do it. Maybe Eric didn't recognize that we were speeding toward a point of no return, but I did.

The week before we were due to leave, I went to meet with Lee Ann. That's when it happened. That's the day my world tilted off its axis.

"You seem to be in a restless mood today, Karlyn," Lee Ann said.

"I'm frustrated. Eric's just not getting it. He's in complete denial about the state of our marriage. Last night he wanted to be intimate, and that's the very last thing I wanted. I wanted to talk. I turned him away and then, of course, I felt guilty about it afterward."

"I thought you wanted more intimacy in your life?"

"I do, but maybe the problem is that Eric's just not the right person to give it to me."

"Have you straight out told him that you'd like to feel more intimacy, and that by intimacy you're not simply referring to sex?" Lee Ann asked.

"Not really."

"We can't expect the men in our lives to be mind readers, can we?"

"No. I guess not."

I watched Lee Ann pour herself a glass of water. She looked at me across the room, and then asked, "Were you ever sexually abused, Karlyn?"

"What?" I said. I knew what she'd asked. It wasn't as if I hadn't heard her. But the question caught me completely off guard.

"I've been thinking about it since you first came in here," she said. "I think it's a fair question to ask. A lot of times these things are buried pretty deep, and it's not so easy to unearth them. Do you remember ever being abused when you were young?"

I gazed out the window at the blue sky and noticed the fronds of a palm tree trembling in the breeze. And then it came flooding back to me. I was eight years old. We were living in Chula Vista and my parents weren't home. I was in the living room playing some made-up game with Kerri when one of my brothers' friends came into the house unannounced. They sometimes did that, looking for the boys, so it wasn't out of the ordinary. Since neither Mark nor Derek were home, he asked us if we wanted to play a game he had made up. He called it the "tickle game," and both Kerri and I were intrigued. Looking back, I can't remember his name or even what he looked like other than that he had stringy hair and his eyes had an odd look. He was a lot older than us, and he laughed a lot. I watched as he tickled Kerri while she was on her back and she squirmed around on the carpet to get him to stop. And then he took Kerri's little legs and began to work them in a sort of breaststroke kick motion. And at first Kerri, all of seven, was giggling and laughing. She was enjoying it. And why not? She was as attention-starved as the rest of us. And then all of a sudden he pulled off her panties, unzipped his pants, and started to lean down toward her. She wasn't laughing anymore. It was all happening so fast. Too fast. She looked over at me with confusion and terror in her eyes. She was just a baby, my poor little Kerri . . .

But wait . . . no . . . that's not right . . . It wasn't Kerri. It wasn't my baby sister at all. He was bearing down on *me*. I struggled with all my might to get away, but I wasn't strong enough. I threw my head back and forth and tried to scream, but a hand went over my mouth. It was Kerri who was watching me now. Our eyes locked. She had an expression on her face as if the tears in her eyes had frozen solid, preventing her from blinking. I winced as this nameless, faceless big kid tried to force himself on me. I started hyperventilating. The pressure was so much that my eyes began to water. I just wanted to get him off me. But he was much stronger than I was. And then there was a noise out in the driveway. It was the sound of a car door being slammed shut. He shoved me away and scrambled to pull up his pants. "To be continued," he mumbled smugly. "Don't say anything. If you say a word about this to anyone, I'll hurt you." He turned his attention to Kerri. "I'll hurt both of you."

I continued to stare out the window at the azure Kona sky. Sometimes the "vog," or volcanic air pollution from Kilauea, colored everything sullen gray. But today the sky was clear. There must have been strong trade winds blowing from the north.

"Karlyn?" Lee Ann asked.

I looked over at her, oddly stoic. I didn't cry. I didn't get angry. I just sat there in silence. For some reason the revelation didn't knock me over as it could have, or as one might think it should have. It was like something I'd known all along but had chosen not to remember. Can a person consciously choose to not remember such a horrible thing, or is it all done on a subconscious level? Is it a reflex for self-preservation? How much control do we have over our thoughts and actions anyway? Was I an alcoholic because it was predetermined? My Higher Power—was he or she or it the one calling the shots? Had I been a victim of abuse because that was meant to be that way too?

I left Lee Ann's office feeling numb. The first thing I wanted to do was go for a swim. I wanted to walk over to the Kailua pier, peel off my clothes, and wade into the water. I didn't want to dwell on what I had uncovered.

I wasn't ready to acknowledge it or even think about it. Not for the time being anyway. I wanted to submerge myself and let the water wash away my fears. I also had clients who needed my help and clinics to set up, and I needed to pack. Besides, I didn't know how to process this information. So I did what I do best—I tucked it back into the box where it came from, shoved it onto the highest shelf in my mental closet, and quietly closed the door. It had been there gathering cobwebs for most of my life anyway, that secret. What could a few more days mean in the long run?

Eric and I had an all-day layover in Vancouver, Canada, on our way to Europe. It was our first time in the city. The weather was crisp, somewhere in the 50s. We strolled down along the waterfront, ending at the picturesque Stanley Park, and sat down. I wanted to broach the subject of my sexual abuse, but was having a difficult time figuring out how best to do it. This was something Eric should know. It would help him understand me, understand why I reacted to situations the way I did, and maybe shed some light on the way I'd been acting toward him. I also wanted to share the revelation with him so that the two of us could come up with a game plan on how to work through this, together. That had always been our strength, our ability to work things out as a team.

For the past few days, more memories had been coming back. At first haltingly, but then, like a swollen river, the recollections started heaving and surging. Over time, in conversations with my siblings, the full truth would come out. The abuse I'd experienced, I came to realize, wasn't an isolated incident. And sadly the truth didn't stop there. One of my brothers was molested by Mr. Cully, our swim coach in Lompoc, when he went to mow the coach's lawn. He reported what happened to our parents, but they didn't believe him. Not only that, but my brother was told to go back to Mr. Cully's house and apologize to him.

The revelation about the abuse explained so much. It was as if a huge cloud overhead had opened up and started raining down pieces of a jigsaw puzzle. As the pieces hit the ground, they bounced a few times and then magically fell into place. And as the picture began to form, I could look back and see the entire arc of my life. Now I understood it. My clinging to my blanket or seeking refuge at the pool. The two things in life that had made me feel safe. I took to the water because it offered the things I needed most—escape and acceptance. There were many missing pieces in my memories of childhood, and now I could see why. Most of all, the picture gradually taking shape explained the aching emptiness I'd always felt inside.

The insanity of it all. Mark took out his anger on Derek. Derek took it out on Mark. The boys took it out on the girls. We girls took it out on each other. We all kept it to ourselves, telling no one outside the family. We had to, because we had nowhere else to turn. From my point of view, that little tomboy knew she was alone. My father, incapacitated by his alcoholism, was impotent. My mother, working overtime to make ends meet and coping with a dysfunctional, painful marriage, was simply trying to endure. It's as if the entire family had been dropped into a well with no ladder or ledge to cling to and were reduced to struggling against one another to try to keep our heads above the surface. How long can a person tread water anyway? No wonder I'd decided to try to become more like a boy when I was little. Little girls were too vulnerable. They were too sensitive. They were targets. Little girls couldn't survive.

It seemed to me that we'd all been contaminated by this black void, my brothers and sisters and I. We all walked around with the darkness in our bellies. Mark and Derek turned to drugs and alcohol to try to fill it. Kirsten swam and earned straight A's and, when that failed, turned to God. Kerri immersed herself in the performing arts. We were all desperately searching for an escape from our shared secret hell.

Is there no end to the fallout from alcoholism? My father should have been there to protect us, but he had emotionally abandoned us long ago. My mother did her best to watch over us, but she too was in survival mode due to my father's drinking. Mark and Derek could have been protective big brothers to the rest of us, but they received minimal nurturing and compassion—again, because of my father's alcoholism—and so didn't have the capacity to offer it to others. And so on, right on down the line.

So Eric and I sat on a park bench to watch the sun go down. I felt as if I'd been staggering around for days beneath the weight of my revelation, numbly going about preparing for our trip, so it was nice to finally take a break. It was a beautiful park, filled with Douglas fir, spruce, and cedar.

"There's something I've been wanting to tell you," I said. "Something that's come up in therapy."

"Okay," Eric said, good-naturedly.

I started to tell him what Lee Ann and I had uncovered. I told him about the abuse and how, after thinking it over for a few days, I was coming to the conclusion that what had happened had colored my entire outlook on life. I had also done some research and found a website for Dr. Laura Berman that offered insight on the long-term effects of childhood sexual abuse.* When I read down the list of symptoms she provides, my mind went into overdrive. That list was describing me! Poor body image. *Check.* Feelings of guilt, shame, isolation, and low self-esteem. *Check.* Sexual confusion or promiscuity as a result of not dealing with the emotions and feelings surrounding the abuse. *Check.* Confusing rape or sexual abuse fantasies. *Check.* Eating disorders, including anorexia and bulimia. *Check.* Drug abuse and alcoholism. *Check.* Poor decision-making in relationships. *Check.* Difficulty with intimacy. *Check.* Self-destructive or even suicidal behavior. *Check.* I was floored. I scored a perfect nine out of nine. Ever the overachiever.

This information put everything in a new light, from my alcohol abuse and bulimia to my swimming successes and failures to my relationship with my mother. It explained how, at the age of almost forty-seven, I was only now beginning to understand myself. But it would take a lot longer to come to terms with the demon now unleashed.

---

* www.oprah.com/oprahshow/Long-Term-Effects-of-Sexual-Abuse

Eric didn't say anything right away. He was probably trying to digest what he'd just heard. But I didn't care about the reason at that moment—all that mattered was that his lack of instantaneous response was *not* what I was looking for. His reaction wasn't quick enough. Maybe I wanted to hear knee-jerk rage, which in hindsight wasn't a fair expectation of him when I hadn't even exhibited knee-jerk rage in Lee Ann's office myself when I was first confronted with the truth. But fair or not, I immediately slammed the mental door shut and snapped, "Never mind!" I shut down the entire line of conversation. And at that point I knew that nothing Eric could *ever* say or do was going to make a difference.

Looking back on it, I realize I blindsided Eric. I'm an extrovert, and I think out loud to solve my problems. Eric is much more introverted, and he thinks before speaking. Of course he wasn't going to respond right away. He needed time to digest my revelation. But I wanted to blame someone, be angry at someone, and by slamming that door and shutting Eric down, I could be angry at him. I was blaming him for my issues— issues I myself was only just starting to deal with—because it was easy. For the rest of the trip, nothing Eric did was right in my eyes. Once we were in Europe, I encouraged him to go on a side trip to Germany. He'd been practicing German (which of course I wasn't supporting), and he had friends he could visit there. The truth was I wanted—*needed*—to be alone. Thankfully, he got the message and left, while I stayed in France and tended to some clinics.

When we got back to the United States, we were like two strangers living in the same house. There was a wall between us, and nothing could surmount it. Eric was too scared to ask me about what we'd started to talk about in Vancouver. He wasn't bringing it up because he was waiting for me to bring it up. The entire sordid topic became untouchable, just as the subject of my father's alcoholism had been when I was growing up. Naturally, I started to simmer and grow resentful. We now owned a very large "elephant," and neither one of us was going to admit it. The lines of communication were completely shut down and broken.

CHAPTER 53

No More Stopping the Tears

O NE OF THE MANY COPING STRATEGIES of a child of an alcoholic is to ignore the elephant in the room. If you don't acknowledge the problem, then it's not there. Eric and I were doing the same thing in regard to the state of our marriage and my childhood sexual abuse. We were back to business as usual and preparing to leave for a three-week Faster Freestyle clinic tour of the East Coast that would include stops in Vermont, New Hampshire, Massachusetts, Connecticut, Maryland, North Carolina, and Washington, D.C. The start of the tour would take us to Stowe, Vermont, where we would meet up with our good friend Charlotte Brynn.

On the drive through the picturesque Green Mountains, neither of us said much. Swimming and work were now the only safe subjects for conversation. I interpreted Eric's unwillingness to talk about the "hot topic" to mean he was just not "deep enough" to understand or comprehend the pain I was experiencing. As a result I became resentful. Instead of taking into account Eric's many good qualities, I focused on the negatives and found countless reasons why our marriage was no longer working. I had already brought up the subject of divorce with Lee Ann. I explained that Eric and I weren't communicating and that the divide between us was so vast that I didn't think it could ever be bridged. When you start wrestling with the idea of a breakup, you can get overwhelmed by the logistics of it all. But "once you make the big decision," Lee Ann said, "the little details usually take care of themselves."

As Eric and I headed toward a park for a hike in the woods, I thought back to all the hikes we'd made together over the years and all the planning we'd done during them. We had plotted how I could go back to school and compete; how I could tackle this or that challenge in the pool; how we could buy a house with Mom; how we could have a family; how we could set up Aquatic Edge. They were strategy meetings, our hikes. More importantly, they were a form of bonding. They were our glue. Sadly, I knew this hike would be different. For the entirety of our relationship, we'd travelled together from one project to the next. But now our marriage had become disjointed and aimless.

The gate to the park was locked, so we moved to the edge of a lake, taking a seat on a log. We were silent for a long time, lost in thought, gazing at the shimmering water.

"Eric, where do you want to be in five years?" I finally asked as I came out of my reverie.

He proceeded to give me a pat answer that didn't reveal much of anything. It was all very neutral stuff—Hawaii, the business, his goals.

"What about you, Spider?" he asked, looking over at me. "Where do you want to be in five years?"

I'm sure he could see the sadness in my eyes. If a solar eclipse had made it completely dark outside, he would have seen it. I took a deep breath and dove into the deep end of our life.

"Eric," I stammered. "Umm, what do we have in common?" I asked instead of answering.

He opened his mouth to say something, but then quickly closed it. And he dropped his head. "Not much."

His shoulders slumped. I could feel his heart sinking. We'd turned that corner. For years, we had been swimming side by side, but now we both realized we weren't going to be doing that any longer. We had been in trouble for a long time, but neither of us had wanted to acknowledge it. Not outwardly. Now our marital problems were out in the open. And I felt his pain. We both started to cry. It had been a long time since I'd cried like that. I cried for Eric and for myself and for the hopes and dreams we shared that would never come to fruition. I cried for the little girl who hadn't been strong enough to fend off her sexual abuser. I cried for the young woman who had wanted to feel loved but felt unworthy, and I cried for the middle-aged woman who wanted to bear a child but was unable to do so. The tears flowed freely. For once, I didn't try to stop them, nor did I back away from the emotions that went with them.

Once Eric and I came to the realization that we would be separating, the conversation between us actually started to flow. Why is life a constant struggle between hope and hopelessness, between what we imagine to be true and what is true? We still hadn't openly addressed the issue of the abuse. That was locked away in the dark room I had made for it. It was something I'd have to work through by myself.

"You can still have kids with someone else," I said later for some reason.

"I don't know if I want to have kids anymore," he said.

"I'm sorry, Eric. There are so many things I'm sorry about."

"Me too," he said. "I'm sorry I couldn't do better. If someone had asked me what the greatest success of my life had been, I would have said our marriage. And now, if someone were to ask about my greatest failure, I'd say our marriage."

We were quiet again for a long while.

"Just so we're clear on this, Karlyn, I love you. I've never stopped loving you. Despite how rough it's been for us the last several months."

"I know," I said. "Thank you for that."

"And if I'm still coaching somewhere down the line—you know, if I'm on deck and you're with someone else or you've remarried or whatever—you can still come to my workouts. Don't ever think that you can't."

That gesture might have seemed small, but it was enormous to me. My eyes began to well up all over again.

CHAPTER **54**

The Island Whispers Truth
to Your Heart

T HERE'S A POINT IN EVERY RACE when you're faced with a moment of truth. The horn sounds, you dive into the water, and you begin swimming across the first length of the pool. You quickly settle into a rhythm. Your primary concern is to stay relaxed, because the best swimming always happens when you're stress free. At first the effort is easy and natural. Everything is flowing in perfect synchronization—each breath, each stroke, each kick. When things are going exceptionally well like that, you're riding so high in the water that you're convinced you can reach up and touch the fluttering backstroke flags overhead.

It doesn't last forever. You know from experience that the sensation of perfection is fleeting. Eventually you begin to tire. Your breathing becomes labored and your limbs start to feel heavy as lactic acid floods your muscles. This is when you're confronted with the moment, both physically and mentally: *What exactly are you made of today?* Backing away from the discomfort would offer immediate relief from the pain, true. But then what? *Can you live with yourself knowing that you didn't give it your very best?* Ultimately, that's what it boils down to—pushing as hard as you can for as long as you can. Triumph and vindication and peace of mind come only to those who can learn to embrace the discomfort and get through it.

Even though we had our fair share of setbacks and challenges, I wouldn't trade my marriage to Eric for anything in the world. He was what newly sober Karlyn needed. He believed in me when I didn't believe in myself. He bolstered my confidence. He supported me. He loved me completely and unconditionally, even when I didn't believe I merited that kind of love. I couldn't have asked for a more amazing life partner and husband, and I loved him more than I've ever loved anyone. But at the end of the day, I couldn't break down the walls I had built up so long ago. The little girl in me was terrified of being vulnerable, and I wasn't yet at a place in my life where I was capable of moving past that.

After he moved out, Eric still came by the house. He'd still take the trash to the dump. He'd still take care of the Endless Pool. He'd still coach Mom and me on Tuesdays. He continued to do so many of those little, everyday things. The difference was that he didn't live with us anymore. What an amazing, strong man he was, to be able to give that.

Before we separated, I picked fights and worked hard to get him to not like me. I wanted him to see how mean and ugly I was so he would stop loving me. Unconsciously, I wanted *him* to be the one to leave *me*. But it didn't work. Day in and day out, Eric just loved me more, and it completely baffled me. It also made me feel guilty. I clearly did not know what "real" love felt like or even looked like, nor did I know how to reciprocate. I grew up believing that love was conditional. It had strings attached to it and you had to earn it, like a grade in school or a medal at a swim meet. *I love you when . . . I love you because . . .* Never just *I love you for who you are.*

Many survivors of addiction live with the inability to accept love on love's terms. If he would just hate me, I reasoned, then maybe I could feel a little better about myself. There would be no reason to feel guilty and no need to be worried about someone else's happiness. But Eric didn't buy into my plan. No matter how rough it was between us during our marriage or how hurt he was feeling, every day he woke up and tried to love me even more.

Competing under the name "Karlyn Pipes" again after my divorce was a strange sensation. Whenever I had competed as "Karlyn Pipes-Neilsen," I felt as if every time I touched the wall and logged a result, Eric was getting well-deserved credit too. Seeing both our names in print was a comforting reminder of the team we'd created together.

Now, though, I was right back to where I had been. Karlyn Pipes was the young age-grouper who'd joined with her teammates at CVAA to break a 9–10 relay record. She was the person who'd won Junior Nationals, swum at University of Arkansas, and broken her first Masters world record at the age of twenty-five. She was scrappy, with a chip on her shoulder the size of Manhattan. She was determined to prove herself to you, and the world, in hopes that you would like her.

But that wasn't me any longer. This new version of Karlyn Pipes was something the world had never seen. I was different because, for the first time in my life, I was gaining comfort with *who I was*. And that comfort wasn't based on *what I did*. I was learning to be authentic. My do-over had turned a corner. I was slowing down long enough for the turbulent waters of my life to calm down, and for the first time I got a glimpse of my true self reflected back to me. And what the surface revealed was someone quite likable.

There's an energy on the island of Hawaii that is distinctly female. In Hawaiian mythology, Madame Pele, the goddess of the volcanoes and creator of the Hawaiian Islands, gives birth to new land every day. Madame Pele possesses a strong spiritual energy, giving her the power to encourage you or to crush you, depending on your attitude toward her. You have a choice. You can choose either to ignore her message and continue in the direction you've been traveling, or you can pause, listen to her wisdom, and seek your true path. If you are in a relationship that is not moving you or your spirit along your path, the Big Island whispers truth to your heart, telling you that perhaps it's time to move on.

Our divorce was difficult on Mom. The three of us had been living together as a family for a decade. Our togetherness had no doubt helped her get over the loss of Lloyd. It had created stability for all three of us. Mom truly loved Eric, and he loved her. Not all men would say that about their mothers-in-law, let alone happily share a home with them for long. As hard as it was for her, though, I think deep down she understood the breakup more than anyone. She herself had made the bold move to divorce Dad in her own quest to lead a more fulfilling life. Now she could see that I was standing on the same staircase she had stood on so long ago. The stairs offer to take you closer to your goal, to your next destination, to a higher place. But forward progress can happen only when you take a leap of faith and relinquish the stair you are standing on. If you don't move, you remain stuck. I was interested in getting unstuck, even if it meant a difficult conversation needed to take place.

Discussing the sexual abuse with Mom was one of the hardest things I've ever had to do. She remembered my brother's accusation about his coach, but not much else. Without using it as an excuse, she reminded me that it was a very different world back then. Adults held all the authority, and it was often assumed that kids made up stories to get attention. In addition, her generation was raised with a "don't ask, don't tell" mindset. If no one said anything, the situation would go away.

I didn't bring up the subject with an intention to make her feel bad. However painful it was, it needed to be discussed so we could both move forward. Little Karlyn might still have a hard time coming to grips with her childhood experiences, but adult Karlyn understood that her mom had done the very best she could in the situation. "You have no idea how horrible I feel that I wasn't there to prevent what happened to you," she told me. "I'm going to have to live with that for the rest of my life. And with your dad being drunk all the time and my being so overwhelmed with managing everything else, sometimes I couldn't even see straight."

"I don't know if I've ever told you this before, Mom, but thank you for leaving him and for taking us with you," I said.

"Clearly I didn't leave soon enough," she said. "I'm so sorry."

"But you *did* leave. That took strength, courage, and a huge leap of faith. That's the important thing," I said, giving her a big hug.

"I'm not sure that I really had a choice," she said after she wiggled out of my strong grip. "I only wish I could have done more to help the boys."

When I finally began to mourn, it was like opening the floodgates. I needed to mourn the end of my marriage, yes. But there was so much more than that. I went for long walks by myself late at night and wept for my brothers' and sisters' lost innocence. I sobbed over my failed relationships, because now I understood why they'd been destined to fail. I cried about all the people I'd hurt during my lost years, because no matter what was compelling me to act the way I did, none of them deserved to be treated the way I had treated them. I wept hardest thinking of the hopes and dreams Eric and I had shared disappearing into thin air. And just when I thought my tears had dried up, I'd think about that little girl who just wanted to be loved but felt she didn't deserve it, and my eyes would well up again.

Between an alcoholic father and sexual abuse, my life was built on a shaky foundation. Deep down inside I felt I was insignificant and unworthy, and I had spent decades trying to prove otherwise. I hadn't felt I could trust anyone to help or protect me, so I had learned to cover up the hurt and do it all myself. The abuse, in particular, revealed so much about what made me tick. It was the root of the deep-seated shame I had felt when I was younger and of the feeling that I was an outsider and didn't belong. It was the catalyst of my self-destructive years. Alcohol and drugs were what I chose to numb that pain. And my eating disorder offered a sense of control over the ugliness I felt inside. If I was thin, people would like me. They'd think I was pretty. They would want to be near me. Pretty was power. Just as with swimming—if I swam fast, if I won, people would like me. Part of me wanted the attention, but another part didn't, because I didn't feel worthy. From the time I was abused to the time I acknowledged the abuse, my life was a constant struggle of discontent and self-rejection.

It took me a long time to work this through, but I finally realized that none of it—the drinking, the eating disorder, the addiction to swimming, the drive to be better than anyone else—was the problem. They were just symptoms of my illness. They masked the pain, but they never cured the cause. It was the lies I told myself that made me sick. And stuck. In order for me to find a new way, in order for me to live authentically, I had to take an aggressive approach and uncover my core wound. I had to let go of the lie that I was undeserving of love. Not only that, but I had to believe that I was indeed lovable, loving, and loved. Only then could true healing begin.

What do you do when you wake up one day and realize that your entire life has been an illusion? No one knew who I was, because I didn't know myself. *The spiritual path holds promise of a better future.* But aren't we, as individuals, the result of all of our experiences, good and bad? And isn't the swimming I do today, for instance, the culmination of a lifetime devoted to the sport? If that's the case, how is it possible to rewrite the script?

Thankfully, the revelations about my abuse didn't cause me to beat a hasty retreat to the bottle. That part of my life, one day at a time and God willing, was over. While the compulsion to drink had thankfully been removed a long time ago, I was acutely aware that my recovery from the aftermath was going to take a lifetime.

I had learned so much in all my years of sobriety, but one lesson became foremost in my thoughts: life is what you make of it. Some days, when you're in open water, the conditions can be extremely challenging. Waves and chop can obscure your view, and the current can be so strong it's difficult to make forward progress. Fighting back or wishing for something different doesn't do any good. Instead, it's a great time to try to relax and practice letting go. You can't control the ocean, but you can control the way you *feel* about it and accept the situation for what it is. This is when you have the opportunity to discover the beauty and grace in *any* experience. And so it is with life. My good friend Dave Dwan once said, "Karlyn, stop pushing so hard and learn to let life unfold."

CHAPTER 55

It's a Break, Not a Breakup

A FTER OUR DIVORCE, ERIC STAYED in Hawaii for another two years. We gave each other plenty of space, which wasn't easy to do on the island. As I continued to work the Program, I began to see Eric in a new light. For most of our marriage, I had been the one dictating the action. That's a common personality trait of alcoholics, the need to control others. And for a long time, I had assumed that Eric went along with "Karlyn's way or the highway" because he lacked the strength to get his own way. In reality, it was precisely his strength that allowed him to give me my way, keeping us together and moving forward. He was resolute in his love for me, and few people could have possessed the confidence and ability he exhibited to maintain the peace in our relationship.

I was finally on a path of self-discovery. As part of the process, I decided to take a rear-view look at our marriage. When a revelation about our relationship bubbled to the surface, I'd call Eric and say, "Why don't you pick me up and we'll go to lunch?" He was always good-natured about it. "If I know you, Spider, you have something you want to talk about." Only Eric would have had that kind of patience, especially after I'd broken his heart, and only Eric could resist the urge to put me in my place, as I no doubt deserved.

Happily, Eric too began to flourish after our divorce. He competed in the Honu Ironman 70.3 Hawaii, a half-Ironman staged in the spring. Not only was he the first male from the Big Island to cross the finish line, he also placed in the top twenty overall against all the professionals. I was so proud of him. While he seemed on the surface to be doing well, I could tell he was growing restless on the island. Soon he embarked on his own personal quest of self-discovery, flying to Europe to spend three months biking that continent's great peaks. On his return, I could tell his time in Hawaii was limited. He eventually moved to Fort Collins, then Loveland, Colorado, where he established Train Smart . . . Race Fast, which is now a successful triathlon coaching and training business. After years of hiatus, he is back on deck coaching Masters swimming. I still believe he is one of the best coaches in the sport, and I refer my clients to him whenever possible. In 2014 I hired Eric to coach me for the Santa Rosa Half-Marathon in California. It was only my second time running this distance, but thanks to his coaching I posted a respectable 1:38 and placed third in the 50–54 age group. When it comes to athletic performance, his is the voice I trust the most.

Just five months after the divorce, in spring of 2010, I embarked on yet another huge East Coast tour. The trip had an aggressive schedule, with a whopping seventeen clinics in twenty-one days. The reward for all that hard work was twofold: I was going to stay with my best friend, Laurie Miller Voke, who lived near Boston, and I would finally have the opportunity to compete at the annual New England Masters Championships, a three-day short course yards meet held at Harvard University. I'd always been interested in that meet, especially since swimmers up and down the Eastern Seaboard make a point of participating in it, but the scheduling had not worked out for me before.

I had just turned forty-eight, and I showed up at Blodgett Pool with the intention of swimming fast. On Friday I swam a respectable 59.20 in the 100-yard backstroke, half a second faster than my teenage time.

I also competed in the 200 fly and the 100 IM, posting the fastest time overall for women of any age. The meet director made a big deal of my presence and a lot of swimmers approached me to offer congratulations, but inside I was aghast at my times. True, there had been a lot happening in my life, but in the past I'd always been able to separate personal distractions from competition. This time, though, something was different. It wasn't so much a lack of focus as a lack of motivation. Even though I was at this big, highly energized competition surrounded by over a thousand enthusiastic Masters swimmers, I felt utterly flat.

I woke up the next morning still feeling uninspired, so I called in sick. Instead of going to the meet, I hit the streets of Boston for some sightseeing. I felt guilty pleasure, like I was ditching school again. It was a beautiful day, and I enjoyed myself immensely. I found it refreshing to see something on a trip other than the inside of a natatorium. On Sunday, I still wasn't feeling it, but I knew I needed to get back to work. I gave myself a quick pep talk, packed my bag, and drove to the Harvard pool. Everyone wanted to know what had happened to me the day before, and I told them I hadn't been feeling well. I had a few low-key, fun races on tap that day—the 100 fly, the 50 back, and the 100 free. Those were events I always enjoyed because they were short and sweet and fun. But when I got into the warm-up pool to prep for my first race, I still felt unmotivated. I stopped at the wall and just hung there for a while, taking in the atmosphere. Acknowledging that my heart just wasn't in it and that no amount of self-talk was going to change that, I lifted myself out of the pool, walked over to the clerk of course, and scratched all my events.

For the rest of the day, I sat in the stands as a spectator. I saw swimmers in all shapes and sizes and from all walks of life get up on the blocks. From the first heat to the last, it seemed that every person was giving his or her best. That did not necessarily mean they *were* the best, but no one seemed to mind. Everyone looked as if they were having fun and enjoying the camaraderie of Masters swimming, even if the clock showed a slower time than hoped for or if a medal was lost. I saw that it wasn't all about winning: it was about suiting up and giving it your all. And maybe the result wasn't what had been hoped for, but in the end, did it really matter? After all, it was *just* a swim meet.

I went back to Laurie's house feeling, once again, as if my world had shifted.

"I'm not sure if I want to race anymore," I said to Laurie. "And that scares me."

"Why would that scare you, Karlyn?" she asked. "You're one of the most courageous people I know."

"I feel as if I've lost touch with myself," I explained. "I mean, who am I if I'm not racing or breaking records? I think I am afraid to let that go."

Laurie took a hard look at me, straightened up, and gave me one of those smiles I have come to know and love.

"Now you listen up. That is a limiting belief," she said with conviction. "The Karlyn I know is capable of so much more. She is a wonderful, giving, and loving human being, and the rest of the world already knows this. She just needs to believe it herself."

Both Laurie and I knew it was time for some soul-searching about my swimming career. It dawned on me that my passion for the sport had diminished. I was simply going through the motions. I was racing because racing was what I did. I had pushed through meet after meet, season after season, nonstop, for over seventeen years. I competed through my father's death, Lloyd's death, my miscarriages, and the breakup of my marriage. It had helped me to cope, the racing. It had helped give my life routine and purpose. It had also brought me accolades and acclaim I never imagined possible. I'd broken over two hundred Masters world records—so many, in fact, that I couldn't remember the details of the majority of them. At what point, I began to wonder, is enough enough?

If I stopped racing, would it all go away? Everything? Outside the pool I was achieving a nice measure of success. I was being asked to give inspirational talks to groups large and small all over the world. I was a two-time presenter at the American Swim Coaches Association (ASCA) World Clinic. My Aquatic Edge Faster Freestyle clinics were fully booked. At home in Kona, I now charged $150 an hour for private sessions in my Endless Pool. The column I wrote for *Swimming World* magazine, "The Pool's Edge," was well received. Sales of the two stroke technique DVDs I had collaborated on with Glenn Mills and Barbara Hummel from GoSwim were going strong.

In addition, my presence on the web expanded greatly after I filmed a series of instructional videos for VASA Trainer, a swimming ergometer that can be used instead of training in a regular pool and helps to add power to a swimming stroke. Some of the VASA Trainer videos have over a million hits. If I searched for my name online, more than 40,000 pages would come up. It boggled my mind.

In the pool, the praise I received boosted my self-confidence and I felt popular, accepted, and appreciated. How was I ever going to give that all up? If I stopped breaking records, would I be forgotten? While it was difficult to imagine separating myself from this very public persona, I knew it was what I had to do. For personal growth and understanding, something had to change. I needed to change.

As I sat in Laurie's kitchen, I gazed down at my busy upcoming race schedule and wondered what it would be like if I simply shook it, like a big Etch A Sketch, and made it all disappear. The year before I'd still been busting it out, setting a total of fifteen world records. But the pace had suddenly become draining. I concluded I needed to take a timeout. And when I finally gave myself permission to step off the blocks, I felt an overwhelming sensation of *freedom*. It was so liberating, in fact, that I wrote a Pool's Edge column about my decision entitled "It's a Break, Not a Breakup."*

It was time to figure out just who the heck I was when I wasn't racing. I would still train. I've always adored that part of my sport and I'm sure

---

* December 2010.

I always will. But it was a tremendous relief that, for the first time in a very long time, I did not have a single goal or championship meet on the horizon. I knew it would take some effort, but I was going to learn how to be comfortable just being myself. And who was that person, anyway? *Well,* I thought, *maybe it's time to find out.*

When I got back to Kona, I resumed swimming with Coach Harry and the kids, but now I didn't concern myself with how fast or even how far I was going. I also did a lot of ocean swimming with my good friend Aimée Kolman and pro triathlete Bree Wee. I took up yoga, went to spin classes, and even tried my hand at belly dancing. What I discovered during my hiatus was that I still really, *really* enjoyed swimming and, surprisingly, I was actually in the water more frequently than before. But my motivation was completely different. I was doing it for fun. I was swimming for me, not for the clock. It was a welcome revelation.

This fresh desire to examine my life coincided with a renewed interest in the Program. For the first time, I began to keep a journal. It's amazing what you learn about yourself when you start to capture your thoughts on paper. Back when I was an age-grouper in my first swimming career, Troy had suggested we each keep a training journal. He wanted us to keep track not just of our workouts and races, but also of how we were feeling. He explained that logbooks were invaluable for gaining insight into what's worked and not worked in the past and for charting future courses of action. We were teenagers and of course complained that we didn't have time to do anything more than what he was already asking of us in the pool. I flat out refused to comply, with the exception of the summer of 1976. A few years ago I uncovered that partially filled spiral notebook, and I am grateful I have it. It provides me a glimpse of fourteen-year-old Karlyn: my hopes and dreams, my times, what I was thinking, and even who I had a crush on. It's a precious snapshot of my life one year before I had my first drink.

As part of the research for her book *Authentic Grit*, life coach Caroline Adams Miller sat down with me for an interview. As I told her my story, she looked at me and declared, "Karlyn, it was alcohol that dissolved your grit." What was so clear to Caroline was a revelation to me. The more I thought about it, the more I realized the truth in her statement. Before alcohol was introduced, I possessed an inordinate amount of determination. Every time I switched teams, I would start at the bottom and willingly work hard to rise to the top. But at the age of fifteen, that all changed.

I'm gritty now, I thought, *so when did it come back? Day Two in rehab, when I was a squashed bug in the gutter looking up. When the need for alcohol was replaced by a glimmer of hope for a better future.* That was when it returned.

Back in 1993, at the onset of the do-over, I finally began regularly keeping that swimming journal, as Troy had suggested years before. I methodically recorded every workout, every set, and even the times I did for each repeat. I logged every yard or meter I swam. As the information in the journals swelled over the years, Eric and I often referred to them to give my training both purpose and direction. I found it curious that I'd suddenly stopped keeping a swimming journal when Eric and I began to struggle with our marriage.

Now I had decided to spend my time and energy on a different journal. At first it was difficult to start writing, especially when it concerned my deep and often dark feelings, but I knew it was necessary. Once I began keeping a recovery journal, one thing became painfully obvious: my obsession with swimming had stalled the personal and spiritual growth aspects of my recovery. In fact, most of what I'd been doing over the last several years now looked like pure avoidance. While my swimming had advanced to a point comparable to a PhD in academics, my emotional recovery in sobriety was that of a kindergartener. But that was about to change.

I began by seeking out a new sponsor. It'd been a long time since I had had someone to hold me accountable. Amanda, one of the most open, honest, and selfless women I've ever met, didn't know a thing about competitive swimming. And that was precisely the point. She didn't need to know a swimming pool from a soccer field to understand that I was entering a new phase in my life. She encouraged me to resume working on my steps, and she volunteered to help in any way she could.

I knew the first hurdle was to come to terms with the Third Step: to have *made a decision to turn our will and our lives over to the care of God as we understood him.* This is where I had become stuck. Since I hadn't had a meaningful relationship with my father, it was hard to comprehend a caring, loving heavenly Father. Deep down I also felt that I was so damaged that I wasn't worthy of love from anyone, let alone God. But Amanda pointed out that I was just the kind of person that God was quite fond of. She suggested that all I needed to do was make a *decision* to give my recovery to a higher power, one of my own understanding. Furthermore, I didn't have to buy into any religion or one-size-fits-all belief system. When I reflected on how I was doing with finding peace and sanity in my life, I realized I was failing miserably. Maybe if I could just let go of my need for control, then God would have the space and freedom to be a better friend, mentor, and coach to me. When I thought about my spiritual recovery in this manner, I finally opened up my heart and decided to give God a try.

While seeking a relationship with a higher power, I also became a voracious reader of self-help books. Matthew Kelly's *The Seven Levels of Intimacy* and Charlotte Kasl's *If the Buddha Dated* had a huge impact on me. I also thoroughly enjoyed *The Soulmate Experience* by Mali Apple and Joe Dunn. Then I discovered Gary Chapman's *The 5 Love Languages,* which led to Melody Beattie's *More Language of Letting Go.* I began to embrace the ideas put forth in books such as Al-Anon's *Courage to Change* and *From Survival to Recovery.* I was desperate for answers and starving for enlightenment, and it seemed I was in the perfect place, mentally and physically, to finally go after both.

The Fourth Step involves getting your butt in a chair and putting pen to paper. Performing a "fearless moral inventory" calls on you to go back to your earliest memories and write a detailed list, in chronological order, of every instance in your life when you experienced some type of discord or resentment, what you did as a result, and how your actions affected you and those around you. It means taking a good hard look at every situation, whether it was with family members, friends, teachers, coaches, coworkers, or anyone else with whom you had interaction, and exploring what the true underlying issues were.

Take my former boss, Steve Lindsey. All these years later, I was still ticked off about the way things ended between us, and I needed to work through exactly why.

Why is he on your inventory?

Because he fired me and at the time it really upset me.

How did Lindsey's letting you go hurt you?

It bruised my ego. It was a financial hit too, because I really needed the income.

Okay, but why do you think he felt compelled to do what he did?

Well, if I want to be perfectly honest with myself, it's probably because I stole from him, drank on the job, didn't show up for work, and took advantage of his kindness and generosity.

So why, then, are you still harboring a resentment toward him for things you did?

And that last question, when I examined it, led to silence. The harsh realization was that I had no one to blame but myself for what had happened with Lindsey. It was the same with just about everyone else on my list. I knew that if I wanted to move forward with my sobriety, I had to take ownership of my past.

Tackling the Fourth Step means taking a good hard look at the "bugs under the rug." We all have rugs in our homes. They offer warmth and comfort underfoot. They are chosen to coordinate with our lifestyle and personal taste. With time, they become so much a part of a room's land-scape that we tend to forget they're there. But that's precisely when and why the problems start. Once we take for granted that a rug is in place, it's only natural to begin to lose sight of what's beneath it. We sweep around it, rarely lifting it to clean. And so we miss things on the under-side. Mold. Mildew. Hidden bugs eating away at it. The floor underneath could be rotting for all we know. Until we actually look under there, we don't know. And that's what the Fourth Step does: it helps you to exam-ine the bugs under your personal rug in the hope that once you discover them, you can liberate yourself from the guilt and shame associated with them and move toward a lighter and brighter future.

Here's the catch to the Program's Fourth Step: it's not enough to simply compile a detailed moral inventory and acknowledge how your shortcomings played a hand in the large haul of anger and resentment you're toting around. The Fifth Step suggests that you share the contents of your inventory and the exact nature of your wrongs with another per-son. At this point you might be thinking, *Whoa. Is that really necessary?* I thought the same thing. It was one thing to write everything down. The prospect of divulging those secrets to someone I knew—well, that was utterly terrifying. No wonder it had taken me so long to have the guts to even make an effort.

But I knew it needed to be done in order to begin to clear the wreck-age of my past. The darkest parts of my life needed to be brought into the light so they couldn't hinder or hurt me any longer. I had heard more than once that out of the Twelve Steps, Steps Four and Five have the greatest power to be cathartic and life changing. More importantly, I was assured that they would help me move forward with my recovery. At this point I had become so uncomfortable with how my life had been—or had not been—progressing that I was willing to go to any lengths to feel better. Even if it meant facing a lot of unpleasantness first.

As I sat with Amanda and carefully went through my list, line by line and page by page, I ran a gamut of emotions. At first I felt ashamed. I was embarrassed by some of the stunts I'd pulled over the course of my life. Then I felt guilt. There were so many people I'd hurt along the way. Then I felt sad, especially at some of the memories I unearthed. Next I felt frightened. I was divulging things in my life that I'd never before shared with another human being, not even Eric or Mom. It was a full-on confession, and I was afraid that by making myself so vulnerable, I would be opening myself up to scrutiny and criticism. Amanda might never again want to associate herself with someone who was as devious, as self-centered, as manipulative, and, well, as *sick* as me.

At one point I paused in my reading and apprehensively looked up into Amanda's eyes. All I saw there was tenderness and empathy. That support gave me courage. And inspiration. And even more determination. It took me nearly six hours to read through my inventory. Amanda didn't say much. Every so often she would ask for clarification or tell me to note a certain situation with a reference in the side bar to a behavior pattern starting to emerge. Special treatment, self-righteousness, and playing the victim dominated the margins of my paper.

As I finally turned the last page, I let out a deep breath. And paused. My bugs were out in the open. My secrets were exposed. And I had not been struck by lightning. I felt an overwhelming sense of relief and, unexpectedly, exhilaration.

"Thank you for sharing that with me," Amanda said.

"Thank you for listening."

"You'll need to make amends to some of the people you've hurt, Karlyn," Amanda said.

"I know."

"It won't be easy."

"Nothing about this step has been easy, but it was worth it," I said, gathering up all the pages. "So now that I'm done, what should I do with this list?"

"A lot of people put a match to theirs," she said.

"As in, actually burn it?"

"If that's too dramatic for you, just throw it away," she said with a smile. "The point of this exercise isn't to demonize you or to memorialize your bad behavior. It's to acknowledge it and to put all those things behind you once and for all. It's time to move forward, Karlyn."

"I-I know," I said. "I'd like that. I'd like that more than anything."

As Amanda rose to her feet to offer me a warm embrace, exhaustion set in. About the only thing I could manage was a smile. It was as if I were fifteen again and I'd just successfully completed the toughest of Troy's main sets. My body, still percolating with what little adrenaline it had left, knew it was okay to finally ease off. That's when the heart rate goes down, the breathing settles, and all of your previously heightened senses begin to fall back to normal. As I began to relax, pleased with the effort I'd put forth, I could feel every cell in my body begin to slowly let go. *Attagirl,* I thought to myself. *Attagirl!*

I had done it. At long last, I had done it. I'd accomplished my Fourth and Fifth Steps, and I was eager to continue the journey.

CHAPTER 56

What Good Was Enlightenment with No One to Share It With?

T HE FURTHER I PROGRESSED ALONG my Twelve Steps, the better I began to feel. Over the course of the next year and a half, many of the axioms I'd heard time and again in the Program began to truly resonate with me. "Let go and let God" became my favorite. The more I released my tight grip on life, the more I began to actually experience it. "We are only as sick as our secrets." Becoming more truthful and open, I found, was key to unlocking self-acceptance and fulfillment. "Practice an attitude of gratitude." I looked for the good in every situation, no matter how challenging. "You will be amazed before you are halfway through," the Promises said, and I *was* amazed. There was a new, more carefree Karlyn emerging who wasn't so domineering or controlling. She was more sensitive to other people's needs and opinions. She was as feisty, competitive, and energetic as ever, but now she was finding it easier to let things go and let life unfold.

The extermination of the bugs under my rug also meant taking a time-out from romantic relationships. It occurred to me that ever since I'd met my first boyfriend, Matt, I'd always had a man in my life. Part of that, I think, was to give me validation and help combat the low self-esteem I'd developed in childhood. I had been divorced and single now for almost two years, and much of the progress I was making in my recovery was because I had allowed myself the time and space to heal. During this time I became much more comfortable with myself and learned to enjoy being alone. Much to my surprise, I realized that I truly liked my own company.

At times I would still catch myself falling into old habits and patterns, especially when it came to swimming. After all, I had spent a long time employing these strategies, and they had become second nature. Case in point was my reaction in June of 2011 when I found out that I had lost my world record in the 400-meter freestyle for the 35–39 age group. I felt a sense of loss, and my ego took a hit. Never mind that I was now almost ten years older and my life was on a completely different path. I still felt crummy about it—until I found out who broke it. It was none other than legendary distance swimmer Janet Evans, who was attempting a comeback for the 2012 Olympic Games. *Wow,* I thought to myself, *that's actually pretty cool!* Not only that, but when I looked at her time, she had broken my record by only a little over two seconds. I visualized us racing in the same pool: me, trailing the great Janet Evans by only a body length. Just the thought of it made me grin. Now instead of feeling the loss of a record, I rejoiced in both of our accomplishments. How things had changed.

In August of 2011 I stumbled across a free twenty-one-day meditation challenge being offered online by Deepak Chopra. I'd never meditated before, even though the Eleventh Step suggests that we seek "through prayer and meditation to improve our conscious contact with God." I was more than willing to give it a try.

The theme of the challenge was "Free to Love," and every morning I woke up to a new meditation in my in-box. Each week the focus would change: we worked on forgiveness and letting go of pain, awakening creativity, and finally opening up the pathway to meaningful love. It was inspiring to imagine thousands of people around the world meditating on the exact same subject each day. As I worked my way through the three weeks, I came to the realization that what I wanted most of all was someone in my life who could take this journey with me. What good was enlightenment if you didn't have someone to share it with?

Every October, the Ironman World Championships roll into Kona like a huge Barnum & Bailey production. Ironman was created back in 1978, almost as a dare, when fifteen participants slugged it out swimming, biking, and running for hours on end to see who was the better athlete. The event quickly evolved into a multi-million-dollar enterprise that today stages dozens of sold-out races around the world. It seems as if every long-distance triathlete's dream is to compete in Kona.

One week before race day, there was an open-water event called the Kukio Blue Water Swim held just north of Kona. Since moving to Hawaii, the Blue Water had become one of my favorite races. The 1.2-mile course is stunning, the race is well organized, and proceeds go to a local charity. A delicious catered brunch and icy cold Kona Brew, for those who choose to imbibe, awaits everyone at the finish line.

Almost as soon as the gun went off in the 2011 race, I began to feel someone's fingertips touching the bottom of my feet. Drafting is commonplace in open-water swimming, so I didn't think much of it. Generally, if you're swimming too close behind the swimmer in front of you, the unspoken rule is to back off a few inches to avoid hitting that person's feet. It's common courtesy. But whoever had decided to hitch a ride with me seemed more than happy to continue whacking my toes and, for some reason, it didn't annoy me.

Halfway through the race, I was in no-man's-land. I'd already been dropped from the lead pack, and the fastest local teenage girl, Madison, had blown past me as if she were late for a school dance. There was not a person in sight, and I was being forced to do extra work pulling along whomever it was who'd become obsessed with the bottom of my feet. Thankfully, a strong young swimmer appeared out of nowhere and confidently cruised past me. I had no idea how someone so fast had ended up so far behind the leaders, but I wasn't about to miss my opportunity. I accelerated enough to slide into his slipstream and then hung on to his draft for dear life. In no time at all, our little three-person pack was moving so quickly that we caught up to Madison and passed her. That meant I was now the lead female. Given the fact that I was still approaching my training with a no-pressure "doing it for fun" attitude, I was surprised to be performing so well in such a fast field of competitors. Now all I needed was a strong finish to seal the deal.

When we came around the last buoy in the final sprint toward home, the guy who'd attached himself to me like a remora pulled up alongside me. We hit the rocky beach at exactly same time. We both stood up and took a few steps side by side. I took a misstep and lost my balance. Much to my surprise, my drafter reached out and steadied my arm so I wouldn't fall. He then proceeded to allow me to sprint up the steep, uneven beach to the finish line ahead of him. Once we crossed the line, we exchanged a smile.

Later, under the spray of the portable showers, I looked over at him. He was really cute, with beautiful eyes that matched the color of the ocean.

"It's a good thing you didn't run up the beach faster than me," I said chidingly.

"Now why would I do that?" he said. "You gave me such a great draft. My name's Brian."

"I'm Karlyn."

"Thanks for the ride, Karlyn. Maybe someday I can return the favor."

As we exchanged another smile, I was attracted to both his looks and his sincerity. I had recently heard in one of my meditations, "There are no coincidences."

I invited Brian to go for an easy swim with me to loosen up after our hard effort. As we swam, I couldn't help but notice how crappy, frankly, his technique was. It was really all over the place and so inefficient that I was having a difficult time figuring out how he'd managed to keep pace with me in the first place. Afterward I invited him to sit at my table for the awards ceremony. As first female, I won a huge haul. It was a nice ego boost. At forty-nine, I knew a top finish like this was probably my last.

Brian and I chatted over brunch and I learned that he was, as I had guessed, in town to compete in the upcoming Ironman. He was single, lived in Northern California, and had partial custody of a teenage daughter. We hung out for most of the day and enjoyed each other's company so much that we set up a casual lunch date for a few days later. We ended up spending a lot of time together that week, and I had a chance to meet his parents and daughter, who had all flown in to watch him race. Brian and I even took part in the annual Underpants Run, a silly Ironman tradition begun as a parody of the European athletes who visit the island and immodestly parade all over town in next to nothing. In the early years of the jaunt, only a few brave souls would show up sporting skivvies and huge grins as they loped down Ali'i Drive. Over time, though, it's become a comedic romp with thousands of athletes flaunting their well-toned bodies in a wide variety of skimpy, colorful, and often group-coordinated underwear.

I couldn't believe how well Brian and I seemed to mesh and how easily we could talk, even about difficult subjects. I was honest with him about my past, my struggles, and about my life growing up as the child of an alcoholic. Brian shared with me that he too had been exposed to the negative effects of alcoholism and suggested we attend an Al-Anon meeting together. So, for our second official date, that's what we did. Al-Anon, a offshoot of the Program, is a support group geared toward those who have been affected by alcoholism but are not necessarily alcoholics themselves.

As I sat through the meeting, I realized that my background allowed me to listen to the messages being shared through three different sets of ears—those of an adult child of an alcoholic parent, those of a recovering alcoholic, and those of someone whose own behavior, I was discovering, was still addictive in nature. I looked around the room and listened to the inspiring stories of those trying to cope in alcoholic relationships or households, and it dawned on me how much my behavior must have hurt, or perhaps even damaged, Eric. It made me wonder why the Program didn't include a suggestion that recovering alcoholics would benefit from attending an Al-Anon meeting. I learned so much.

The week leading up to an Ironman competition is all about resting your body and trying to keep your mind off the grueling task ahead. I proved to be the perfect distraction for Brian, and I could tell we were both feeling the same spark. He even nicknamed me his "island girl." Brian was smart, playful, and self-assured, and we went on some memorable training swims in the ocean. As we stroked together, side by side, I remembered yet another of the Program's sayings: "Expect miracles." I was ready for a miracle. I was two years post-divorce, ready and eager to find love, and Brian had quite literally swum straight into my life.

Brian had his best Ironman performance ever and after the race indicated that he wanted to include me in his future plans. We decided to celebrate by visiting Maui for some R & R. He seemed to be shaping up to be the perfect boyfriend. He was attentive, affectionate, athletic, and fun to be with. We went for more scenic swims, low-key runs, and even tried our hand at surfing. Most importantly, we talked—*really* talked. The type of heart-to-heart, spiritual conversations I had been yearning for. The two of us shared our hopes and dreams and even felt comfortable enough to share some of our deepest, darkest secrets. I told him all about my father. I also told him about the challenges I'd overcome to reach this point in my life, including the abuse I'd unearthed. In turn, he confided to me that both of his parents were children of alcoholics and how he was happy to be emerging from a difficult three-year relationship. His honesty touched me.

I was ecstatic. This was becoming exactly the type of relationship I had longed for. The feelings I was having for Brian were growing, and I again had to credit the Program. If I hadn't tackled that Fourth Step, I knew none of this would be happening. In the past, I didn't possess the capacity for these types of feelings. But now, because of all my hard work, I felt I was ready for it.

When Brian returned to the mainland, it gave us both an opportunity to catch our breath. Our time together had been so unexpected, so heady and exhilarating, that it was surreal. The good news was that Brian and I both loved to travel, and we were blessed with flexible jobs, plenty of free time, and the type of financial stability that afforded us the opportunity to wander the globe to our hearts' content. We realized that few people share that type of good fortune and how exciting it would be to explore it together.

CHAPTER 57

My "Happily Ever After"
Fantasy

W HEN SPRING CAME ALONG, I continued to hold on to the notion that Brian and I were meant to be together. I had scheduled another series of clinics on the East Coast, and Brian surprised me by flying out to Boston for my fiftieth birthday. Our relationship was changing me both inside and out. For instance, I had been living in Kona for seven years and not once had I straddled a bike and peddled the Queen K, or Queen Ka'ahumanu Highway, where the bicycle portion of the Ironman is held. True, I'd done some biking over the years, but I'd never looked at the sport as a means of training or even a source of fun. My head was still completely immersed in the pool. But one day Brian coaxed me out for a steady 25-mile ride. The feeling of the wind rushing past my cheeks, the speed, and the road beneath my wheels opened up a new world to me. I was hooked.

My swimming schedule was already more flexible, and now that I'd become enamored with cycling, I discovered I no longer needed to be tethered to a pool. It's amazing what a person can see from the seat of a bicycle. And you can talk! Unlike swimming, where your face is underwater much of the time, on a bike you can spin for hours just chatting away. I started to take up more running as well. Nothing crazy—I certainly wasn't logging marathon-like miles—but I found that running offered yet another great alternative to the water.

Unfortunately, something else was changing as well—Brian was starting to get moody and impatient with me. Anger seemed to be his default response more and more frequently. I also began to sense an underlying tension—an expectation on Brian's part. He seemed to want me to be someone other than who I was. Sure, he loved to brag about my world records and swimming accomplishments to anyone who would listen, but he rarely said anything complimentary to me. Looking back, I often felt he was more interested in his triathlon training than in me. In the bedroom, lovemaking for him was little more than an act. It seemed no different from an obligatory training run, bike ride, or swim workout.

Early in our relationship I had seen red flags but had chosen to ignore them. Like the very first time I picked him up at the airport in Kona. We'd been seeing each other for only a little over two months, but we'd spent nearly half that time together and had visited Maui, St. Maarten, and several places on the mainland. I was excited to see him, and on the way to the airport I bought a fragrant lei to welcome him back with. I also wrote out his complicated last name on a piece of paper and thought it would be cute to hold it up when he disembarked, much like a chauffeur picking up an unfamiliar client.

As I waited for him to pass through the security doors, my insides were fluttering in anticipation. Ten minutes later, he casually strolled toward me. His emotions were completely unreadable behind his sunglasses. He grinned at the silly sign, which I was holding upside down, dispensed a chaste kiss, and asked, "Well, did you miss me?" If Brian was happy to see me, he didn't show it. His message was clear: tone yourself down, Karlyn. Put a lid on your effervescent and affectionate self, because that's not my style. I slipped into my people-pleasing mode and cooled myself down right away.

When I talked to him about some of my concerns, he seemed to listen, but it didn't make an actual difference. Here I was in a "committed relationship" with Brian, and yet I had absolutely no idea where the two of us stood. I chalked it up to fallout from his most recent relationship and continued on trying to please.

I began to think, well, if I changed some of the things he's complaining about, like my exuberance, or my loud voice, then maybe he'll love me and we can live happily ever after. I was falling back into the role of the little girl who tried everything to get her parents' love and acceptance. It was obvious my insecurities were rearing their ugly heads. It was my fantasy of a happily ever after driving me. I'd become fixated on the notion that Brian and I were meant to be. That our coming together had happened for a reason.

I saw many of Brian's shortcomings, but I loved him anyway. Brian rarely spoke words of affection or said "I love you," but that didn't stop me from frequently bolstering his confidence and expressing my love for him. I kept showing up to the plate. I saw so much potential in him. Call it tenacity. Call it foolhardiness. Whatever you want to label it, I was all in. *Maybe this could work out,* I kept telling myself. *It's meant to be.*

As I struggled in my relationship with Brian, I took the opportunity to lean more heavily on both the Program and Al-Anon to find comfort and strength. It was strange to be at Al-Anon meetings and know I was sitting there more because of Brian than because of anything else. And he wasn't even an alcoholic.

I also took my hurt and disappointment to the most comfortable place I knew—the water. When I aged up to the 50–54 age group, I was moving ahead with a swimming comeback. I teamed up once again with ACBB and went to the French Nationals in Angers. I swam six races and broke three world records. I went to a couple of meets later that year and broke a few more records. By year's end I had performed well enough to be selected as one of the 2012 Masters Swimmers of the Year. But the racing in the pool had changed. Sure, the water still felt great, but the magical feeling I usually experienced when I touched the wall was, once again, missing.

At a suggestion from Brian, I decided to give triathlon a try. To some it might seem as if I were jumping from the frying pan into the fire training three sports instead of one, but I was having a ball. I was excited to be doing something new and novel, and I had very few expectations. I was swimming, biking, and running for fun. Janet and Grant Miller, the owners of Bike Works in Kona, set me up with a great bike and racing kit, and I was ready to go. In March of 2013 I competed in a local race called the Lavaman Triathlon, a huge event attracting over 1,500 athletes from all over the world. In my first attempt at the Olympic distance (1.5k swim, 40k bike ride, 10k run) I won my age group in a respectable time of 2:25 and was the tenth woman overall. I even qualified to compete at the USA Triathlon National Championships, though I politely declined. Testing the waters a bit more, a few weeks later I placed first in the aquabike category at the Silicon Valley Triathlon in California. Triathlon made me feel like a kid again. I was having so much fun that I often startled my competitors in the bike portion by spontaneously letting out a loud "Wheeeee!" as I peddled down the road.

During this time my relationship with Brian remained status quo. On the surface and to all our friends, it looked ideal. My mind and heart, however, seemed to be always in a state of confusion. On one hand, Brian made a huge effort to spend time with me, whether that was in Hawaii, California, or anywhere else we decided to meet up. I kept thinking, *Well, he's showing up. That must mean he loves me.* At other times I would bear the brunt of his discontent when his anger would boil over, which it did easily. About what, I was never sure. Whenever I privately began considering a break-up, Brian would somehow sense my ambivalence and do something sweet or loving, and I would talk myself into staying. Maybe my love would "fix" him, and then I would have the attentive, affectionate, loving partner I desired.

In keeping with our globe-trotting lifestyle, in May 2013 Brian and I planned a trip to Riccione, Italy, located on the Adriatic Coast about a hundred miles south of Venice. We stayed at the Belvedere, a four-star hotel and spa that caters to cyclists. It's a fabulous hotel, and the owner, Marina Pasquini, ensures that all your needs are taken care of, including providing expert cycling guides to take you all over the Emilia-Romagna, Tuscan, and Umbrian countrysides. Brian invited some of his friends along, including triathlon legends Scott Molina and Gordo Byrn, to experience the riding as well as Marina's wonderful cuisine and hospitality.

Each day the hotel guests broke into at least three groups of riders, including the Race group, for those who wanted to hammer on the bike from beginning to end; the Road group, for mid-range cyclists who wanted a good workout but weren't quite as fast as those in the Race group; and the Panorama group, for those folks who were more interested in enjoying the scenery than in hard riding. While the biking was spectacular, Brian and I weren't getting along. His anger and moodiness toward me worsened with each passing day. Things got so bad that I finally found the strength and said I wanted out of the relationship. I needed a break, I said.

When I told Brian my feelings, his temper flared once again. After he calmed down, he asked me to stay. Against my better judgment, I put my suitcase away and geared up to ride. Brian, Scott, Gordo, and some of the other guys headed off in one direction, and I went with two women on another route. I really loved cycling, and my confidence on the bike was growing. I took off ahead of my riding partners and was taking a curve in the middle of a descent when my back wheel hit a wet spot. As I began to slide I tried to correct the mistake, but it was too late. I was going down.

I stuck out my left arm to brace myself, and my hand took the brunt of the fall. I could tell right away I had completely screwed up my wrist. As I sat in a heap by the side of the road waiting for my riding partners to reach me, the first thought in my mind was *Brian is going to be mad.*

That's how badly our relationship had deteriorated—I was more worried about his reaction than about my broken wrist.

After the crash, everything became a blur. The hours spent in an Italian emergency room, the x-ray revealing the shattered bone fragments resembling a box of Chiclets gum, Brian's unexplained absence at the hospital, the rescheduled flights back home, the emergency surgery on Oahu, the seven pins inserted into my wrist . . .

The end of our roller-coaster relationship arrived in an email a few weeks later. For almost two years Brian and I had become experts at coordinating our schedules to maximize our time together. But when it came time for him to let me know it wasn't working out for him, he fell back on impersonal communication. "I am sorry this has to be from so far away, via an email," he wrote, "but I do not know of any other way to truly express what I need to say . . . I am truly sorry for the pain I might have caused, might be causing now, and might cause in the future . . . I will miss you every day . . . "

CHAPTER 58

Seeking Out
Lessons from the Pain

I N THE END, ALL YOU CAN DO is try to make sense of it all. You seek out lessons from the pain. And my breakup with Brian hurt. It hurt a lot. Looking back on it, Brian made me feel insignificant and under-valued throughout our relationship. In many ways, he treated me as my father had when I was young. That sense of familiarity—that was why I became so enamored with him, even though the clues were all there that he was the wrong match for me. It was yet another instance of my being unable to break free from the shackles of my past.

What I finally came to terms with was that just as my father hadn't deliberately set out to hurt me, neither had Brian. He, like my father, was simply trying to survive. Brian had learned his relationship skills from his parents—the same parents who had learned their own elabo-rate coping skills growing up in alcoholic households. I knew what that meant—I'd learned some of those same skills. Maybe Brian's parents were just trying to survive too. Aren't we all, in the end?

While I was recovering from the bike accident and the breakup, I went back to work with Amanda. I was now on my Seventh Step, which focuses on humility. It suggests we humbly ask God to remove our short-comings so we can move away from an egocentric life. We had already acknowledged our powerlessness in the face of addiction. Now we were flat out asking for our higher power's help.

In retrospect, I was catapulted into decisive action by the broken wrist and the ugly end of my relationship. Both had left me in pieces. Something needed to be done, but what? Was I doomed to keep repeating the same mistakes? Why had every relationship, even ones that started with such good intentions, ended up on the side of the road in a heap? How did I stop the cycle? I was so raw and broken that I was willing to do just about anything to get past this pain. It was time, I knew, to finally address the issue of my sexual abuse.

I spoke to Amanda about it, but she explained that the Program isn't equipped to offer that type of assistance. She instead recommended Teri Callaghan, a therapist in Kona who specializes in EMDR treatment, or eye movement desensitization and reprocessing.*

It turned out that Teri, Earth motherly and a bit on the hippie side, was just what I needed. Her calm demeanor and quiet wisdom enabled me to connect with her quickly and, more importantly, to trust her. I was forthright about my history and about where I viewed myself in both my recovery and my life in general. I described at length my relationship with Brian and the emotional upheaval of our breakup.

"Just when I thought I was finally making progress in my recovery, this happens," I said. "I was convinced that all the hard work I've been doing was finally going to bear fruit."

---

* "EMDR is a psychotherapy developed by Francine Shapiro that emphasizes disturbing memories as the cause of psychopathology. It is used to help with the symptoms of post traumatic stress disorder (PTSD). According to Shapiro, when a traumatic or distressing experience occurs, it may overwhelm normal coping mechanisms. The memory and associated stimuli are inadequately processed and are stored in an isolated memory network. . . . The goal of EMDR is to reduce the long-lasting effects of distressing memories by developing more adaptive coping mechanisms." en.wikipedia.org/wiki/Eye_movement_desensitization_and_reprocessing

"So you thought Brian was the one?" Teri said.

"I was convinced of it, Teri. I wanted someone I could swim with and travel with and share a life with. That's exactly what I'd asked for in my meditation challenge."

"And Brian sailed into your bay just like Captain Cook sailed into Kealakekua Bay for the first time back in 1779. The indigenous Hawaiians he came in contact with believed that he was the one too, didn't they?"

I studied her, contemplating the parallel she was drawing. The native Hawaiians had been expecting the arrival of a god. That expectation was part of their belief system. When Captain Cook arrived on the Big Island in a seemingly supernatural vessel, they embraced him and worshipped him. They put their own well-being on hold to cater to this deity from another world. I could see what Teri was getting at. I'd reacted the same way when Brian swam into my life. It was only natural that he, like Captain Cook, would relish all the attention and then eventually take advantage of the arrangement. Captain Cook, as it had turned out, was far from a deity.

"I guess what you're trying to say, Teri, is that I was as gullible as the native Hawaiians."

"I don't think wishing and hoping for something in and of itself makes someone gullible," Teri said.

"But I should have paid better attention to the warning signs," I said. "If I had, I would have seen right away that Brian certainly wasn't the right guy for me."

"But he was, Karlyn. That's what you're not understanding. He may not have been the romantic interest that you wished for, but he played an invaluable role in your growth. Brian is what's known as a pivotal facilitator. These are people who are sent into your life to teach you something. When it's time for them to go, they leave right away. Poof! They're outta here. After they've gone, you discover that their presence has made you move in a different direction."

As I sat there considering what Teri was saying, I scratched beneath the opening of my pink plaster cast. It felt good to address the itch. It would feel even better, I knew, to get the darn thing off in a few more weeks.

"So Brian was a teacher of sorts?" I asked.

"Unwittingly," said Teri.

"Dang, that was the hardest class I ever took."

"Maybe. But look what you got out of it, Karlyn. You're finally ready to confront your demons. You're here. If Brian hadn't swum into your life and turned your world upside down, I doubt that the two of us would be sitting in this room right now," she explained.

"I would simply have continued to do the same thing over and over again, expecting a different result," I mused. "That's one of the definitions of insanity."

"You've got that right. Without this experience, however painful, you wouldn't have had any incentive to do anything differently. You weren't hurting enough to want to change."

"I wasn't *broken* enough to change," I corrected.

"Maybe that would be a better way of phrasing it," she said, offering me a smile.

Teri's EMDR treatment was life changing. It was life affirming. Within a relatively short period of time, I was able to desensitize my emotional state to much of the trauma I had experienced both with Brian and in my childhood. I was also finally free of the residual guilt and shame I had been harboring regarding my sexual abuse. I didn't forget about it; I just didn't hurt the way I used to whenever those memories came up.

During this process, I realized I had been selective about which of the bugs under the rug I was addressing. I had overlooked the most obvious ones because they were the scariest. Confronting sexual abuse is scary, but the consequences of living a life without acknowledging the reality are even worse. I had lived an entire life filled with fear of those bugs! Now, with Teri's help, I had scooted them out of their hiding place and they were gone for good, taking with them their power to hurt me.

The Program's Eighth and Ninth Steps are about identifying those you have harmed with your addictive behavior and those to whom you are able to make amends. For many, the Ninth Step, addressing atonement, is the most daunting. The only legitimate way to move forward and to grow in your recovery, the Program urges, is to make a good faith effort to repair the damage you caused in the past. I used the information I had gathered in my Fourth Step to generate a list of all the people I would contact and offer to make things right with. It's one thing to apologize to your mother for screwing up. *Mom, I'm sorry for stealing money out of your purse when I was seventeen because I wanted to go buy beer with my friends. I'm sorry for lying to you about going to swim practice all those mornings and for skipping out on school and for forging your signature on sick notes . . .* On a difficulty scale, 'fessing up to Mom probably rated only a six or seven, particularly since she was the one who had helped get me into rehab in the first place. But the others? Some of those amends would rate a difficulty of a solid ten.

As I looked back over the course of my life, so many of those whom I'd harmed seemed inaccessible and unapproachable. Steve Lindsey I could track down. I could and would apologize to him for taking advantage of his generous and forgiving nature. I could even offer to pay restitution for the money he'd lost because of my behavior, although putting a dollar amount on that would be near impossible. Chuck Chase, my supervisor when I was a state lifeguard, and my bosses at the navy base—I could find them as well. What about Chris, whose test I'd cheated from during our lifeguard examination, or Beth and Cathy, whom I'd let down during our around-the-island relay swim? Did I need to apologize to them for showing up to the race hungover? So many names, so many uncomfortable memories.

"What if I simply posted a blanket apology on my Facebook page?" I asked Amanda. "Would that count?"

I knew the answer even before Amanda opened her mouth to respond.

"Is that how you would want to receive an apology, Karlyn? If someone had taken advantage of you, would that be the best way for them to make amends?"

I shook my head no.

"I know it can seem overwhelming and completely unrealistic," Amanda said. "If it's any consolation, when I went through my list of amends, I felt the exact same way. But just the fact that you're wrestling over these questions and formulating a game plan means you're committed to continuing your recovery. You won't believe how good it feels to get these things off your chest. Only you can judge how far you need to take this."

List in hand, I took a deep breath and went to work. The Internet and Facebook made it relatively easy to locate people, so I began in earnest to contact the people from my past and extend heartfelt apologies. Some, like Murly, were surprised by my admission. "I knew something was going on, Karlyn, but I had no idea of the extent of your drinking problem. You hid it so well." He wished me well, and we're still friends to this day. Keeney and Raapman were gracious.

At the time I reached out, Steve Lindsey was living on a sailboat in Mexico, and I was unable to connect with him. I hope one day I will have the opportunity to do so in person. As for Mike Troy, he accepted my apology with a tinge of guilt for being unaware of the struggles I faced outside the pool. "I never knew any of this, Karlyn," he said via email. "It makes me feel like I failed you." I reassured him that his coaching and guidance had made a positive and lasting impression on me, and that I was blessed to have had him as my coach.

Amanda was right. It did make me feel better to unburden some of the guilt I'd been lugging around for so many years. I never realized how heavy the load was.

CHAPTER 59

You Gave Me Life Not Once, but Twice

I N JULY OF 2013 I FLEW TO COLORADO to meet with Eric. He looked great. He'd been training hard and was fit and healthy. His triathlon training business was doing well, and I was happy for him. He's always been a first-rate coach, and I had no doubt in my mind that he would be successful in any endeavor he chose.

We sat in a park near the picturesque Cache La Poudre River. It seemed apropos, meeting one another in nature again like this. When I had called Eric from Kona to ask him if we could meet face-to-face, I could hear his voice tense up on the other end of the connection. "Spider, is there, uh, anything I need to know about?" he questioned. "Don't worry," I said, reassuring him. "But can you bring a box of tissues when we meet?" Now the box sat between us. I studied him for a long while. We'd been through so much together, he and I.

Finally I said, "I got a little taste of what it was like to have been you, Eric." I told him about the relationship I'd been through and how I'd felt as if nothing I could do was right or good enough. I told him how Brian often responded in anger, and about how I would say to him, "I'm just trying to love you. I don't get it. Why are you so angry with me?"

Eric didn't say anything at first. He just nodded his head.

"I'm sorry, Eric," I said, as I started to cry. "I'm sorry for everything I put you through. One day toward the end of our marriage, you told me, 'Karlyn, you treat me with less respect than you do a complete stranger.' You were right. And you didn't deserve that. No one ever deserves that, especially not someone who was such a big part of my life for so many years."

"Maybe I should have stood up to you more," he said. "Maybe things would have turned out differently for us."

"It might not have worked," I said, reaching for one of the tissues. "If you back a Pipes girl into a corner, it's not going to be pretty. No, this isn't about how you handled the situation. It's about how I handled it. It goes back to that sense of entitlement I've always wrestled with. I thought I was above dealing with my issues."

"You didn't need to fly all the way out here to tell me this, Spider," he said quietly.

"Yes, I did. Apologizing to you in person is the very least I could do."

I listened to the soothing murmur of the river and gazed at the rugged Front Range in the distance. *Can there possibly be anything as therapeutic as sitting in a place like this?* I wondered. I inhaled deeply, as if I were determined to make all the clean air and beautiful surroundings a permanent part of my being. At fifteen I had wanted nothing to do with Colorado. Now, all these years later, I wanted to breathe it deep into my soul.

"So was this Brian thing a case of relationship karma?" Eric finally asked with a smile. "You're the spiritual one. Is that what this was all about?"

"I don't know whether it was or wasn't. I just know that for a long time I was a lousy friend and wife to you. I was too focused on my swimming and too obsessed with the records. That's the thing about alcoholics. It's all or nothing with them."

"But look at everything you were able to do, Karlyn. There's no way you could have done any of that without that type of commitment and focus."

"There's no way *we* could have done any of that, Eric. You deserve as much of the credit as I do. All those world records are under Pipes-*Neilsen*. We were a team. Don't ever forget that."

"It was a heckuva ride, wasn't it?"

I nodded.

"I don't regret it, you know," Eric said. "All those years together—I don't regret them at all."

"Neither do I," I said. "I wouldn't trade what we had for anything in the world. Thank you for trying to love me."

"I didn't try to love you. I *did* love you."

"Well, thank you for that, then, because I know that type of devotion is pretty damn precious. I didn't used to know that, but now I do."

After Colorado, I flew directly to Costa Rica, a country that reminds me of my Hawaiian home. Not only does it have beautiful beaches, lush tropical rainforests, and stunning volcanoes, but it also exudes a spiritual energy that I knew would allow me to continue to heal my wounds. I was visiting for practical reasons too. I had an appointment with my favorite dentist, Dr. Simon Flikier. Trained at Boston University, he now had a successful practice, the Flikier Institute of Oral Rehabilitation, in San Jose, Costa Rica. The damage done to my teeth by years of throwing up had taken a long time to repair. Visiting Dr. Simon meant I could get my dental work done at about half of what it would have cost in the States.

After my dental appointments, I hit the road. As I drove around in my rental car, I had no idea where I was going or sometimes even where I was. *This is a good time to relinquish control,* I thought. I didn't bother using a GPS. I didn't want an itinerary or a timetable. I just wanted to wander and enjoy the complete freedom of doing so. I visited waterfalls, hiked, and enjoyed some thrill-seeking adventures like zip-lining down the slopes of the Arenal Volcano. Now I was meandering toward the ocean, following the signs. Or trying to. If I found myself at a dead end, I'd just laugh, turn around, and negotiate my way back to the main road.

I eventually found myself in a little town called Puntarenas. I checked into a quaint, family-run hotel and, since it was late afternoon, the first thing I did was amble over to the beach to watch the sunset. As the sun went down, the sky was suffused with vibrant pinks, reds, oranges, and magentas. It was stunning—one of those sunsets that reminds you that you're part of something bigger than you can ever imagine. As I sat in awe and wonder, I was once again filled with an overwhelming sense of gratitude.

My hotel had a swimming pool, no bigger than the campground pool I'd swum in at the Lake Henshaw retreat the first weekend of my sobriety, but it was inviting and the water was warm. Having made my way back from the beach, I slipped into the pool, closed my eyes, and floated on my back. As night settled, I drifted, soaking in the peace and feeling giddy at the stillness and my weightlessness. Throughout the course of my life, water has always been my friend. As is the case with any great relationship, ours has had its share of ups and downs. But even during the most challenging times—even when I turned away from her, resented her, and renounced her—the bond we had was unbreakable.

All of a sudden, something threatened to disrupt my serenity. I could sense light. I opened my eyes to a preposterously huge full moon. It was immense, the biggest I'd ever seen. I glanced around the pool and realized I was alone—this was *my* moon. This moon was a gift, meant in that moment to be experienced by me and me alone. As I watched, my moon continued to inch its way higher into the inky sky. I was awestruck at how it lit up the darkness, how it bathed me in its light.

Don't worry, Karlyn, a voice inside me said. *It's going to be okay. Everything's going to be okay.* As I lay there, I could feel the shattered pieces of my body and soul slowly start to fuse back together. All of the dark memories of poor choices, the sadness and guilt, the loss and loneliness, the hurt—it all began to trickle away. All of that was "before." Being in this pool, illuminated by this magical moon, was "now."

It's going to be okay, the voice whispered again. *You're going to be okay.* And at that moment, I finally let go.

When I arrived back home from Central America, exhausted from my long flight, I found that Mom had left me a surprise on my bed—a new pillow. As I picked it up, my eyes began to fill. This was not just any pillow. I have no idea how she did it, but Mom had found fabric identical to what she'd used to sew my Night-night all those years ago. Not only that, but she had kept the little bear appliqué from the original blanket for all these years—for what reason, I do not know. But there it was, on the center of that satiny smooth pillow. It made my insides melt, the idea that while I was away on my healing trip she'd been sewing this present for me. The old Karlyn would have politely accepted the gift and gone to sleep. But life was different now. I rushed into Mom's room and woke her up. I squeezed her in my arms and told her how much the gift meant to me. She smiled and told me she loved me. Mom and I had had an interesting relationship—from two people who could barely stand each other to roommates to best friends. I hugged her again before I retreated to my room to get ready for bed. As I crawled beneath the covers and lay my head on my new pillow, the hard edges of the world became soft again.

April 17, 2014, was a birthday night for me. Birthday nights in the Program are festive affairs. If you had happened to walk by before the meeting started, you would have heard animated voices punctuated with loud bursts of laughter and thought there was a party going on. And there was. Page 132 of the Big Book states, "We are not a glum lot," and nothing could ring more true on these special nights. Birthday meetings include the presentation of chips for those celebrating sobriety anniversaries. These meetings are huge and well attended, and those marking milestones are invited to the front of the room to share their experience, strength, and hope. The first to be recognized are those who have one year under their belt, the next are those who have two years, and so on, until the person with the most time gets up before the crowd and speaks.

One by one, people moved to the front of the room to address the crowd. Some for just a few moments, others for longer. As I listened to each person share a bit of their story, I felt fortunate to be a part of this fellowship. It was touching to be surrounded by so many people fighting the good fight when it came to their health and well-being, staying sober one day at a time. Each of us in recovery was a walking miracle, including me. How else can you explain that after drinking for approximately 4,748 days straight, one day I was able to stop, and I have not picked up a drink since?

My name was one of the last to be called. Amanda, beaming, went up first to introduce me. After a few words, she asked me to come up. When I reached her, she gave me a hug, a flower lei, and presented me with my chip. Everyone in the room applauded. Twenty-one years! How the time had flown by. The chip was passed around the room. Tradition holds that everyone who handles it transfers some of their own positive energy into it.

I looked at the attendees and couldn't help but remember the first time I nervously rose to my feet at Sharp Cabrillo Hospital to admit that I was an alcoholic. I had felt anguish and shame that day. Today I was filled with peace and gratitude. In an odd way I wish everyone in the world were an alcoholic. Not an active one, but one in recovery. The Program showed me a better way to live. Not just to survive, but to thrive. Looking back, it's amazing to see how a series of small changes added up to make such a big difference. While it may not have been the most efficient route, I took my recovery at my own pace. Thankfully, the Program and the fellowship were there for me, waiting patiently.

"I wanted to be the one who broke the record for getting through the steps the fastest," I announced to the crowd. "You're looking at someone who had it all figured out. I was going to buzz through them in no time at all. But I stand before you here tonight, a humble woman with twenty-one years of sobriety, to let you know that it actually took me twenty years and ten months to complete all of my steps. Imagine that," I said, shaking my head with a smile. "It may be a record, but it's not quite the one I was after."

Heads nodded and some of the attendees chuckled. It was the kind of non-threatening, knowing laughter that comes only to those with familiarity, to those who know.

"But the important thing is that I stuck with it," I continued. "I stuck with it and I did it. It's been a wild ride and an amazing journey, and thanks to the help of the fellowship and to the thousands of people like you whom I've met over the years, I'm here."

The room began to break into applause, but I held up my hand—the hand with my mended wrist—to pause the clapping.

"One last thing," I said. "There's someone in the audience today who deserves the most credit for helping me become the person I am today."

I looked across the sea of faces and found her—my mom. It was the first time that I'd invited her to attend a meeting. I hadn't been sure if she would accept the offer, but she did, with no questions asked and not a second thought. Now there she was, sitting in the back of the room, tears streaming down her face.

"You gave me life, Mom," I said, addressing her directly. "You gave me life not once, but twice. Thank you. I never would have been able to do this without you. Thank you for who you are, for what you've taught me, and for everything that you've done for me over the years. I'm so lucky to have you as my mother. I love you."

CHAPTER 60

The Courage to Be Myself

F OLLOW YOUR PASSION AND YOU will find your purpose. So much of my life had been empty, void of passion and drowning in addiction and self pity. A life lived without passion is a slow death, addict or not. When I stopped being a victim of my circumstances and let go of anger and resentment toward myself and others, my passion was reborn. It breathed life back into me. After I reached out and accepted help from others, my purpose, once submerged on the sea floor, buried in muck and debris, broke free and began to rise. When this purpose finally reached the surface, it became crystal clear where my energy and focus were going to flow next. Share. Help others. Be of service. Inspire. Give.

I've recently gained a deeper appreciation for *The Wizard of Oz*. Dorothy discovers that the happiness and contentment she was searching for were inside her all along. She just had to believe. Isn't it the same for all of us? It's our own limiting beliefs that ultimately hold us back from becoming the best versions of ourselves. This certainly has been the case with me. My voyage toward a new life didn't start when I stopped drinking; it truly began when I embraced the meaning and message of the Serenity Prayer.

God, grant me the serenity to accept the things I cannot change . . . At a very early age I had been tossed into the deep end where it was sink or swim. I did both. Instead of being resentful of this, today I am grateful. My life, the way I lived it, made me the person I am today. The worst time in my life turned out to be the most valuable, which shows me that every experience provides the opportunity to learn and grow. I also gave myself permission to let go of the guilt and shame I harbored surrounding the poor choices I'd made. I have been set free.

The courage to change the things I can . . . I became aware of how I ran my life through the "good/bad" filter. You know the one I'm talking about—the filter you use to judge everything you do. I turned that filter off and have been working at letting go of critical self-judgment. I know I hurt myself more than others, so I've learned to be kinder to *me* and to forgive myself. As for my hidden "bugs under the rug," the Program suggested I seek outside help, and the result was life changing. I still remember the traumatic events of my past, but the memories no longer have the power to hurt me. I also still catch myself from time to time reacting to life's circumstances from a place of fear. When I do, I try to stop and realize that "little Karlyn" in survivor mode is likely trying to run the show. At that point I have a choice: I can either regress back to old patterns and stay stuck, or let go and trust.

And the wisdom to know the difference. Life is a series of holding on and letting go, and the discomfort and pain associated with both. Once I stopped fighting everyone and everything and learned to let life unfold, life became much sweeter. Pushing into resistance might feel productive, but it usually means it's not meant to happen. I have faith now that when something doesn't work out, it's for a good reason. Almost always, there's a better option coming soon.

And where are my addictions now? They are never very far away, shimmering just below the surface of my life. It doesn't matter whether I have twenty-two years of sobriety or just two days; if I *choose,* my next drink is only as far away as the kitchen cupboard or the nearest liquor store. I know that my addictions will always be a part of me, and I'm okay with that. Thanks to the tools I've learned in the Program, my addictions don't control me. While I will never underestimate their power, I have made friends with them and can even laugh about them. But in all seriousness, I stand before you and can honestly say, "Hello. My name is Karlyn, and I am a alcoholic. A *grateful* alcoholic."

In swimming technique, there's a sweet spot that every swimmer hopes to find. It's a magical place where you are one with the water, gliding along in a beautiful liquid dance. On the surface, it looks easy. But underneath you know it requires work to make it appear so effortless. It takes trust that the water will support you. It takes awareness that your old habits no longer serve you. It takes willingness to do something different. It takes being open to change. It takes time, practice, and patience. And often, it requires a do-over. But do-overs need not be as extreme as mine. They can be as simple as a shift in perception, a change in attitude, or simply a new way of looking at an old situation. Over time, a series of small ripples can build up to a big wave of change. That's the beauty of a do-over: in every experience you have opportunity to say, "I'm doing it over." Whether it's a conversation, a relationship, or even the next pull of your swimming stroke, there are no limits to how many do-overs are available to you. Do it over, or do it the same? The choice is yours.

Epilogue

W AS THIS REALLY HAPPENING, or was it a dream?
It was a festive affair. The tables were tastefully decorated and the stage was adorned with a colorful display of flags from around the world. It was both a celebration of the new and a reunion of the old. Each year since its inception in 1963, hundreds of decorated and talented athletes from each aquatic discipline—swimming, diving, water polo, synchronized swimming, and open-water swimming—as well as coaches and other pioneers of the sports apply to be recognized and honored. Only twelve are selected each year. The energy in the hall was electrifying.

The ballroom lights dimmed, and almost immediately the animated conversations of over five hundred guests quieted down. Bruce Wigo, president and CEO of the International Swimming Hall of Fame, took the stage.

"It gives me great pleasure to welcome you to the enshrinement of the honorees of the International Swimming Hall of Fame class of 2015."

On cue, twelve people stood up. I was one of them.

As I rose, my body responded as if I were ready to step up onto the blocks and race. My pulse quickened, my heart thumped in my chest, and my vision narrowed. I scanned the room, seeking. It was easy to pick out my "team." At the banquet table sat many of the angels who had influenced my life so positively. There were John Baker, Coach Pat, Patti and Harry, my girlfriends Laurie and Maggie, Uncle Bill and Auntie Gracie, and even Janet Neilsen, Eric's mother. And of course, there was Mom. She beamed.

Out of the corner of my eye I caught a shadow and looked in that direction. There *they* were, all of them. The greats who had come before me and had since moved on. Duke Kahanamoku, Esther Williams, Gertrude Ederle, Johnny Weissmuller, and many more stood quietly in the recess of the room emanating an energy that penetrated every cell of my body. *Welcome, Karlyn. We are so pleased you have been invited to join us. Your induction is well deserved,* Duke said. Goose bumps covered my skin as a wide smile spread across my face.

John Naber, 1976 Olympian and four-time gold medalist, took the stage as master of ceremonies, and the enshrinement began. One by one each honoree was introduced, and then a video presentation recapping their life rolled on a massive screen. When each video concluded, the honoree went up on stage to give an acceptance speech and receive a red satin sash and a beautiful award.

By the time it was my turn, my nerves had settled down and I felt a comfortable sense of calm, even though I knew what was coming next. My name was called, and my video began.

There I was on the blocks at my first swim meet at age six, earning a medal; as a sprouting teenager with Mike Troy; with my Coronado high school team accepting a championship trophy; at a college meet at Arkansas. The video then jumped to my Masters career, college swimming at Palomar and CSUB, and rolled right up to present day. To an audience familiar with aquatic greatness, the sheer width and breadth of my swimming accomplishments may have seemed preposterous. Over two hundred Masters world records spanning three decades, world records in every stroke and every distance, the oldest NCAA champion, and an open-water specialist. The list went on. Even to me, the person who had swum each and every one of those races, it boggled my mind. I still wonder how I did it. I still wonder, why me?

Unnoticed by the crowd, the video had a gap. The lost years weren't recorded. Only close friends and family knew the circuitous route I had taken to reach this moment in time. But that was about to change. I stood under the spotlight on center stage and took a deep breath.

"It is indeed quite an honor to be here," I said with shaking hands and a quavering voice. "It's the pinnacle of every swimmer's career to be able to accept this prestigious recognition. In movie terms, it's an Oscar." Heads nodded in agreement.

"There is one chapter, however, that the video omitted. It's the most important chapter of my life because it has formed the person I am today." I took another deep breath. "Before I became the decorated athlete you see today, I was a helpless, hopeless alcoholic drinking a liter of vodka a day." My heart skipped a beat. The secret was out. The room went totally silent.

"I am grateful to be alive, grateful for the many people who believed in me before I believed in myself. Some of them are here in this room to help me celebrate," I continued, gaining momentum. "The person I want to thank the most is here too. Adrienne Pipes—Mom—would you please stand up?" On shaky legs she stood, and I addressed her directly. "Mom," I said with tears streaming down my cheeks, "you gave me life twice. From the bottom of my heart, and with all that I am, thank you.

"I also owe a debt of gratitude to my best friend," I continued once my voice returned. "You never judged me. You gave me purpose, you rekindled my passion, and you allowed my talent to shine. But most importantly, you healed my broken soul.

"So please, raise your water glasses. I would like to make a toast to my best friend, and to what brings us all together on this very special night. Here's to water."

Inspirational Speaking Engagements
with Karlyn Pipes

Karlyn Pipes is an internationally acclaimed inspirational speaker. Drawing from the challenges she faced to rise from the depths of addiction and self-destruction to her induction in 2015 into the

International Swimming Hall of Fame, Karlyn's odds-defying comeback story will inspire, entertain, and engage audiences of all ages and from all walks of life.

Invite Karlyn to create a custom-themed inspirational talk for your next business conference, school, university, church, or team event. Email **karlynpipes@gmail.com** or visit **karlynpipes.com**.

Aquatic Edge
Swim Technique Workshops

Karlyn is also a swim technique guru. Through Aquatic Edge, Inc., she offers single or multiple-day workshops, pool and open water swim camps, and private instruction worldwide. For inquiries about hosting an Aquatic Edge Faster Freestyle, Multi-Stroke, or Open Water workshop in your area, or to set up a camp or private lesson in Kona, Hawaii, email **aquaticedge@hawaii.rr.com**.

For swimming technique tips, instructional videos, and swimming related articles, visit **aquaticedge.org**.

38359530R00211

Made in the USA
San Bernardino, CA
04 September 2016